P9-DTB-567

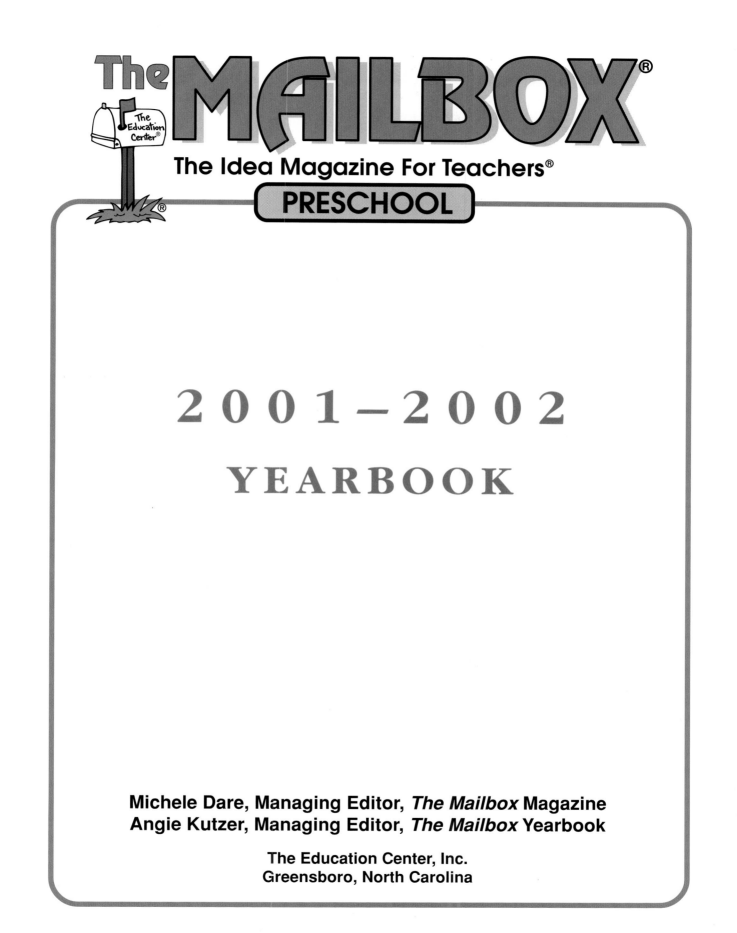

The MAILBOX®

The Idea Magazine For Teachers®

PRESCHOOL

2001–2002
YEARBOOK

Michele Dare, Managing Editor, *The Mailbox* Magazine
Angie Kutzer, Managing Editor, *The Mailbox* Yearbook

The Education Center, Inc.
Greensboro, North Carolina

The Mailbox® 2001–2002 Preschool Yearbook

Founding Editor in Chief: Margaret Michel
Managing Editor: Michele M. Dare
Executive Director, Magazine Publishing: Katharine P. S. Brower
Editorial and Freelance Management: Karen A. Brudnak
Editorial Training: Irving P. Crump
Curriculum Director: Karen P. Shelton
Copy Editors: Sylvan Allen, Karen Brewer Grossman, Karen L. Huffman, Amy Kirtley-Hill, Debbie Shoffner
Traffic Manager: Lisa K. Pitts
Staff Artists: Pam Crane, Nick Greenwood, Clevell Harris, Rebecca Saunders (SENIOR ARTISTS); Theresa Lewis Goode, Ivy L. Koonce, Sheila Krill, Clint Moore, Greg D. Rieves, Barry Slate, Stuart Smith, Donna K. Teal
Cover Artist: Lois Axeman
Typesetters: Lynette Dickerson, Mark Rainey
Editorial Assistants: Hope Rodgers, Jan E. Witcher
Librarian: Dorothy C. McKinney

ISBN 1-56234-516-8
ISSN 1088-5536

Copyright ©2002 by The Education Center, Inc.

All rights reserved except as here noted. No part of this publication may be reproduced or transmitted by any means, electronic or mechanical, without written permission from the publisher. Please direct written inquiries to the address below. Permission is granted to the original purchaser to reproduce pages for individual classroom use only and not for resale or distribution. Reproduction for an entire school or school system is prohibited.

The Education Center®, *The Mailbox*®, *Teacher's Helper*®, *The Mailbox*® *BOOKBAG*®, *Learning*®, The Idea Magazine For Teachers®, and the mailbox/post/grass logo are registered trademarks of The Education Center, Inc. All brand or product names are trademarks or registered trademarks of their respective companies.

Printed in the United States of America.

The Education Center, Inc.
P.O. Box 9753
Greensboro, NC 27429-0753

Look for *The Mailbox*® 2002–2003 Preschool Yearbook in the summer of 2003. The Education Center, Inc., is the publisher of *The Mailbox*®, *Teacher's Helper*®, *The Mailbox*® *BOOKBAG*®, and *Learning*® magazines, as well as other fine products. Look for these wherever quality teacher materials are sold, or call 1-800-714-7991.

Contents

Thematic Units and Special Features

Preschool Is out of This World!

Get ready to blast off into a new year of preschool with these space-themed ideas!

by Ada Goren

All systems are go...for a great year in preschool!

A Note From Mission Control

Introduce yourself to your new students and their families with a note sent to their homes before school begins. Make one copy of the open newsletter on page 10; then write a short letter introducing yourself and giving information about the year ahead. Duplicate your letter to make a class supply. Send a letter to each child in your class, with a sprinkle of star-shaped confetti in the envelope. If desired, send along the note and rocket pattern on pages 11 and 12 (see "Astronaut Introductions" below). Have youngsters complete the project and bring it to school on the first day.

Astronaut Introductions

Looking for a way to get to know your little astronauts? Duplicate and cut out the rocket pattern on page 12 for each child. If desired, send home the pattern and a copy of the note on page 11 before school begins. Or complete the projects on the first day of school. Working with one child at a time, read aloud the unfinished sentences on the rocket and ask her to complete them. Later, share each child's responses during a group time so that your youngsters can begin to learn about one another.

Prepare for Liftoff Preschool Friends!

Door Decor

Your young astronauts will know they've come to the right place when they see this rocket ship door decoration! To make it, cut two triangular flaps and a rounded triangle top from bulletin board paper in the color of your choice. Attach the pieces around your door to resemble a rocket, as shown. For added effect, cover your door with silver paper. Cut a flame shape from orange bulletin board paper and use clear Con-Tact covering to attach it to the floor in front of your door so that it resembles the engine fire of the rocket. Then use die-cut letters to spell out a welcome message on the door. For a final touch, cut a supply of stars from yellow construction paper and create a path from your school entrance to your doorway.

A Glittering Galaxy

Every one of your new students is a star, so why not show it? Duplicate the star name-tag pattern on page 11 onto yellow paper for each child. Write a child's name on each nametag, cut them all out, and then decorate the edges of each one with glitter glue before laminating the tags for durability. Punch a hole where indicated in each laminated name-tag; then use a safety pin to attach it to the child's clothing.

To make an attendance board, cover a bulletin board with black background paper. Add a title similar to the one shown and use pushpins to display the nametags around the title. As each child arrives at school, remove her nametag from the board and pin it to her clothing. A quick look at this board will tell you who's absent—just look for the stars left in the sky!

A.J.

Adam Josie Jose Blake
Sara Alex
Mrs. Wade's Shining Stars
Tasha
Matt Ben Kate

Twinkle, Twinkle, Flash, Flash

Encourage your little stars to shine as they sing this getting-to-know-you song. Give each youngster a small flashlight and have him practice flashing the light on and off. Then invite all your new students to sit in a circle and flash—or twinkle—their lights as you sing the song. Have the named child stand on cue and then sit again when you repeat the verse for another child.

(sung to the tune of "Twinkle, Twinkle, Little Star")

Twinkle, twinkle, preschool star.
How we wonder who you are!
[Erin], are you here today?
Stand up tall and then we'll say:
"Welcome, welcome, preschool star!
We're so glad you're who you are!"

Marvelous Moons

Little ones won't have to wait until nighttime to see the man in the moon when they create these crafty moons! To make one, shape a small ball of colored Crayola Model Magic into a crescent shape. Or use a moon-shaped cookie cutter. Next, use a drinking straw to poke a hole at one end. Then press on a wiggle eye and small pieces of Model Magic to make a smile for the moon. Allow the project to air-dry. Tie a length of yarn through the hole and then hang the moons around your room.

Books Are a Blast!

Shuttle your junior astronauts over to your group area for a storytime look at these space books!

Me and My Place in Space
Written by Joan Sweeney
Illustrated by Annette Cable

Big Silver Space Shuttle
By Ken Wilson-Max

Martian Rock
Written by Carol Diggory Shields
Illustrated by Scott Nash

Roaring Rockets
Written by Tony Mitton
Illustrated by Ant Parker

I Want to Be an Astronaut
By Byron Barton

Hush, Little Alien
By Daniel Kirk

Zoom! Zoom! Zoom! I'm Off to the Moon!
By Dan Yaccarino
(See pages 132–133 for teaching ideas to accompany this book.)

Helmet Headbands

Ready to explore your school or center on your annual first-day tour? Suit up your young space enthusiasts in these headbands first! To make one, cut out the center of a thin white paper plate; then staple the remaining plate rim to a sentence strip that has been cut in half lengthwise. Attach a flag sticker over the staple; then staple the sentence strip to fit a child's head. Invite each child to wear her helmet headband as you blast off on your tour!

Preschool Really *Is* out of This World!

Are your little ones loving Planet Preschool? Invite them to tell you just what they like about it in this class book! First, duplicate the book cover on page 13 onto white paper. If desired, use a photocopier to enlarge the cover. Color the cover with a silver crayon and then cut it out. Cut a class supply of white paper pages to match the book cover's shape. To make each child's page for the book, have him put on his astronaut helmet headband (see above); then snap a head-and-shoulders photo of him. Mount the developed photo on a prepared book page. Next, explain to your preschoolers that the phrase "out of this world" means that something is really wonderful. Then have each child tell you what is out of this world about preschool. Record his response on his book page. Stack the pages behind the cover and then staple them together on the left side.

Encourage each child to shuttle the class book home for a night. His parents will be able to see the names and faces of all his classmates *and* read their stellar descriptions of preschool!

Preschool Is out of This World!

Max thinks preschool is out of this world because he loves to play at the sand table.

Alex
(child's name)
is a
preschool STAR!

Mrs. Baker
(teacher signature)

9-10-01
(date)

Mission Accomplished!

Congratulate your new students on soaring through their first days of preschool with these awards! Duplicate the award on page 13 onto white paper to make a class supply. Personalize an award for each child. Then invite youngsters to color the stars on their awards with glitter crayons in the colors of their choice. Send home the finished awards to let parents know their little ones are doing a heavenly job at preschool!

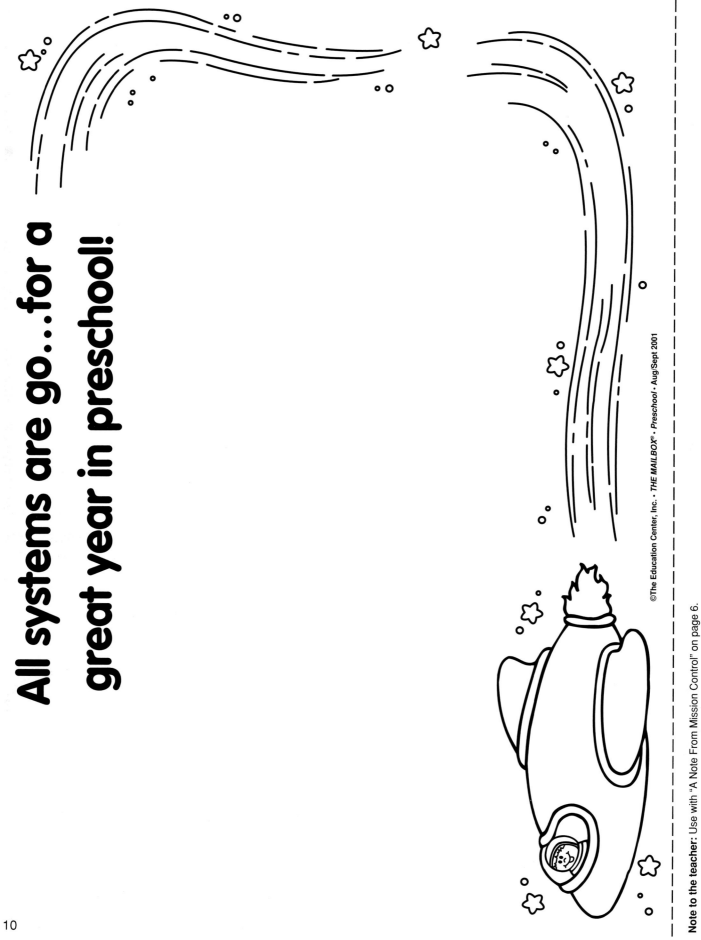

All systems are go...for a great year in preschool!

©The Education Center, Inc. • THE MAILBOX® • Preschool • Aug/Sept 2001

Note to the teacher: Use with "A Note From Mission Control" on page 6.

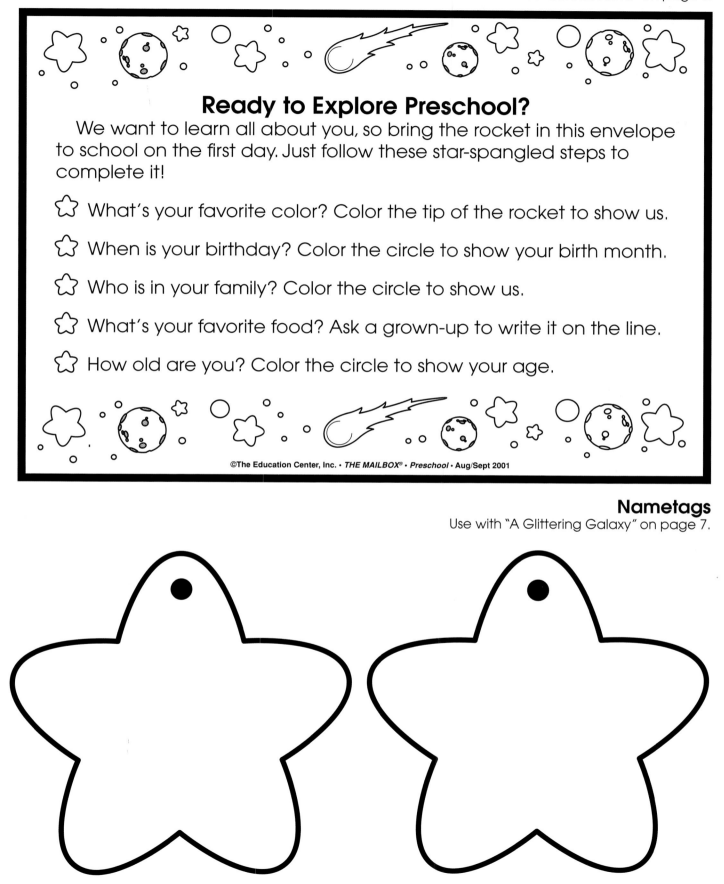

Ready to Explore Preschool?

We want to learn all about you, so bring the rocket in this envelope to school on the first day. Just follow these star-spangled steps to complete it!

☆ What's your favorite color? Color the tip of the rocket to show us.

☆ When is your birthday? Color the circle to show your birth month.

☆ Who is in your family? Color the circle to show us.

☆ What's your favorite food? Ask a grown-up to write it on the line.

☆ How old are you? Color the circle to show your age.

©The Education Center, Inc. • THE MAILBOX® • Preschool • Aug/Sept 2001

Rocket Pattern

Use with "Astronaut Introductions" on page 6.

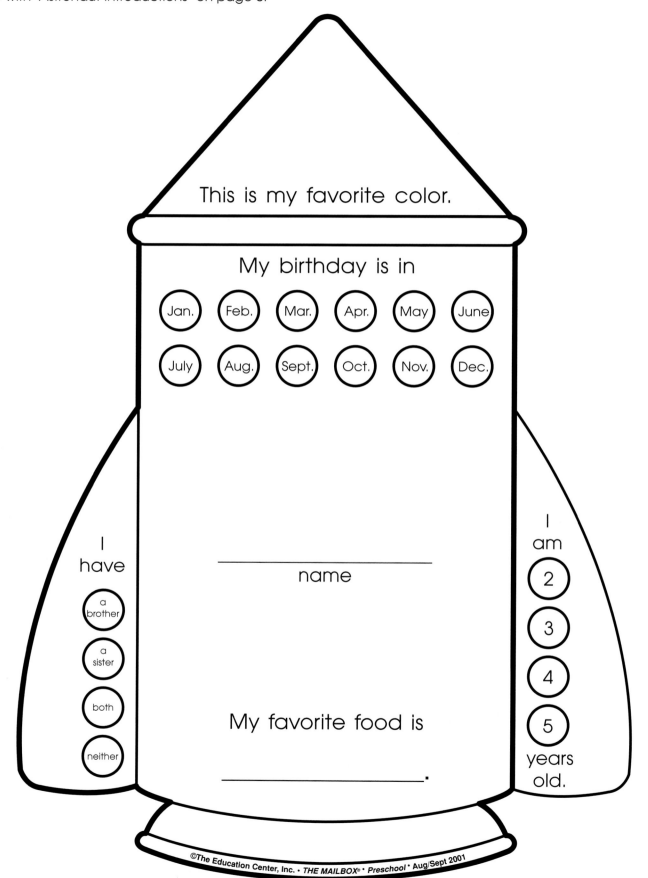

This is my favorite color.

My birthday is in

Jan. Feb. Mar. Apr. May June

July Aug. Sept. Oct. Nov. Dec.

I have

a brother

a sister

both

neither

_____
name

My favorite food is

_____.

I am

2

3

4

5

years old.

©The Education Center, Inc. • THE MAILBOX® • Preschool • Aug/Sept 2001

Preschool *Is*
out of This World!

©The Education Center, Inc. • THE MAILBOX® • Preschool • Aug/Sept 2001

Award
Use with "Mission Accomplished!" on page 9.

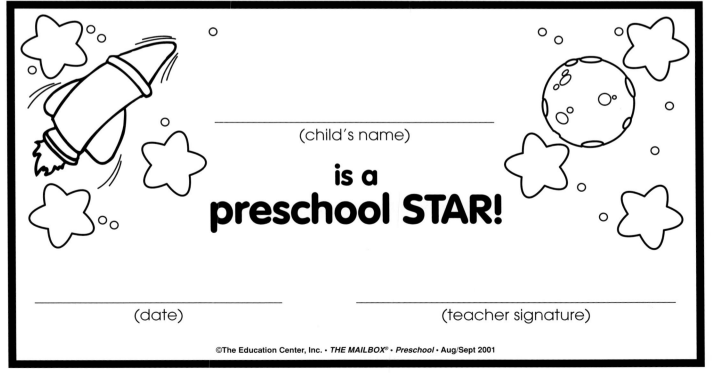

_____
(child's name)

is a
preschool STAR!

_____   _____
(date)   (teacher signature)

©The Education Center, Inc. • *THE MAILBOX® • Preschool •* Aug/Sept 2001

Investigating APPLES

Teaching science is a snap with this crop of exploration ideas involving apples!

ideas contributed by Julie A. Koczur

What Do These Have in Common?

Introduce your apple study with a group activity that gets youngsters thinking. In advance, gather the following items: apple seeds, a box of apple juice, a container of applesauce, and several apple stems. During your group time, pass the items around for students to examine; then ask your youngsters what all of the items have in common. Lead them to discover that the items all came from apples. Then invite students to discuss what they know about apples. *observing, comparing, hypothesizing, communicating*

An Unusual Apple Tree

Youngsters will learn a crop of information in this unit, so record your apple discoveries on a display that shows off what they know! Mount a large tree cutout on a wall in your classroom. After completing each investigation on page 15, discuss the results with your class. Write students' conclusions on apple cutouts and place them on the tree. As your students' knowledge ripens, so will this apple tree display! *recording information*

Some red apples are sweet.

All apples have seeds.

Apples float in water!

Apple peels are hard to chew.

Apple seeds are in the middle of the apple.

Some red apples are sour.

Peel Appeal

To prepare for this activity, gather two apples of the same variety. Peel one apple and save a portion of the peel. During group time, show students the two apples and have them discuss the similarities and differences. Lead your little ones to notice that one apple is missing the peel; then pass around the peel for students to examine. Next, have each child taste a peeled apple piece and then an unpeeled apple piece. Invite your youngsters to discuss the differences in taste and texture; then record their discoveries as directed in "An Unusual Apple Tree" (see page 14). *observing, comparing, communicating*

Red, Ripe Apples

Red is a sure sign that an apple is ripe. But do all red apples taste the same? Invite youngsters to discover the answer with this activity. To prepare, gather a variety of red apples, such as Red Delicious, McIntosh, and Rome Beauty. Set aside one of each type for students to examine. Slice the remaining apples for students to taste.

To begin the activity, have a small group of students examine the whole apples. Lead students to discover that all of the apples are red. Ask your youngsters if they think all of the apples will taste the same; then have each child taste each type of apple. Your little ones may be surprised to discover that the apples taste very different! After discussing the results, place students' conclusions on the apple display. (See "An Unusual Apple Tree" on page 14.) *observing, comparing, classifying, hypothesizing, communicating*

Floating Apples

Try this apple adaptation of the classic sink-or-float investigation. Invite a small group of students to your water table. Discuss the concepts of *sink* and *float.* Then place two objects in the water: one that will sink and one that will float. Allow students time to examine the objects; then ask your little ones if they think apples will sink or float. Provide each child with a small apple and have her place it in the water. Record the investigation results as directed in "An Unusual Apple Tree" on page 14. *observing, hypothesizing, testing, communicating*

Seed Study

Stir up some apple excitement with this seed study. Slice an apple in half to expose the seeds. Have a small group of students use plastic magnifying lenses to examine the apple. Lead your youngsters to discover the seeds in the apple; then ask each child if he thinks all apples have seeds. Next, divide students into pairs. Provide each pair with a different type of apple. Cut the apple in half and then give each child in the pair one half. Have him examine the apple for seeds and then count any seeds he finds. After the investigation, record students' conclusions on the display. (See "An Unusual Apple Tree" on page 14.) *observing, hypothesizing, counting*

Preschoolers in the Spotlight!

Learn all about your preschoolers with this self-esteem unit, which will make each of your youngsters feel like a star. Ready? Lights, camera, action!

ideas contributed by LeeAnn Collins—Director, Sunshine House Preschool, Lansing, MI

Introducing...

Ask any savvy star—at large gatherings, introductions are a must! So get your group acquainted with this activity. In advance, photocopy the stage pattern on page 19 to make a class supply. Cut out each one and then write a parent note similar to the one shown. Send the note and stage home with each child. After each stage has been completed and returned, mount it on a bulletin board titled "The Stars of [your name]'s Class." Each day during group time, remove one or two stages from the display. Invite the children featured on those stages to stand while you introduce them to the class. Ladies and gentlemen! Introducing…

Dear Parents,
We are beginning a unit called "Preschoolers in the Spotlight!" Enclosed you will find a stage pattern. Please take a few moments with your preschooler and complete the stage with information about your little one. Then have your child draw a self-portrait in the middle of the page. We will hang the completed stages on a bulletin board in our classroom, and each day one or two students will be spotlighted. Thanks for your help!

Names in Lights

Every aspiring star longs to see her name in lights. So give youngsters a taste of superstardom with this name-recognition activity. To prepare, help each child write her name on a strip of construction paper. Then have her glue yellow construction paper lights around the edges. Next, have the child use a gold-glitter glue pen to decorate the lights. If desired, add a photograph of the child to the strip to help her recognize her name. Mount the strips on a wall or bulletin board.

To begin the activity, gather your youngsters in front of the display. Play some lively music and dim the lights in your classroom. Shine a flashlight on a child's name, read the name, and have her stand up as the class cheers. Continue in this manner until each child has had a chance to see her name in lights. Bravo!

Hands in Cement

A handprint in cement is a true sign of stardom! So invite your rising stars to make handprints using a cement substitute—Crayola Model Magic modeling compound. To make one print, help a child use a rolling pin to flatten a ball of Model Magic compound. Be sure the flattened ball is thick enough to make a deep print. Have the child press his hand in the modeling compound to leave a print. When the compound is dry, use a permanent marker to label it with the child's name. Then invite the child to use glitter pens and paint to decorate the area surrounding his print. Set all of the prints at a center. Then let your little ones have a ball examining the prints, comparing them, and trying them on for size. What a perfect opportunity to discuss concepts such as *bigger, smaller,* and *same!*

Hollywood Walk of Fame

Your preschool stars will be thrilled to give their very first interviews with this unique movement activity. In advance, obtain a working microphone or make a pretend one by taping a Styrofoam ball to a paper towel tube. Next, cut out a large star shape from bulletin board paper and then laminate it. Have your youngsters stand in a circle; then tape the star to the floor between two children. Play some marching music and direct your youngsters to walk around the circle. Stop the music and have students stand still. Hand the microphone to the child standing on the star and encourage her to say a few things about herself, such as her favorite food, a place she likes to visit, or something she has learned to do. When she has finished her interview, begin the activity again.

Tickets to Stardom

Just how do your little stars measure up? Find out with this measurement activity. In advance, purchase a large roll of raffle tickets (available at party supply stores). Use the tickets to measure the height of each child; then cut off the length of tickets equivalent to his height. Write his name on the tickets and then tape them to a wall so that the bottom edge touches the floor. Mount the tickets in sequence according to height; then gather students together to examine and discuss the ticket display. Be sure to save the tickets on the display and then measure each child again at the end of the year. My, how you've grown!

Applause! Applause!

How are your youngsters special? Help them remember with a song that builds self-esteem! Have students stand as directed in the song; then have the standing stars receive a round of applause. What should your little ones do while receiving the applause? Bow, blow kisses, and say, "Thank you!" of course!

(sung to the tune of "Mary Had a Little Lamb")

[Brown-haired stars], please stand up now.
Stand up now. Stand up now.
[Brown-haired stars], please stand up now.
This song is just for you!

Sing additional verses, replacing the underlined words with other phrases, such as *blue-eyed stars, four-year-olds, little girls,* or *little boys.*

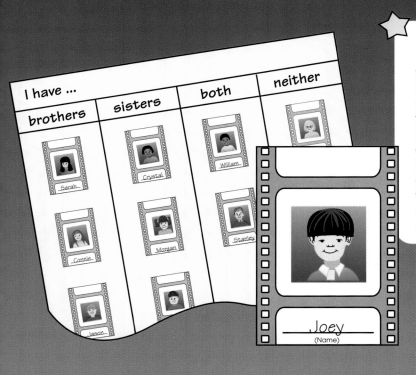

Film Shoot

Family graphing—take 1! Learn which of your youngsters have brothers and sisters with this unique graph. In advance, duplicate the pattern on page 20 to make a class supply. Cut out each pattern. Glue a child's photograph in the center. Write his name on the pattern and then laminate it for durability. Next, use bulletin board paper to make a large graph similar to the one shown. Provide each child with his filmstrip and invite him to tape it onto the graph to show the children in his family. After each child has had a turn, discuss what the graph reveals.

Superstar Sorting

This sorting activity gets two thumbs-up! To prepare, follow the directions in "Film Shoot" to make another set of filmstrips with photographs. Place the photographs in an area and invite students to sort them by hair color, eye color, and gender.

That's a Wrap!

What's the perfect way to wrap up your superstar studies? Show a movie starring your little preschoolers! Videotape students engaged in various activities, and also film individual shots of each child. Then have a movie premiere and show the completed video. Hey, you ought to be in pictures!

Spotlighting Me!

Name _____

I am _____ years old.

My birthday is _____.

My hair is _____.

My eyes are _____.

I like to eat _____.

I can _____.

©The Education Center, Inc. • *THE MAILBOX®* • *Preschool* • Aug/Sept 2001

Filmstrip Pattern
Use with "Film Shoot" and "Superstar Sorting" on page 18.

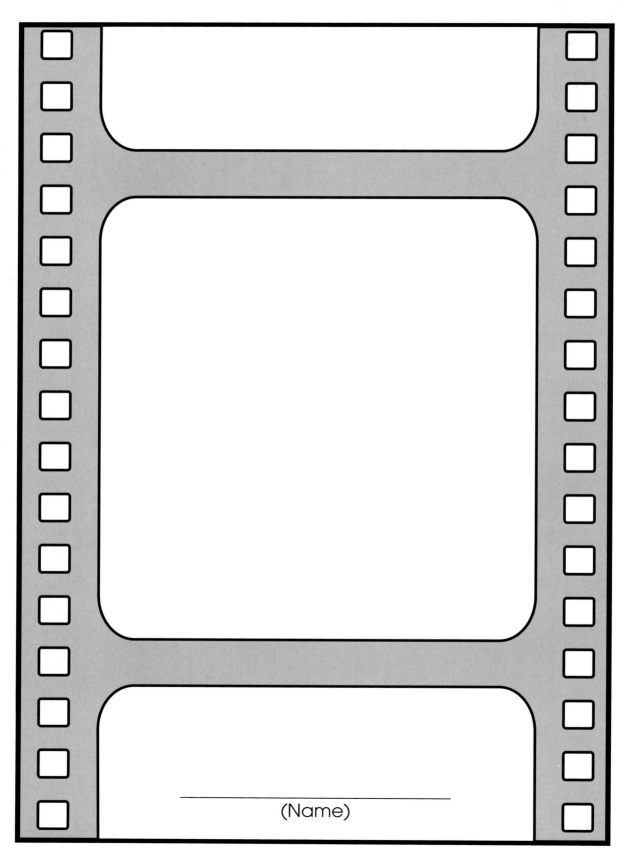

_____
(Name)

©The Education Center, Inc. • _THE MAILBOX_® • _Preschool_ • Aug/Sept 2001

A Closetful of Colorful Monster Ideas

Use these friendly monster ideas to help teach your preschoolers all about colors. Your little ones will be experts before you can say "Boo!"

Group Time

There Are Monsters in Here!

Youngsters will be tickled pink when you begin your color study with this amusing monster hunt. In advance, photocopy the patterns on page 26 to create nine monsters. Color the monsters the same color. Laminate them and then cut out each one. Before students arrive in the morning, hide the monsters around your classroom. Then begin your group time by singing the first verse of the song shown. Invite students to find the hidden monsters and then bring them back to the circle. Display the monsters. Count them with your youngsters and then sing the second verse of the song. For an added challenge, hide several sets of monsters in different colors. Sing the song and have students find only the colored monsters mentioned in the song.

(sung to the tune of "Ten Little Indians")

One [red], two [red], three [red] monsters.
Four [red], five [red], six [red] monsters.
Seven [red], eight [red], nine [red] monsters.
Find where they're hiding right now!

One [red], two [red], three [red] monsters.
Four [red], five [red], six [red] monsters.
Seven [red], eight [red], nine [red] monsters.
We found where they were hiding!

Cele McCloskey, Head Start of York County, York, PA

Movement

Monster Movements

To prepare for this musical monster activity, cut out large construction paper monster feet in a variety of colors. Be sure each foot is large enough for one or two children to stand on. Laminate the feet and then tape each one to the floor of your circle time area. Play a lively musical selection, such as "The Monster Mash," and invite students to dance to the music. Stop the music. Call out a color and direct each child to stand on a footprint in that color. Those monsters sure do have big feet!

Angie Kutzer
Burlington, NC

Five Little Monsters

Thrill your youngsters with this monster mitt and poem! To make a mitt, gather five pom-poms in five different colors. Glue a pair of wiggle eyes to each pom-pom and then use self-adhesive Velcro to attach them to an old glove as shown. During your group time, slip on the monster mitt and begin reciting the poem below. Five little monsters…

Five little monsters sitting on the floor.
The [red] one said, "Let's knock on someone's door."
The [green] one said, "Let's act a little scary."
The [white] one said, "Why are we so hairy?"
The [blue] one said, "I hear a funny sound."
The [pink] one said, "There's no one else around."
Then "WOOSH" went the wind and "EEK!" someone said.
So five little monsters ran under the bed.

craft idea by
Lori Burrow, Meridian, CA

Purple Hair, Yellow Eyes…

If you could make a monster, what would it look like? Use this small-group activity as a stand-alone idea or as a follow-up to Ed Emberley's book *Go Away Big Green Monster!* To prepare, use different-colored permanent markers to draw a monster face outline and monster features, each on a separate overhead transparency (as shown). Set up an overhead projector and place the monster face transparency on it. Invite each child in the group to choose a feature and place it on the projector. When the face is complete, review the different-colored features on the monster. Then remove the features from the projector one by one. Bye-bye purple hair!

Angie Kutzer
Burlington, NC

This Monster Says...

Identifying colors will be a scream with this lively song and activity! In advance, duplicate the monster patterns on page 26 to create a class supply. Have each child color a monster one color and then tape a craft stick to the back of it. During circle time, invite a child to show his monster stick puppet to the group. Have the class identify the color; then encourage your youngsters to join the monster in singing the song shown. (For the colors purple, yellow, and orange, sing the variation.) After singing the last line, invite the child to tell the class what his monster says. Continue the activity until each child has had a chance to show off his monster. Boo!

(sung to the tune of "Alouette")

I'm a monster.
I'm a big [blue] monster.
I'm a monster.
And this is what I say…

Variation:
I'm a monster.
I'm a [purple] monster.
I'm a monster.
And this is what I say…

Fingerpainting, Monster Style

It's true! Monsters love fingerpainting just as much as preschoolers do! So invite your youngsters to try this color-mixing activity—the monster way. To make one monster masterpiece, invite a child to wear a set of plastic monster fingertips or fingernails (available at party supply stores). Provide the child with a sheet of fingerpaint paper and two spoonfuls of fingerpaint that will blend to make another color. Drop the paint onto the paper and direct the child to use her monster fingers to mix the colors together. What fiendish fun!

adapted from an idea by
Lori Burrow
Meridian, CA

The Better to See You With!

What's the best part of a great big monster? His great big eyes! Create a set of monster-eye manipulatives by painting different-colored irises on Ping-Pong balls. When the paint is dry, invite students to sort the eyes by color into clean, empty egg cartons. The eyes have it!

Lori Burrow
Meridian, CA

Monster Cutups

This small-group activity reinforces color recognition, body-part recognition, and following directions. In advance, make different-colored copies of the monster pattern on page 27. Laminate the monsters and then cut apart each one on the bold lines. Set the patterns at a center and invite three children to the area. To begin the activity, direct each child to find a different-colored monster part. For example, ask one child to find blue feet, one child to find a yellow body, and one child to find a green head. Then have the group work together to assemble the colorful creature. When students are familiar with this activity, invite a pair of children to use the center independently. Have one child give directions to the other child; then have them switch roles. "Make a monster with purple feet, a green body, and an orange head!"

Ada Goren
Winston-Salem, NC

Furry Findings

Dogs and cats aren't the only ones that shed. Monsters do, too! Invite your youngsters to clean up after these critters with this color-matching idea. To prepare, duplicate the monster patterns on page 26. Color each monster a different color. Cut out the monsters and then glue each one onto a small paper bag. Place the bags near your sensory table; then fill the table with rice and lengths of yarn in the same colors as the monsters. Direct each child to sift through the rice to find lengths of "monster fur." Then have him place the fur in the matching monster bag. These monsters aren't scary—they're hairy!

Roxanne Dearman
North Carolina School for the Deaf
Charlotte, NC

Monsters Lay Eggs, Too!

Color-matching skills will be hatching at this fine-motor center. To prepare, gather several plastic Easter eggs in a variety of colors. Next, make a matching monster for each egg by gluing wiggle eyes and felt features to a large pom-pom. Set the monsters and eggs at a center; then invite your youngsters to place each monster inside the matching egg.

adapted from an idea by
Roxanne Dearman
Charlotte, NC

Color Tracking

Keep track of which colors your youngsters have mastered with this assessment idea. To begin, duplicate the award on page 28 for each child. Program each award with a different child's name; then place the awards in an easily accessible location. Each time a child learns a new color, invite him to color the appropriate monster on his award. When the child has mastered all of the colors, encourage him to take the award home to show his family what he knows. Daddy and "Mummy" will be so proud!

purple orange
brown
black

Hooray!

Taylor

white knows all of these colors! blue

yellow red

I Scream Sundaes

Learning all those colors is a monstrous task! So wrap up your color unit by treating each child to a monster's favorite snack—an I Scream Sundae! To make one, place a scoop of lime sherbet in a plastic bowl. Add a squirt of whipped cream. Then top the sundae with some colored sprinkles and a Gummy worm. Have each child identify the colors in her sundae and then invite her to dig in. There's nothing scary about this snack, but it _will_ give your youngsters the chills!

Lori Burrow
Meridian, CA

Monster Patterns

Use with "There Are Monsters in Here!" on page 21,
"This Monster Says…" on page 23, and "Furry Findings" on page 24.

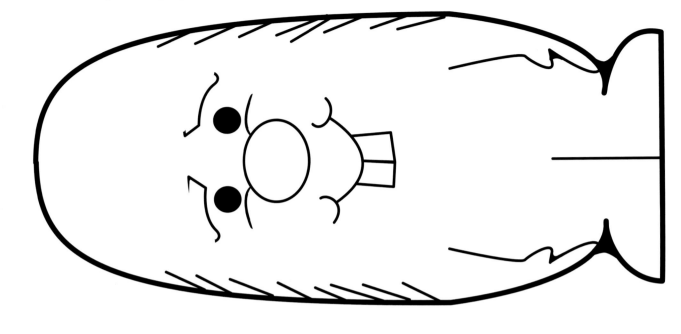

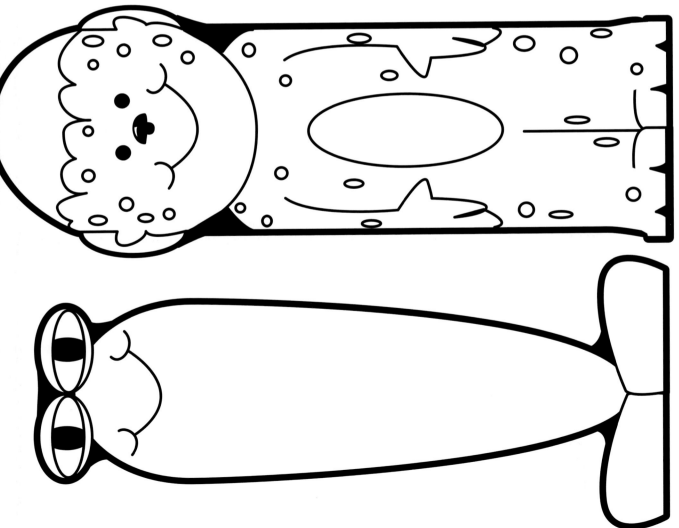

 ©The Education Center, Inc. • *THE MAILBOX®* • Preschool • Oct/Nov 2001

purple

orange

brown

black

Hooray!

_____

knows all of these colors!

white

blue

yellow

red

green

pink

©The Education Center, Inc. • THE MAILBOX® • Preschool • Oct/Nov 2001

Note to the teacher: Use with "Color Tracking" on page 25.

'Twas the Night Before...

Christmas, Hanukkah, and Kwanzaa! With all the hustle and bustle, the holidays must be around the corner! So use the ideas on the following pages to introduce your little ones to a variety of seasonal symbols, treats, and traditions. Happy holidays!

ideas contributed by Lucia Kemp Henry and Suzanne Moore

Christmas

Invite your youngsters to participate in these Christmas preparations and they're sure to learn a "ho, ho, ho" lot!

Center Idea

The Stockings Were Hung by the Chimney With Care

Hanging stockings is a sure sign that Christmas is fast approaching! With this idea, your youngsters will get into the spirit of the season while developing spatial-reasoning and fine-motor skills. Place three self-adhesive hooks on a wall in a center. Set three different-sized stockings in the area along with toys in various sizes. Invite your little ones to discover which toys will fit into which stockings; then have them hang the stockings on the hooks. Encourage older students to hang the stockings in sequence from smallest to largest. It's beginning to look a lot like Christmas!

Craft

Oh, Christmas Tree!

The celebration of Christmas wouldn't be complete without a decorated tree. Use this craft idea and invite each child to create a miniature tree of her own. To make one, use pinking shears to cut out two four-inch-tall green tagboard tree shapes. Sandwich a craft stick by taping it to one shape and then gluing the other shape on top of it as shown. Invite a child to decorate the tagboard tree with holiday stickers, sticky dots, and glitter glue. When the glue is dry, help the child insert the craft stick into a Styrofoam ball half. Display your youngsters' trees on a table; then add cotton batting around the base of each tree to create a winter wonderland.

A Great Gift Idea!

After hanging stockings and setting up a tree, one more thing is a must for Christmas—presents! Invite each child to create a holiday candleholder to give to a special someone. To make one, pour one-third cup of dried red beans and one-third cup of dried peas into a 16-ounce plastic container. Mix the beans and peas together; then stir in one tablespoon of white glue. Next, cover the bottom of a 2" x 4" pillar candle with plastic wrap and press it into the mixture so that it forms a ring around the candle. Allow the mixture to dry overnight. Remove the candle and plastic wrap. Pop the bean mixture out of the container and the candleholder is complete!

Cookies for Santa

One of the most important Christmas preparations is making sure a snack is available for jolly ol' St. Nick! Set up this center and have students prepare plates of craft-foam cookies for Santa. Place a large and a small paper plate at a center. Then cut out and decorate large and small craft-foam gingerbread cookies. Place the cookies in a container and set it at the center along with the plates. Invite each child to sort the cookies by size onto the appropriate plate. For added learning fun, set some crayons and paper near the center and encourage youngsters to write a note to Mr. Claus. Cookies and a note for Santa! No wonder he's so jolly!

Reindeer Toast

Santa's eight reindeer work hard on Christmas Eve. So invite each child to salute Rudolph and company by making a reindeer toast! To make one, toast a piece of bread; then spread peanut butter over it. Use a plastic knife to cut the bread and arrange the pieces as shown. Then add two raisin eyes, a maraschino cherry nose, and pretzel stick antlers. With this snack idea, you're likely to hear little ones saying, "Excuse me, I'd like to make a toast…."

...Hanukkah

Your youngsters will be all aglow as they participate in these Hanukkah-themed activities.

Group Activity

Hanukkah Is Here!

To prepare for this circle-time activity, follow the directions in "Lovely Lights" (below) to create a class menorah. Assemble the menorah without the paper flames; then display it in your circle-time area. To begin the activity, place a paper flame in the *shammash* and sing the song shown. Then provide a child with a paper flame and direct him to place it in the first candle. At the end of the day, remove the flames from the candles. Repeat the activity the following day, adding one more flame and singing the song accordingly. Continue the activity each day until all eight candles are lit. On certain days, light more than one candle for those days when students will not be in school.

*The **shammash** is the tallest candle on the menorah and is used to light the other candles.*

(sung to the tune of "For He's a Jolly Good Fellow")

It's time to light the candles.
It's time to light the candles.
It's time to light the candles,
For Hannukah is here!

For Hannukah is here!
For Hannukah is here!
It's time to light the candles,
For Hannukah is here!

Let's light [one] pretty candle(s).
Let's light [one] pretty candle(s).
Let's light [one] pretty candle(s),
For this special time of year!

Center Idea

Lovely Lights

One cup, one candle, one flame. Reinforce one-to-one correspondence with this center idea that has youngsters assembling a pretend menorah. To prepare, use the pattern on page 36 to make nine construction paper flames. Paint eight toilet paper tubes blue. To make the shammash, cut a paper towel tube in half and paint one of the halves blue. When the paint is dry, place each tube inside a nine-ounce paper cup wrapped in foil. To make a menorah, line up the cups as shown with the shammash in the middle. Invite students to light the menorah by placing one flame inside each tube. For older students, separate the cups, candles, and flames. Then direct them to assemble the menorah by placing a tube in each cup and a flame in each tube.

Love Those Latkes!

Potato latkes are a traditional Hanukkah treat. Try this simplified recipe and give your youngsters a taste of Jewish tradition.

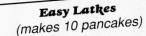

Easy Latkes
(makes 10 pancakes)

Ingredients:

2 c. packed frozen shredded hash browns
3 eggs, beaten
1 tbsp. flour

1 tbsp. plain bread crumbs
1 tsp. salt
$1/2$ c. oil

Spread the hash browns on a clean cutting board to thaw. Pat the thawed hash browns dry with a paper towel. Mix the hash browns, eggs, flour, bread crumbs, and salt in a bowl. In a large skillet over medium heat, heat the oil until hot. Drop tablespoons of the mixture into the oil; then gently press them with a spatula to make $1/4$-inch-thick pancakes. Brown the pancakes on one side; then flip them over and brown the other side. Drain the pancakes on paper towels. If desired, serve with applesauce or sour cream.

On the Hunt for Hanukkah Gifts

Eight days of Hanukkah means eight small gifts for little ones! Stir up a little excitement at your sensory table by filling it with Styrofoam packing pieces and then hiding eight small gift wrapped boxes in the table. Invite your youngsters to search for the boxes and then sort them by size, wrapping paper, or bows. Or program each box with a different number from 1 to 8 and have students place the boxes in numerical order. There are a whole lot of learning opportunities wrapped up in this center!

Gelt Guessing

Gelt, the Yiddish word for money, also refers to chocolate coins that many children receive during Hanukkah. This estimation activity has students preparing pretend sacks of gelt for the giving! In advance, make several yellow copies of the gelt patterns on page 36. Laminate the patterns. Cut them out and then place a self-adhesive magnetic strip on the back of each one. Next, photocopy the sack patterns on page 37. Cut out the sacks and then tape them onto a magnetic board or a cookie sheet. Place the coins around the sacks; then display the board in your circle-time area. To begin the activity, invite students to guess how many coins will fit onto the smallest sack. Place the coins on the sack and then count them with your youngsters. Continue in this manner with the medium-sized sack and the large sack. After completing the activity, open up a real sack of Hanukkah gelt and treat each child to a tasty gold foil–wrapped chocolate coin. Happy Hanukkah!

...Kwanzaa

This colorful collection of Kwanzaa ideas is just right for a preschool celebration!

Group Activity

The Colors of Kwanzaa

Use this group activity to help youngsters become familiar with the traditional colors of Kwanzaa—red, black, and green. To begin, teach youngsters the song below. Then provide each child with a red, black, or green streamer. After naming a Kwanzaa color, have students with that color streamer sing the song and wave their streamers in the air. Continue the activity until all the colors of Kwanzaa have been named.

(sung to the tune of "Jingle Bells")

Colors bold, colors bright
Shine this time of year!
The color [black] is all around,
For Kwanzaa time is here!

Repeat, replacing the underlined word in turn with *red* and *green*.

Display

Umoja Means "Unity"

One of the principles of Kwanzaa is *umoja* (oo-MOH-jah) or unity. Invite little hands to unite and create a class Kwanzaa flag. To prepare, place shallow pans of black, green, and red paint on a newspaper-covered table. Have each child make several handprints in each color on a large sheet of bulletin board paper as shown. When the paint is dry, display the completed flag in your classroom as a festive reminder of umoja.

Kwanzaa Candles

Mishumaa (mee-SHOO-mah) are the seven candles of Kwanzaa. The red, black, and green candles are arranged in a distinct pattern on the *kinara,* the Kwanzaa candleholder. Set up this center to help your youngsters become familiar with the mishumaa and also to reinforce visual-discrimination and color-matching skills. In advance, collect seven toilet paper tubes. Paint three tubes red, three tubes green, and one tube black. When the paint is dry, tape a construction paper flame to the inside of each painted tube so that it resembles a candle. Display a color picture of a kinara at the center; then set the candles near the picture. Invite each child to use the picture to guide him as he places the Kwanzaa candles in the proper pattern.

Sesame Sweets

Benne cakes are a popular Kwanzaa treat with a special ingredient for good luck—sesame seeds! If you have a parent who enjoys baking, enlist his help in making these tasty treats for your students to sample.

Benne Cakes
(makes approximately 24 cakes)

Ingredients:

nonstick cooking spray
1 c. brown sugar
1/4 c. softened butter
1 beaten egg
1/2 tsp. vanilla

1 tsp. lemon juice
1/2 c. flour
1/2 tsp. baking powder
1/4 tsp. salt
3/4 c. sesame seeds

Preheat the oven to 325°. Lightly oil the cookie sheet. Mix brown sugar and butter until creamy. Stir in the egg, vanilla, and lemon juice. Then mix in the remaining ingredients. Drop the batter by rounded teaspoons about two inches apart on a cookie sheet. Bake for about 15 minutes or until the edges are browned.

A Gift of Corn

In Kwanzaa tradition, ears of corn are symbolic of children; one ear represents one child.

Kwanzaa gifts, called *zawadi,* are often handmade. Invite each child to create a crafty ear of corn to give to a special someone. To make one, press orange paint fingerprints onto a 4" x 1 1/2" yellow craft-foam corn shape. When the paint is dry, glue several dried kernels onto the shape. Next, glue a few small crepe paper pieces to the end of a jumbo craft stick. Then use craft glue to attach the stick to the back of the corn so the crepe paper resembles the husk. Place a self-adhesive magnetic strip on the stick and the gift is complete!

Flame Pattern
Use with "Hanukkah Is Here!" and "Lovely Lights" on page 32.

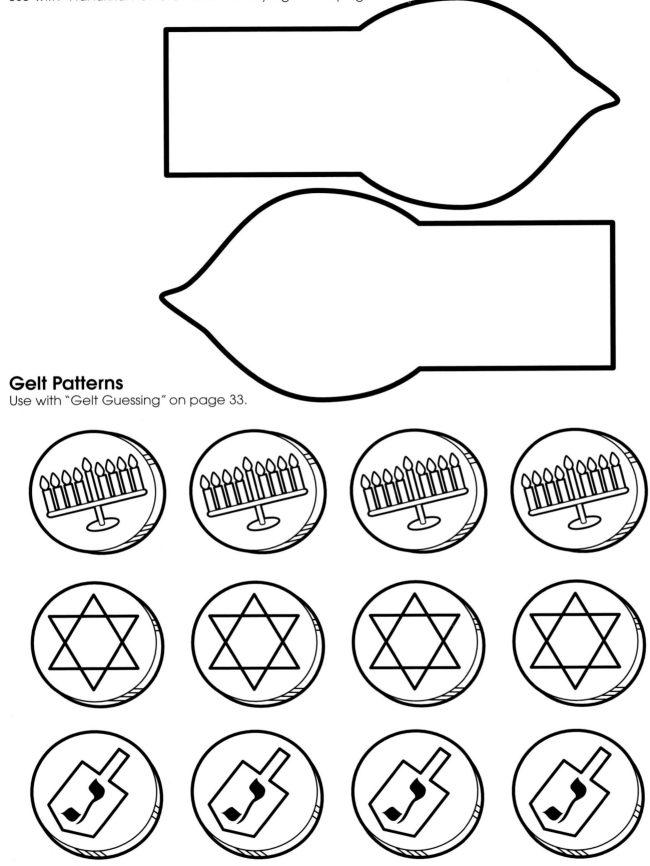

Gelt Patterns
Use with "Gelt Guessing" on page 33.

©The Education Center, Inc. · THE MAILBOX® · Preschool · Dec/Jan 2001–2

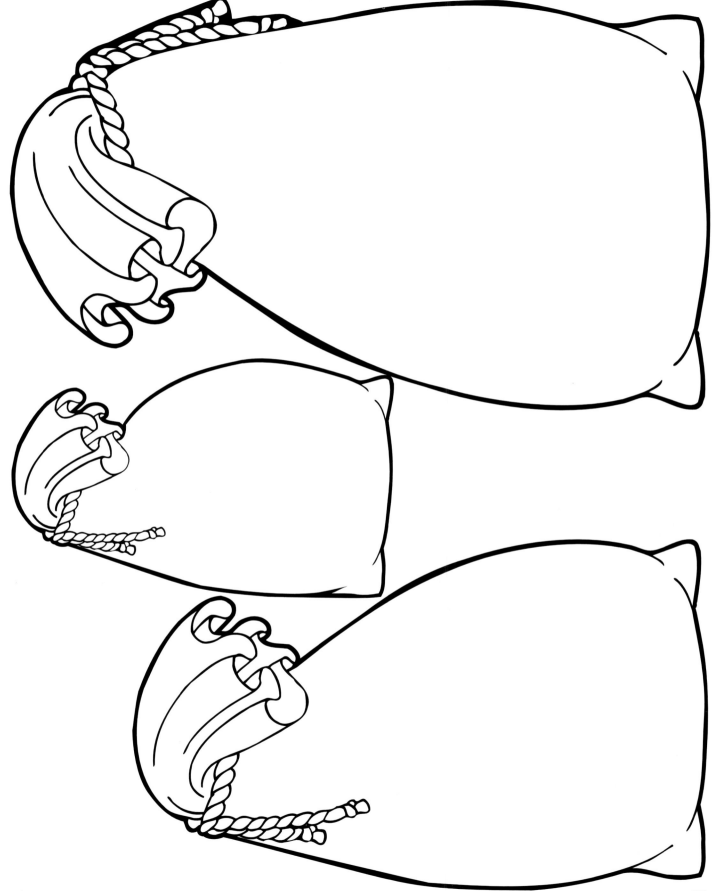

Weather Wise

"Who-ooo" knows about the weather? Your little ones will after you share the fun ideas and activities in this unit!

by Ada Goren

Weather Wear

Begin your weather unit with a sorting activity that will get your students thinking about what they wear in different types of weather. To prepare, label three boxes as shown. Gather a variety of children's clothing and accessories appropriate for the three types of weather.

Set up the three boxes in your group area. Show youngsters one item at a time and ask a child to place it in the box that shows the corresponding type of weather. Talk about why the various items are worn or used in each type of weather. After the sorting is finished, place the items in your dramatic-play area for youngsters to use independently.

hot ☀   cold ❄   rainy 💧

Storytime

Reading Up a Storm

The forecast calls for good books galore at storytime! Add to your weather theme by donning sunglasses, a rain hat, or a pair of woolly mittens as you share some of these selections!

It's Raining, It's Pouring
By Kin Eagle

What Can You Do in the Rain?
What Can You Do in the Sun?
What Can You Do in the Snow?
All by Anna Grossnickle Hines

What's the Weather Today?
By Allan Fowler

Rain
By Robert Kalan

The Wind Blew
By Pat Hutchins

The Snowy Day
By Ezra Jack Keats

We like the sun.
It's lots of fun!

We like the snow.
It's cool, you know!

We like raindrops.
We think they're tops!

Picture-Perfect Weather

Different people enjoy different types of weather. What kind of weather do *your* students like best? Find out when you create this display, which doubles as a weather-preference chart. Begin by dividing a bulletin board into three sections. Label each section with the weather icon and rhyme shown. Next, gather a pair of sunglasses, a pair of mittens and a scarf, and a child's umbrella. Ask one child at a time to tell you which of the three types of weather she likes best. Then take an instant photo of her dressed for that weather. After everyone has voted, post the photos in the appropriate sections of the bulletin board. Gather your little ones around to view the photos. As a class, count the number of children who prefer each type of weather. What's the favorite weather in your classroom?

Weather Wheels

Is the weather outside frightful or delightful? Your young weather watchers can make a daily report to their families with the help of these weather wheels. To prepare, duplicate page 42 to make a class supply. Have a child color the wedges on his copy as desired before cutting them out. Direct him to glue the four wedges to a white paper plate as shown. Then help him cut out the arrow and attach it to the center of the plate with a metal brad. Encourage little ones to take their weather wheels home and post them in a prominent place. Each day, a child can report on the weather he observes by pointing the arrow to the corresponding section on the wheel.

Weather Tunes

Start each day of your weather unit with a sing-along! These kid-friendly ditties cover the weather from sunny to stormy, and the motions and special effects will have your weather watchers wiggling and giggling!

Sunshine
(sung to the tune of "You Are My Sunshine")

Outside there's sunshine.	*Use arms to form circle sun overhead.*
There's lots of sunshine.	*Use arms to form circle sun overhead.*
And not a cloud in	
The sky so blue!	*Shade eyes and look upward.*
So let's go outside!	*Point thumb toward door.*
Let's not stay inside!	*Shake index finger "no."*
I'll spend my sunny days with you!	*Point to self, then others.*

Pam Crane

Do You Love the Snow?
(sung to the tune of "Do Your Ears Hang Low?")

Do you love the snow?	*Put both hands over heart.*
You can play in it, you know!	*Point to others.*
You can make a big snowball	*Use both hands to form big circle.*
Or a snowman really tall!	*Indicate "tall" with one hand.*
You can travel on your skis,	*Pretend to grip ski poles and move hips.*
Make an angel if you please!	*Wave both arms as if making snow angel.*
Do you love the snow?	*Put both hands over heart.*

Lightning and Thunder

Give each child a flashlight and an aluminum pie pan to use for the sight and sound effects in this song. Dim your classroom lights to get the stormy mood just right!

(sung to the tune of "If You're Happy and You Know It")

Can you see the lightning flashing in the sky?	*Flick flashlight on and off.*
Can you see the lightning flashing in the sky?	*Flick flashlight on and off.*
Can you see the lightning flash? Then it's followed by a crash!	*Bang hand against pie pan.*
Can you see the lightning flashing in the sky?	*Flick flashlight on and off.*

I Love Windy Weather
(sung to the tune of "I'm a Little Teapot")

I love windy weather!	*Put both hands over heart.*
See it blow.	*Shade eyes and look around.*
Watch the trees move to and fro.	*Put both arms up and sway body.*
Feel it on my face and in my hair.	*Touch hands to face, then hair.*
How I love that playful air!	*Put both hands over heart.*

41

Weather Wheel Patterns

Use with "Weather Wheels" on page 39.

sunny

snowy

rainy

cloudy

©The Education Center, Inc. • *THE MAILBOX®* • *Preschool* • Oct/Nov 2001

Snap!
Button!
Z-z-z-i-p!

Looking for a way to help your little ones dress for success? With this collection of ideas, teaching self-help skills will be a snap…and a button…and a zipper!

ideas by Lucia Kemp Henry

Jackets Required

Buttons, zippers, snaps. So many types of fasteners! Help your students sort it all out with this circle-time activity that involves their own jackets and coats. To begin, invite each child to put on his jacket and come to the circle. Discuss why we should keep our coats buttoned, zipped, or snapped in chilly weather. Have each child identify the type of fastener on his jacket; then let the sorting begin! Place three large Hula-Hoop toys on the floor. Or use lengths of yarn to make three large circles. Designate one circle for zippers, one for buttons, and one for snaps. Direct students to sort themselves by fasteners and stand in the appropriate circle. Then count the number of children in each group. "Fasten-ating"!

Laundry Learning Center

To prepare for this center, gather a supply of baby clothes with a variety of snaps, buttons, and zippers. (Ask parents for donations, or check thrift stores and yard sales.) Wash the clothes and then place them in a laundry basket. Place the basket in a center along with a variety of stuffed animals that will fit into the clothes. Invite each child to put the clothing on the animals and then fasten the zippers, buttons, or snaps. To add a little zip to this activity, invite each child to sing "A Snappy Song" (page 44) as she works.

A Snappy Song

What's the best way to refine those self-help skills? Practice, practice, practice! So invite your youngsters to act out this lively tune and get those little fingers snapping, buttoning, and zipping!

(sung to the tune of "Down by the Station")

Chorus:
Snap, button, zipper,
See them on my clothing!
I can button, snap, and zip
All by myself!

See how I can zip up
All the little zippers.
Zip, zip! Zip, zip!
Off I go!

Repeat Chorus

See how I can snap up
All the little snappies.
Snap, snap! Snap, snap!
Off I go!

Repeat Chorus

See how I can button
All the little buttons.
Button, button! Button, button!
Off I go!

Snap to It!

Snap! Snap! Snap! That's the sound you'll hear at this matching center. In advance, gather a supply of old shirts with snaps. (Check thrift stores, or ask parents for donations.) Snap up each shirt; then cut off the snap plackets. Next, cut each placket into different lengths. Unsnap the plackets and place them in a basket at a center. Invite each child to explore the strips and snap together the different pieces. For older students, have each child match the snaps by fabric design and length. Then have her snap the strips together.

Zip-a-dee-doo-dah!

Jeans, jackets, pocketbooks, pencil pouches. They all have zippers! Stock a center with a variety of zippered items such as these. Then invite youngsters to zip and unzip away! Zip-a-dee-doo-dah! Zip-a-dee-ay! My, oh my, what a wonderful way…to practice zipping!

Mary Lester

Mr. Snowman's Size Seminar

He's an expert on small, medium, and large. So let Mr. Snowman teach your preschoolers about sizes. They'll think he's cool!

by Ada Goren

Snowball Sorting

Every snowman begins with the basics—snowballs. Set up a center where your youngsters sort Styrofoam snowballs by size. Fill a sensory tub or table with three different sizes of Styrofoam balls. Provide three different-sized buckets nearby. Have youngsters drop the small balls into the small bucket, the medium balls into the medium bucket, and the large balls into the large bucket. For an authentic touch, invite the children to wear mittens while they work.

○ large

○ medium

○ small

A Step-by-Step Snowman

It's easy to build a snowman—just listen to the step-by-step instructions! Encourage your youngsters to build their own paper snowmen with these snowman kits. To make one, fill a small plastic bag with the following items: white paper circles in three sizes—small, medium, and large; two craft sticks; two small black pom-poms; one small orange pom-pom; and a black paper hat. Give each child a snowman kit and guide youngsters to first remove the largest paper circle, then the medium one, and then the smallest one. Have them place the circles on the tabletop to form a snowman shape. Ask, "What items in your bag would make good arms? How about eyes? A nose? A hat?" After your students have added all the items to their snowmen, invite them to disassemble them and take their snowman kits home to rebuild for their families.

Cindy Hubbard—PreK, Bunche Early Childhood Development Center, Tulsa, OK   45

Does That Nose Come in a Large?

It takes more than getting the snowballs in the right order to make a really fine snowman—the accessories must be the proper size! Help your little ones match sizes as they dress some snowmen on your flannelboard. To prepare, make three copies of the snowman pattern on page 47: one regular copy, one enlarged by 20 percent, and one reduced by 20 percent. Also make a copy of the snowman accessories on page 48. Cut out the patterns, color the accessories as desired, and prepare all the pieces for use with your flannelboard. Put the three snowman patterns on the board, along with the three nose patterns. Ask student volunteers to match the noses to the snowmen by size. Then continue with the other accessories until all three snowmen are dressed and dapper!

Introducing His Friends, the Flakes

For a poetic lesson in sizes, make a set of Mr. Snowman's friends, the Flakes! Simply laminate three different-sized doilies. Add sticky-dot eyes to each one; then tape on a craft stick handle to turn each doily into a snowflake puppet. Invite three children to stand in front of the group, each holding a puppet, as you recite this poem. As youngsters become more familiar with the poem, invite the puppeteers to recite the speaking parts.

Three white snowflakes, fancy-free,
Each as pretty as could be.
The first one said, "I'm so small—
The smallest snowflake of us all."
The second one said, with a twinkle in his eyes,
"I'm bigger than you. I'm medium size."
The third one said, "Hey, this is fun!
Can you see I'm the biggest one?"
Three white snowflakes in the sky,
Small, medium, and large all say, "Goodbye!"

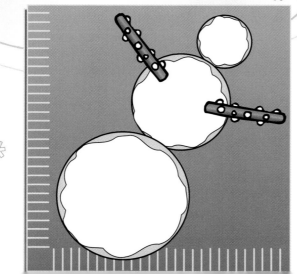

Pam Crane

Snowman Snack

Celebrate your preschoolers' size savvy by having them make a special snack that resembles Mr. Snowman himself! For each snack, you'll need a mini Ritz cracker, a regular Ritz cracker, and a larger round cracker, such as a water cracker. To make the snack, spread soft cream cheese on each of the three crackers; then arrange them on a plate or napkin to resemble a snowman. Break a pretzel stick in half and add one half to each side to make arms. Now he's complete and it's time to eat!

46

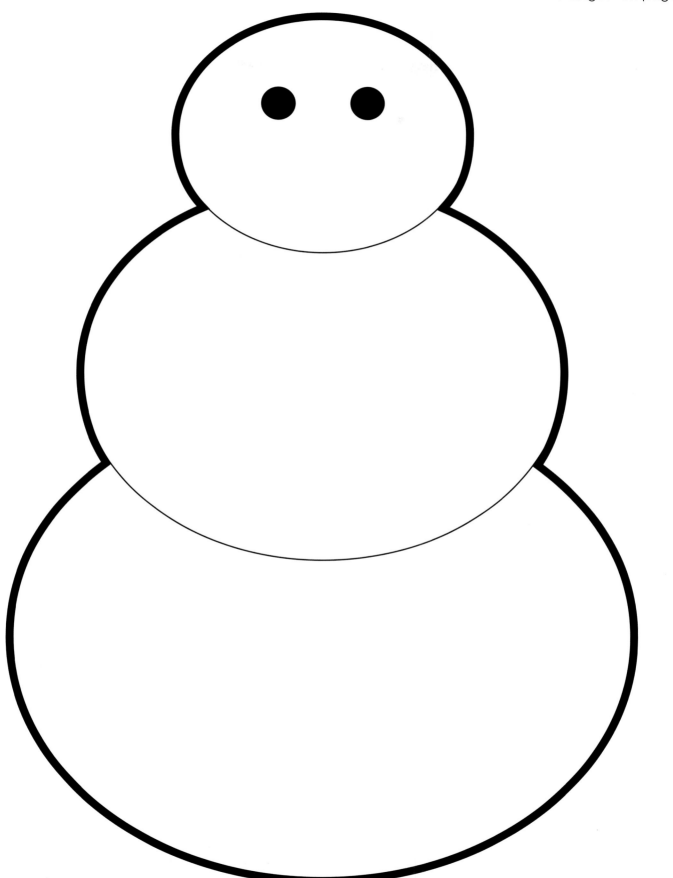

Snowman Accessories

Use with "Does That Nose Come in a Large?" on page 46.

©The Education Center, Inc. • THE MAILBOX® • Preschool • Dec/Jan 2001–2

Celebrating Friendship With Dr. King

Looking for a way to honor civil rights leader Dr. Martin Luther King Jr.? Use these activities to foster friendship among your preschoolers, and on Martin Luther King Jr. Day (January 21), your youngsters will truly have something to celebrate!

ideas by Carol Plaut

Take My Hand

Get your youngsters in the spirit of Martin Luther King Jr. Day with a circle-time activity that also reinforces name recognition. To prepare, laminate a picture of Dr. King and then place a piece of self-adhesive felt on the back of it. Next, label a class supply of felt hand cutouts, each with a different child's name. Give each child her hand cutout; then place the picture of Dr. King on your flannelboard.

To begin the activity, sing the first two lines of the song shown. Have the mentioned child sing the third and fourth lines of the song and place her hand cutout on the flannelboard around the picture of Dr. King. Then invite the class to sing the last four lines of the first verse. Repeat the activity until all of the children's hands have been placed around Dr. King. Then have the class sing the second verse of the song and wish Dr. King a happy birthday!

(sung to the tune of "Are You Sleeping?")

Verse 1

Teacher: Where is [Kayla]'s hand?
Teacher: Where is [Kayla]'s hand?
Student: Here it is!
Student: Here it is!
Class: Let's put our hands together
In fair and stormy weather.
We are friends.
We are friends.

Verse 2

Class: Happy birthday,
Happy birthday,
Dr. King!
Dr. King!
We put our hands together.
We'll honor you forever.
Man of peace.
Man of peace.

One World, Many Faces

Kelli • Sam • Ashley • Kyle • Stephan • Caroline • Tamika • Jan • Drew • Robbie • Natasha • Jackson • Austin • Jamal • Chris • Vickie

We Are the World

Dr. King had a dream that one day all people would be able to live together in peace and harmony. Help your youngsters envision Dr. King's dream by having them make this unique collage of the world. To begin, help students cut out magazine pictures of different faces. Then have them glue the pictures onto a large sheet of bulletin board paper. Direct your youngsters to overlap the pictures so that the entire sheet of paper is covered. When the glue is dry, cut the paper into the shapes of continents. Then glue the continents onto a large blue paper circle to resemble the earth. For added interest, cut out photographs of each child and invite him to blend it into the collage. Display this wonderful world on a bulletin board; then add a title and a personalized handprint of each child. Just look at all the different faces that make up the world!

Swing Your Partner Round and Round

Step right up! This square dance adaptation fosters friendship as your preschoolers discover things that they have in common. In advance, arrange a class supply of chairs, plus a few extra, in a circle. Invite each child to sit in a chair. Next, have students switch seats by giving directions such as "If you have a sister, find a new seat" or "If you like pizza, find a new seat." When your little ones feel confident about switching seats, demonstrate a square dance turn and encourage students to twirl with a partner before sitting in a new seat. Add some lively music and let the friendship dance begin!
Bow to your partner….

Pam Crane

Circle of Friends

Promote peace and love in your classroom with this idea that displays all the friendly gestures your preschoolers demonstrate. In advance, use the pattern on page 52 to create a supply of child cutouts in a variety of colors. When one of your little ones demonstrates an act of kindness, such as sharing a toy or helping another child, write it on a cutout and display it on the wall. Hang the cutouts so that the hands are joined and, before long, you'll notice a circle of friends forming around your classroom!

I'm an Ambassador!

As your celebration winds down, encourage youngsters to continue carrying out Dr. King's dream by naming each child an Ambassador of Goodwill and providing him with a badge. Use the pattern on page 52 to make an ambassador badge for each child. Have an official ceremony and pin a badge onto each child's clothing. Then send your little ambassadors on their first mission and have them complete the activity described in "Good Tidings We Bring!"

Good Tidings We Bring!

This sweet gift is sure to spread love and cheer to the lucky recipients! In advance, ask parents for donations of Hershey's Kisses or Hershey's Hugs. Make a class supply of gift cards similar to the one shown. Help each child sign her name on a card. Punch a hole in the card and thread a length of ribbon through the hole. Next, have the child count out five Kisses and five Hugs. Help her wrap the candy in clear cellophane and tie the ribbon with the card around the top. Have your little ones wear their badges (see "I'm an Ambassador!") and present their gifts of goodwill to staff members or students in another class. Afterward, be sure to treat your youngsters to some Hugs and Kisses of their own! Good work, little ambassadors!

Ambassador of Goodwill

In honor of Martin Luther King,
This gift of love to you I bring:
Lots of Hugs and Kisses!
Sam

Child Pattern
Use with "Circle of Friends" on page 51.

Badge Pattern
Use with "I'm an Ambassador!"
on page 51.

Ambassador
of Goodwill

©The Education Center, Inc. • *THE MAILBOX®* • *Preschool* • Dec/Jan 2001–2

From Poems to Peanuts!

Important Contributions of Black American Citizens

During February, celebrate Black History Month by taking a look at some of the many achievements and contributions made by Black American citizens. From jazz music to poems to peanuts, your preschoolers will enjoy the hands-on interaction they'll get with the following activities!

ideas contributed by Roxanne LaBell Dearman—PreK
North Carolina School for the Deaf, Charlotte, NC

Peanut, Peanut Butter!
George Washington Carver *was a famous scientist who developed over 300 products that could be made using peanuts. Can you imagine lunchboxes without peanut butter sandwiches?*

What goes together as well as peanut butter and jelly? Peanut butter and preschoolers! Use the following recipe to make a batch of peanut butter for your students to sample. Mr. Carver would be proud! *sensory experience*

peanut butter recipe by Linda Anne Lopienski
Asheboro, NC

Be sure to check for student peanut allergies before using the recipe below.

Ingredients:
2 c. roasted, shelled peanuts
2 tsp. oil
1 tsp. sugar

Place the peanuts, oil, and sugar in a blender and blend until smooth. Serve with bread or crackers.

Peanut Butter

Jelly

A Pleasing Poet

Maya Angelou is a famous Black American writer. She has written a children's book, autobiographies, and poems. One of her most famous works is "On the Pulse of Morning," a poem written for President Clinton's inauguration. The poem ends with two simple words, good morning.

Bacon frying. Birds singing. What do your little ones like about the morning? Invite each child to tell what makes her happy in the morning. Write students' responses on a sheet of chart paper to create a class poem; then end the poem with the words *good morning*. Display the poem on a wall or bulletin board and add student-made suns and smiley faces. *creative expression, literacy*

Good Morning!

Eating Toast.
Pancakes.
My mom
wakes me
up.
Yawning.
Stretching.
Good Morning!

Bebop!

*Where would jazz music be today without the influence of saxophone player **Charlie Parker**? His song "A Night in Tunisia" has been labeled the anthem of bebop, a style of jazz music. Check your local library for copies of Parker's recordings. Play samples for students to hear and then complete the following activity.*

Introduce your youngsters to Charlie Parker by reading Chris Raschka's lively book *Charlie Parker Played Be Bop*. With catchy rhythms and unexpected phrases, the text of Raschka's book effectively mimics the sound and style of bebop. After reading the book, play a Charlie Parker selection and invite students to move to the music. Boppity, bippity, bop, bang! *gross-motor skills*

I Scream, You Scream

*In 1897, **Alfred Cralle** invented the ice-cream scoop. Thanks to Mr. Cralle, we can now serve up sundaes lickety-split!*

Celebrate the invention of the scoop at your sand table! In advance, wet the sand in the table to a molding consistency. Place a variety of ice-cream scoops and plastic bowls near the table. Then invite each child to visit the area and scoop up some sandy sundaes! *fine-motor skills, gross-motor skills*

54

Can't Beat the Eggbeater!

Willis Johnson's invention of the eggbeater can't be beat! Just think of all the goodies that can now be made more easily. Thank you, Mr. Johnson!

Get ready for some frothy fun at your water table. In advance, collect several rotary eggbeaters. Place a generous amount of bubble bath in your water table; then invite your preschoolers to use the beaters to whip up some frothy bubbles. As your little ones use the beaters, encourage them to observe the changes occurring in the water and bubble solution. *science observation skills, gross-motor skills*

Red Light, Green Light!

*Credit is given to **Garrett Morgan** for inventing the traffic light. Without this invention, we sure would be in a jam!*

What will this traffic-light activity yield? Color recognition, practice with following directions, and musical expression! To prepare, cut out large red, yellow, and green construction paper circles. Tape each circle onto a jumbo craft stick. After discussing the meaning of each traffic signal, provide each child with a handheld musical instrument. Direct students to play their instruments every time you show the green construction paper circle, slow their playing every time you show the yellow circle, and stop playing every time you show the red circle. *color recognition, following directions, musical expression*

From my rocket I might see a star, a moon, and a planet.

To Infinity and Beyond!

Dr. Mae Jemison *is not your average physician. In 1992, she became the first Black American woman to explore space. The accomplishments of Dr. Jemison are out of this world!*

To prepare for this activity, gather several reference books with pictures of outer space. Then make a class supply of the rocket pattern on page 56. Show your youngsters pictures from the books and discuss what Dr. Jemison might have seen as she explored outer space. Provide each child with a rocket pattern and a $3\frac{1}{2}$" x 8" strip of orange construction paper. Direct the child to glue the orange paper to the bottom edge of the rocket and then cut slits in the paper to create rocket flames. Encourage each child to think of something she might see while exploring space and then draw it on her rocket. Have her dictate a phrase about her illustration; then write her response on the line provided. *fine-motor skills, creative thinking, literacy*

Rocket Pattern

Use with "To Infinity and Beyond!" on page 55.

©The Education Center, Inc. • *THE MAILBOX® • Preschool • Feb/Mar 2002*

UNDER THE BIG TOP

Where's the greatest place on earth to find shapes? At "The Greatest Show on Earth"—the circus! The following high-flying circus activities will have your youngsters shaped up on shapes. So come on everyone! Let's join the circus!

ideas contributed by LeeAnn Collins—Director
Sunshine House Preschool, Lansing, MI

assessment

KEEPING TRACK OF IT ALL

Before beginning the activities in this unit, invite a friendly clown to help you keep track of the skills that each child masters. To prepare, make a class supply of page 63; then label each sheet with a different child's name. As each child masters a skill, color the corresponding ball on her sheet. When all of the balls have been colored, invite the child to color the clown. Photocopy the sheet to keep for your records and then send the colored sheet home with the child.

reciting simple rhymes

LIONS, TIGERS, BEARS!

Oh, my! Open up your circus act by teaching youngsters this call-and-response chant. When students are familiar with this activity, invite a child to recite your lines and lead the group in the chant.

Teacher: Elephants, ponies, and clowns.
Students: At the circus!
Teacher: Acrobats flip up and down.
Students: At the circus!

Teacher: Lions, tigers, and bears.
Students: At the circus!
Teacher: Triangles, circles, and squares.
Students: At the circus!

Teacher: Cotton candy and capes.
Students: At the circus!
Teacher: Let's find some wonderful shapes!
Students: At the circus!

I SPY

Challenge your little ones to spy all the different shapes at the circus with this center idea. In advance, use a photocopier to make copies of the patterns on page 64. Color the patterns. Laminate them and then cut out each one. Set the patterns in the center along with three embroidery hoops to represent circus rings. Or use lengths of yarn to create the rings. Invite each child to find the shape in each pattern and then sort the patterns into the rings by shape.

matching basic shapes
walking heel-to-toe

WALKING A TIGHTROPE

The tightrope walkers at the circus are always a popular act. So invite your youngsters to practice walking a tightrope—the preschool way! In advance, place lines of masking tape on the floor of your circle time area. Then tape construction paper shapes to each line of tape as shown. Next, cut out paper shapes to match those on the floor and then place them in a paper bag. To begin the activity, have a child pull a shape out of the bag, find the matching shapes on the floor, and then walk heel-to-toe across the line of tape between them. Continue the activity in this manner until each child has had a turn to walk a tightrope.

HERE COMES THE CIRCUS TRAIN

All aboard! What better way to reinforce shapes than to have youngsters create this circus train! To prepare, use the patterns on page 65 to create a supply of animal cutouts. Provide each child with a sheet of construction paper and two black paper circles. Have the child create a train car by gluing the black circles to the paper as shown. Invite the child to choose an animal cutout and glue it onto the car. Then direct him to color the animal and draw the shape of his choice around it. For younger students, provide shape tracers to help them reproduce the shape.

When each child has completed a car, tape a train engine cutout to a wall and attach the cars to the engine. Gather your group around the train and invite each child to identify some shapes on it. Just look at how your preschoolers are shaping up!

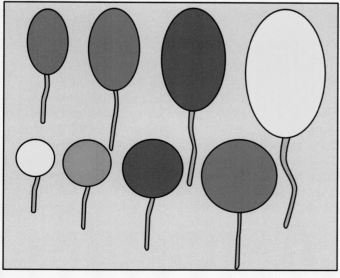

BUNCHES OF BALLOONS

At the circus, balloons are abundant! At this center, size-seriation skills and shape discrimination will balloon! To prepare, cut out a set of felt ovals in a variety of sizes. Hot-glue a length of yarn to each oval to create a pretend balloon. Place the felt balloons near your flannelboard and invite each child to line up the balloons from smallest to largest. For an added challenge, add a set of circular balloons to the oval balloons. Have students sort the balloons by shape and then arrange each set by size.

identifying basic shapes
developing gross-motor
skills

PRETEND PIE TOSS

Every clown knows that a pie in the face is just part of the job! Invite your preschoolers to join in some light-hearted circus fun with this small-group activity. To pre-pare, create construction paper clown faces similar to the ones shown. Laminate the faces and then use double-sided tape to attach them to a wall. Next, cut out circle shapes from sponges to make pretend pies. Place the sponges a short distance away from the clowns. Invite a small group of children to the area. Have a child toss the "pie" at the clowns and then identify the shape of the clown that was hit (or nearly hit). Repeat the pie practice with a different child. Any way you toss it, this activity is sure to be a hit!

matching basic shapes
developing fine-motor skills

PEANUTS! POPCORN!

The best thing about the circus is the snacks! Set up this sensory table filled with pretend peanuts, and youngsters will feel as if they're under the big top. In advance, cut out a supply of small tagboard shapes. Fill your sensory table with Styrofoam packing peanuts and then hide the shapes in the peanuts. Place several empty, unused popcorn boxes near the table; then label each box with a different shape. Invite students to find the shapes and then sort them into the appro-priate popcorn boxes. For added fine-motor fun, have students use small tongs or tweezers while they work.

triangle

circle

rectangle

square

singing simple songs
developing gross-motor
skills

HIGH-FLYING FEATS

Trapeze artists train for years, but with a parachute and some sponges, you can create some high-flying feats of your own! In advance, cut craft sponges into a variety of shapes. Have students hold the edges of a parachute and then place the sponges in the middle. Sing the song shown and instruct your little ones to gently shake the parachute. As you sing the last line, have youngsters quickly raise and lower the parachute to send the sponges soaring!

(sung to the tune of "Daring Young Man on the Flying Trapeze")

Oh, they float through the air
With the greatest of ease.
Circles and ovals
Fly high in the breeze.
Triangles, rectangles,
And squares, if you please.
The shapes are all flying away!

Amelia

At the Circus
March 14, 2002

creating designs
with shapes

FRAME IT IN COTTON CANDY!

If you're planning a field trip to the circus, here's a sweet way to create a keepsake. Take a photo of each child at the circus. After developing the photographs, tape each one to the back of a tagboard frame. Provide each child with two cotton balls and two 1 1/2-inch pieces of a drinking straw. Direct the child to glue each straw to a cotton ball (so that it resembles cotton candy) and then glue the cotton balls to the frame. Label the frame with the child's name, the date, and a title similar to the one shown. Invite the child to add colorful construction paper shapes to the frame. Add a strip of magnetic tape to the back; then have the child take the frame home to spark a family discussion about shapes and the circus!

61

SEND IN THE CLOWNS!

To prepare for this flannelboard activity, use a photo-copier to create an enlarged copy of the clown pattern on page 63. Lay the pattern under a piece of white interfac-ing (available at your local fabric store). Then use a black crayon to trace the pattern onto the interfacing. Cut out the resulting clown; then cut out a variety of felt shapes small enough to fit onto the clown.

To begin the activity, provide each child with a shape and help her identify it. Next, place the clown on your flannelboard. As you sing the song shown, direct the chil-dren holding the mentioned shape to place it on the clown. After singing, count the number of shapes on the clown. Remove the shapes and then sing the song again using a different shape.

(sung to the tune of "This Old Man")
The circus clown
Came to town,
Wearing [circles] all around.
There were [circles] on his head
And [circles] on his toes.
He wears [circles] wherever he goes!

ANIMAL TRAINERS IN TRAINING

This snack idea will give your little ones a taste of what it's like to be a circus animal trainer! To begin, provide each child with a Ritz cracker, a triangular Triscuit, and a graham cracker section. Identify the shape of each cracker and then have the child spread peanut butter on each one. Next, provide the child with an animal cracker. Name one of the three cracker shapes and have each child stand his animal on that shape. Continue the activity in this manner, directing youngsters to stand their animals on the different shapes. After a few rounds of tricks, invite each little trainer to take a bow and then eat!

matches shapes

walks heel-to-toe

draws shapes

seriates by size

sorts by shapes

creates designs with shapes

counts objects

discriminates oval and circle

sings songs

recognizes shapes

recites rhymes

identifies shapes

©The Education Center, Inc. • THE MAILBOX® • Preschool • Feb/Mar 2002

Circus Patterns
Use with "I Spy" on page 58.

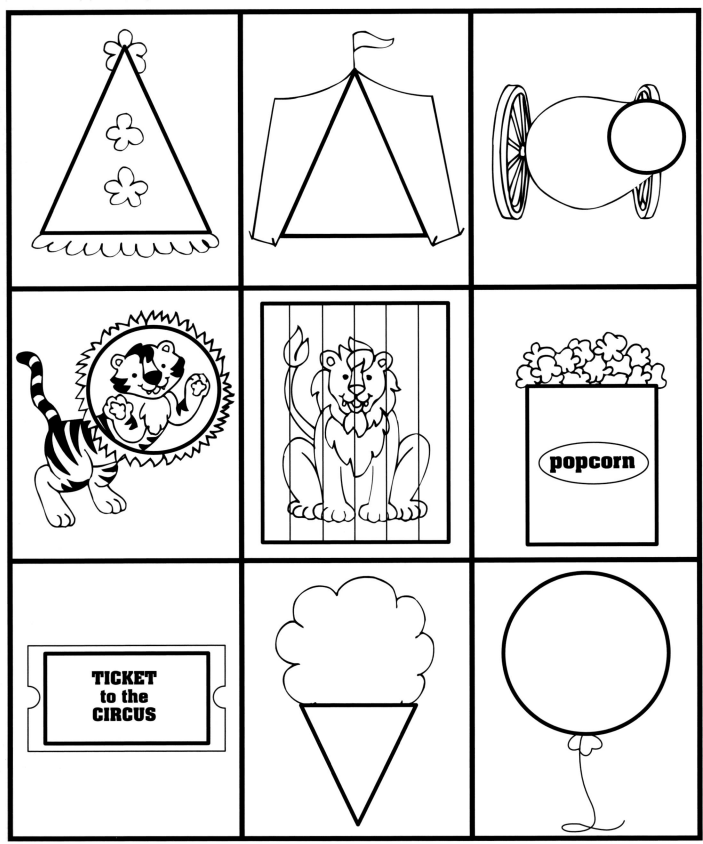

popcorn

TICKET
to the
CIRCUS

©The Education Center, Inc. • *THE MAILBOX* • *Preschool* • Feb/Mar 2002

Every Chick Counts

Need some math ideas that you can count on? Use this collection of chick-themed activities and teaching math skills will be as easy as 1, 2, 3!

ideas by Sue Fleischmann—Preschool, Holy Cross School, Menomonee Falls, WI

Here a Chick, There a Chick

Going on a chick hunt is a great way to motivate youngsters and get them counting! In advance, use the pattern on page 70 to make a supply of chick cutouts. Be sure to make enough chicks for each child to have at least one. Then hide the chicks throughout your classroom. For added fun, scatter a few yellow craft feathers around the room. To begin the activity, show students a paper chick and explain that several more chicks are hiding in the classroom. Play some lively music and invite your youngsters to search for the remaining chicks. When the music stops, bring your group together to count each child's chicks. If desired, make a graph similar to the one shown. Have each child place his chicks on the graph. Then use terms such as *more, less,* and *equal* to discuss what the graph reveals. ***counting, comparing numbers of objects, vocabulary***

Counting Chicks

| Kate | Tara | Nick | Teddy | Christy |

Bouncing Baby Chicks

A few old tennis balls and a parachute are all you need to put some bounce into a counting lesson. In advance, use paint pens to draw eyes, wings, and a beak on each ball. When the paint is dry, have each child hold the edge of a parachute. Place the tennis ball chicks in the middle of the parachute. Sing the song shown and have youngsters shake the parachute to make the chicks "hop." After singing the last line, invite a child to say a number. Have the class count out loud as they shake the parachute and make the chicks "hop" that many times. Continue the activity until each child has had a chance to say a number. ***meaningful counting, gross-motor skills***

(sung to the tune of "The Wheels on the Bus")

Little baby chicks hop up and down,
Up and down,
Up and down.
Little baby chicks hop up and down.
How many times?

Little Chick, Little Chick

There's nothing like an entertaining action poem to get your little chicks cheeping! To prepare for this activity, use the pattern on page 70 to make five chick necklaces, each labeled with a different number from 1 to 5. During your group time, invite five children to stand in front of the class. Provide each child with a chick necklace and identify its number. As you recite the poem below, have each little chick perform an action as directed in the poem. *number recognition, listening, gross-motor skills*

Little chick, little chick, number one,
Flap your wings and have some fun.
Little chick, little chick, number two,
Reach way down and touch your shoe.
Little chick, little chick, number three,
Nod your head for us to see.
Little chick, little chick, number four,
Jump up high, right off the floor.
Little chick, little chick, number five,
Dance around and do the jive.

Chicks Ahoy!

Keep math skills afloat with this water table idea. To prepare, use permanent markers to draw beaks, eyes, and wings on each of 15 Ping-Pong balls. Place the Ping-Pong ball chicks in a container and then set it near your water table. Next, label the sides of five small plastic margarine tubs, each with a different number from 1 to 5. If desired, also program the inside of each tub with a corresponding set of dots. Float the tubs in the water table. To use the center, a child reads the numeral on each tub and then places the correct number of chicks in it. Rub-a-dub-dub! The chicks are in the tub! *number recognition, creating sets to match numbers*

Birds of a Feather

Sharpen one-to-one correspondence skills with this fine-feathered center idea! To prepare, paint five toilet paper tubes to resemble chicks. When the paint is dry, program the front of each chick with a different number from 1 to 5. Then poke small holes in the back of each chick to correspond with the number programmed on the front. Set the chicks at a center along with a supply of craft feathers. To use the center, a child identifies the number on each chick and then places a feather in each hole on the back of the chick. *one-to-one correspondence, number identification, fine-motor skills*

Take Five!

Here's a snack activity chock full of counting and fine-motor fun! To begin, read the recipe card shown. Gather the necessary ingredients and supplies, and arrange them at a table for easy student access. Invite each child, in turn, to wash her hands and then join you at the snack table. Help her count out each ingredient and place it in a resealable plastic bag. Have the child seal the bag and then give it a good shake to mix the ingredients. After enjoying her snack, invite your little chick to make a second batch of feed to share with her family. Slip a copy of the recipe inside the bag. Seal the bag and send it home. *counting objects, fine-motor skills*

Fun Feed

5 miniature marshmallows
5 pieces of Chex cereal
5 pieces of Honeycomb cereal
5 small pretzels
5 Goldfish crackers

Seal the ingredients inside a plastic sandwich bag and shake!

Nine, Ten—Big Fat Hen

To prepare for this play dough activity, use the pattern on page 70 to make ten hen cutouts. Color the hens. Program each one with a different number from 1 to 10; then laminate the cutouts for durability. Place the hens and a container of yellow play dough at a center. To use the center, a child identifies the number on a hen and then makes that many play dough chicks. He sets the chicks near the hen and then repeats the activity with a different hen. *number identification, creating sets to match numbers*

One Little, Two Little...

The following toe-tapping song will add a little rhythm to this counting lesson. In advance, cut out ten felt chick shapes. Line up the chicks on a flannelboard; then sing the song shown, touching each little chick as you count. When students are familiar with this activity, set the chicks near your flannelboard for youngsters to use independently. *counting objects*

(sung to the tune of "Ten Little Indians")

One little, two little, three little chickies.
Four little, five little, six little chickies.
Seven little, eight little, nine little chickies.
Ten little chickies say, "Cheep! Cheep! Cheep!"

Chick Booklet

After teaching youngsters the song above, invite each child to make a song booklet filled with little fingerprint chicks! To make one booklet, program ten 9" x 6" sheets of construction paper similar to the ones shown. Have a child identify the number on each booklet page. Then have him dip a finger into yellow paint and make the corresponding number of prints on each page. When the paint is dry, use permanent markers to draw eyes, feet, and a beak on each print. Stack the pages in order between two covers; then staple the booklet together. Write a title and the child's name on the front of the booklet. Then have the child add fingerprint chicks to the cover as desired. When the booklet is complete, encourage your little one to sing the song and count the chicks on each page. *number identification, literacy*

Counting Kudos

Mother hens (and other caretakers) will have something to cluck about when their little chicks bring home this counting certificate! Use the pattern on page 70 to make an award for each child; then program it according to the child's ability. Encourage the child to take home her award and share her counting know-how with her family. *home-school connection*

69

Chick Pattern

Use with "Here a Chick, There a Chick" on page 66 and "Little Chick, Little Chick" on page 67.

Hen Pattern

Use with "Nine, Ten—Big Fat Hen" on page 68.

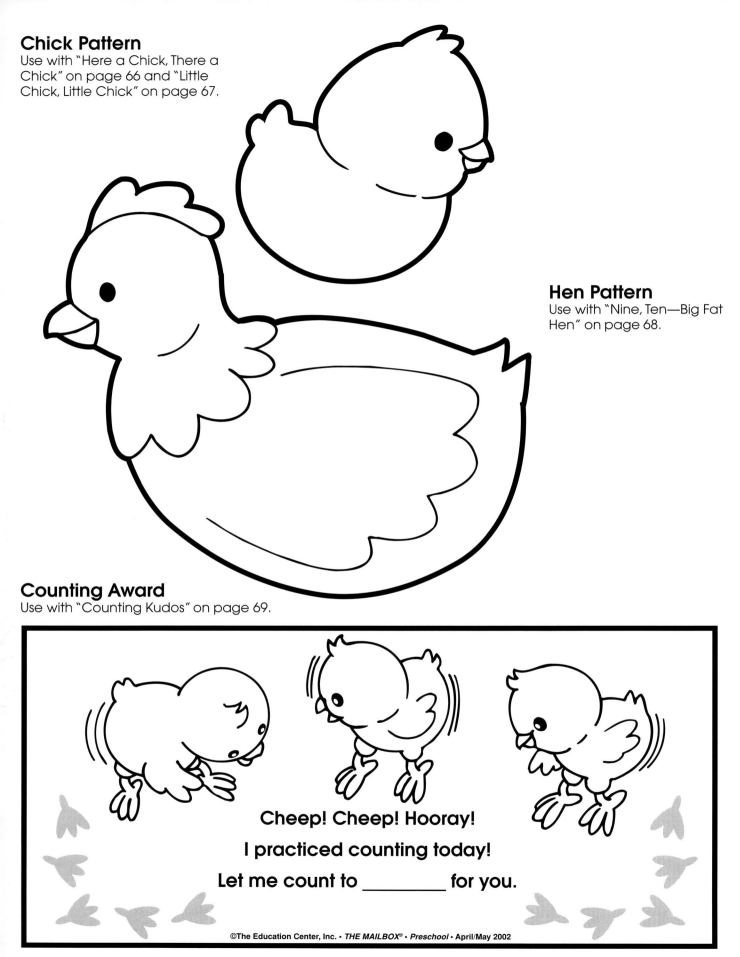

Counting Award

Use with "Counting Kudos" on page 69.

Cheep! Cheep! Hooray!

I practiced counting today!

Let me count to _____ for you.

©The Education Center, Inc. • THE MAILBOX® • Preschool • April/May 2002

©The Education Center, Inc. • THE MAILBOX® • Preschool • April/May 2002

SANDWICHES? SUPER!

If your little ones have an appetite for learning, serve up some of these sandwich-related activities. From music to math, you'll find they're a tasty combination of skills and fun!

by Ada Goren

SINGIN' ABOUT SANDWICHES

Start your study of sandwiches by teaching your preschoolers this delicious ditty. Seat youngsters in a circle and sing the verse together. Then go around the circle and have each child name a type of sandwich she likes to eat.

(sung to the tune of "Twinkle, Twinkle, Little Star")

Chicken salad or grilled cheese,
Peanut butter, if you please.
Ham or turkey, tuna fish,
Or bologna, if you wish.
Any sandwich is a treat!
What kind do you like to eat?

Sandwiches
grilled cheese
peanut butter and jelly
turkey
roast beef
peanut butter and banana
hot dog
hamburger
ice cream

HOW MANY ARE THERE?

Chances are your youngsters have a few standard favorites when it comes to sandwiches. But just how many types of sandwiches are there? Explain to your little ones that a sandwich can be any type of bread with a filling. Then ask them to try to think of as many types of sandwiches as they can. List the sandwiches on a sheet of bread-shaped bulletin board paper. Display the list throughout your sandwich unit and invite little ones to add to it as they like.

Let's Go to a Sub Shop!

Plan a field trip to a local restaurant that specializes in sub sandwiches so your preschoolers can see professional sandwich makers in action. If you're lucky, your tour will include some sample sandwiches! Afterward, have little ones help you create a thank-you note that resembles a sub. Cut two elongated ovals from 12" x 18" sheets of white construction paper. Color one cutout with a tan crayon and then write the message shown, personalizing it for your class. Next, duplicate the sandwich ingredients on pages 76 and 77 onto appropriate colors of paper. Have each child choose a cutout and dictate a message about the field trip for you to write. Add her name to her message. Then glue all the cutouts to the plain white oval, having them overlap a bit on the edges. Staple the colored oval on top of the ingredients to make a thank-you sandwich!

I liked watching you slice the meat on the big cutter.
Allison

I liked the smell of the bread cooking.
Drew

I liked tasting the green peppers. They were good!
Austin

I liked the way you chop up all the food.
Katie

I liked the big oven you have.
Graham

I liked eating my ham sandwich with pickles!
Tai

The drink machine was fun.
Sarah

I liked your great big refrigerator!
Claire

...our great big ...e sacks!
Joe

I liked watching the man make sandwiches. He is fast!
Dominick

Thanks!
Our field trip was "sub-perb"!
from Mrs. Hogan's four-year-olds

Jose's
bologna, cheese, and lettuce on wheat
sandwich

Sandwich Mobiles

Have youngsters show off their personal preferences with these sandwich mobiles. Duplicate the sandwich ingredients on pages 76 and 77 for each child. Encourage older preschoolers to cut out the two bread slices and to color and cut out any other ingredients they want to put on their sandwiches. (Precut the pieces for younger preschoolers.) Each sandwich chef may leave his bread white or, if he likes wheat bread, color it brown. Help him stack his ingredients between his two bread slices in a vertical line on the tabletop. Then turn all the cutouts facedown. Lay a length of yarn atop the cutouts and tape it to each one. Then flip the finished mobile back over. Label the top bread slice with the child's name and a description of his creation as shown. These mobiles will make a delectable display of individuality!

A Sandwich Smorgasbord

Is all this talk of sandwiches making you and your students hungry? Then it's time to eat! First, check for student food allergies or dietary restrictions. Then have a parent volunteer or an assistant help you prepare a few different types of sandwiches for your youngsters to sample. Make just one or two of each type; then cut the sandwiches into small pieces for tasting. Encourage little ones to try each type of sandwich; then have each child choose his favorite sandwich from the smorgasbord. Record youngsters' favorites by making a graph.

To prepare the graph, cut a large piece of poster board into the shape of a bread slice. Print the types of sandwiches along the bottom of the slice. Then give each child a sticky note with her name on it. Have her stick the note above the type of sandwich she prefers. Count the votes and examine the graph to see what it reveals.

Which sandwich do you like best?

PB&J	tuna	turkey	bologna
Alex			Stacy
Pam			Rena
Tanny		Kerri	Chase
Jose	Ann	Michael	Sonnetta
Theo			

Sandwiches for Dessert?

If there's any room left in youngsters' tummies, help them prepare some ice-cream sandwiches for dessert! Open a carton of vanilla ice cream and allow it to soften. When you are ready to make the sandwiches, give each child two round, flat cookies on a paper plate. Provide a melon baller and show each child how to scoop out some of the softened ice cream and place it in the center of one cookie. Have him top the ice-cream ball with the second cookie and then squeeze the cookies together gently. Mmm! Crunchy cookies and frosty filling—what a *cool* sandwich!

VANILLA ICE CREAM

SANDWICH PUZZLES

No matter what's inside, little ones are likely to be particular about how their sandwiches are sliced. Triangles? Rectangles? Squares? Make some sandwich shapes to challenge your preschoolers' perceptual skills! To begin, cut out four large bread-slice shapes from a piece of poster board. Cut one slice in half to make two rectangles, one in half diagonally to make two triangles, one into four squares, and one into four triangles. Place all the pieces in a zippered plastic bag and place the bag in your math center. Encourage a child to remove all the puzzle pieces from the bag, sort them by shape, and then assemble the four puzzles to make four whole sandwiches. (For younger preschoolers, you may want to use only two puzzles at a time.)

PEANUT BUTTER AND JELLY PAIRS

No sandwich unit would be complete without paying tribute to that childhood favorite—peanut butter and jelly! Read aloud Nadine Bernard Westcott's *Peanut Butter and Jelly: A Play Rhyme.* Invite youngsters to join you in the traditional chant about making a PB&J. Then try this art activity to encourage creativity *and* cooperation!

Cut out a large construction paper bread-slice shape for each child. Then tint some brown tempera paint with a little yellow and white to resemble the color of peanut butter. Stir a bit of grape or berry-flavored gelatin powder into some purple paint to add a fruity smell. When you're ready to paint, have youngsters pair up. Give each child a bread-slice cutout. Have one child paint her slice with "peanut butter" (brown paint). Have the other child paint her slice with "jelly" (purple paint). Then have the youngsters press their two slices together to make a peanut butter and jelly sandwich! Pull the paintings apart and have little ones observe the unique results! Write each child's name on her dry painting and display this mouthwatering artwork for all to see!

Jennifer

TOMATO, HAM, TOMATO, HAM...

Introduce older preschoolers to simple patterns using the sandwich ingredients on pages 76 and 77. Duplicate the patterns onto appropriate colors of paper to make several copies of each ingredient. Make patterning cards by gluing some of the cutouts onto tagboard strips in simple ABAB patterns, such as *tomato, lettuce, tomato, lettuce* or *bologna, cheese, bologna, cheese.* Laminate the patterning cards and the extra ingredient cutouts and place them in a center. Invite a child to choose one card at a time and continue the pattern with the extra ingredient cutouts.

LETTER-SOUND SANDWICHES

Your little ones have talked about what goes into *real* sandwiches, but how about some silly sandwiches? This sandwich-making activity will set letter-sound reinforcement on a roll! Provide each child with colored copies of the roll patterns on page 78. Have the child choose a letter; then help her write the uppercase letter on the top of the roll and the lowercase letter on the bottom. Direct the child to glue the top and bottom to a sheet of paper as shown. Next, have her look through old magazines to find items that begin with that letter. Have her cut out the pictures and glue them between the top and bottom of the roll. Have your preschoolers share their sandwich creations during a group time. A sandwich with bells, bacon, and bears? How silly!

Sandwich Ingredients

Use with "Let's Go to a Sub Shop!" and "Sandwich Mobiles" on page 72 and "Tomato, Ham, Tomato, Ham..." on page 75.

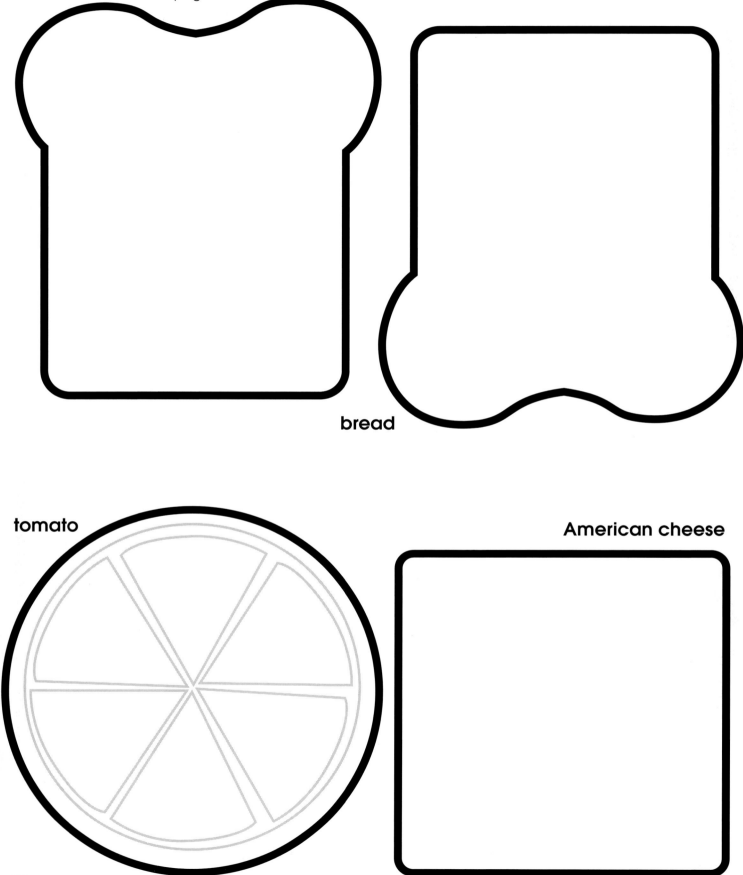

bread

tomato

American cheese

©The Education Center, Inc. • *THE MAILBOX® • Preschool •* April/May 2002

Sandwich Ingredients

Use with "Let's Go to a Sub Shop!" and "Sandwich Mobiles" on page 72 and "Tomato, Ham, Tomato, Ham..." on page 75.

ham

bologna

lettuce

Swiss cheese

Sandwich Roll Patterns
Use with "Letter-Sound Sandwiches" on page 75.

top

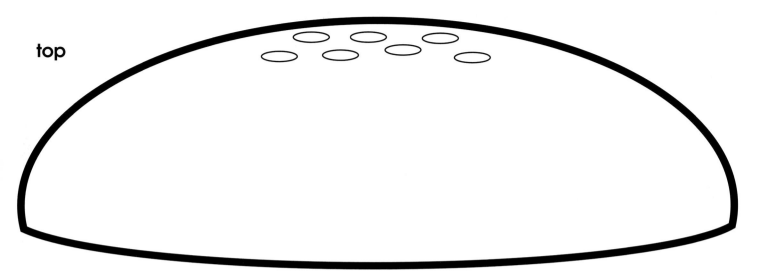

bottom

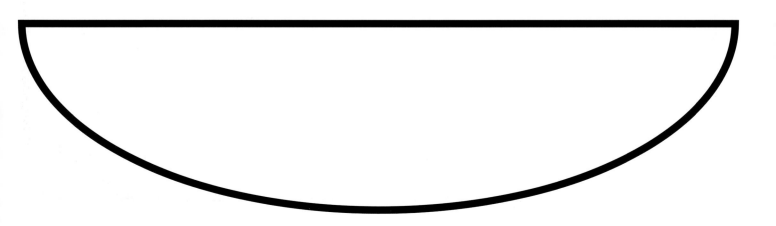

©The Education Center, Inc. • *THE MAILBOX*® • *Preschool* • April/May 2002

A Preschool Parade!

We're having a preschool parade to celebrate our nation's birthday on _____ at

(date)

_____.

(time)

Please dress your child in red, white, and blue clothing on that day. And be sure to join us for some patriotic fun!

©The Education Center, Inc. • THE MAILBOX® • Preschool • June/July 2002

A Patriotic Preschool Parade

Hip, hip, hooray for Independence Day! Celebrate our nation's birthday with a preschool parade that will have your little ones marching, singing, and learning to the beat of the band!

by Ada Goren

A Parade Is...

Begin your parade planning by finding out what your youngsters know about parades. Ask if anyone has been to a parade. What did he see? List students' responses on your chalkboard or on a sheet of chart paper. Share *Parade* by Donald Crews or *Thump, Thump, Rat-a-Tat-Tat* by Gene Baer to get youngsters thinking and talking more about parades. Then break the news—your class will be holding its own parade to celebrate the Fourth of July!

jugglers
bands
clowns
people waving

Marching Mania

Marching is essential for a good parade—and it's a great gross-motor workout, too! Teach your preschoolers the chant that follows and show them how to high-step all around your classroom. After a few repetitions of the chant, turn on some great marching music, such as a selection from John Philip Sousa or the song "76 Trombones" from the musical *The Music Man.* Invite youngsters to march around to the music. And be sure to keep your music selection handy because you may wish to use it during your real parade!

One, two, three, four—
Stomp your feet upon the floor!
Five, six, seven, eight—
Knees up high; that's really great!

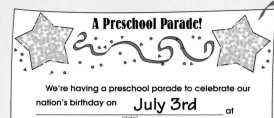

A Preschool Parade!

We're having a preschool parade to celebrate our
nation's birthday on **July 3rd** at
(date)
2:00.
(time)

Please dress your child in red, white, and blue clothing
on that day. And be sure to join us for some patriotic fun!

An Invitation

Of course, the parents of your petite patriots will want to see them in action on parade day! So make a copy of the invitation on page 79; then fill in the date and time for your parade. Duplicate the programmed invitation to make a class supply; then have each child color her invitation. If desired, have the child add glitter glue to the stars on the invitations before sending it home.

Birthday Banner

Here's a lesson on letters that will also help you make a red, white, and blue banner perfect for the front of your parade! Explain to your preschoolers that the Fourth of July is like a birthday for the USA. Then have them help you construct a banner with birthday wishes for America. In advance, cut a long length of white bulletin board paper. Die-cut capital letters from red and blue construction paper to spell out the message "Happy Birthday, USA!" Then write the same message on a large sheet of paper (in matching capital letters). Have youngsters sit on the floor with you, and spread the banner out in front of the group. Point out on your sheet of paper the first letter of the message—*H.* Place three die-cut letters in front of the group: an *H* and two other letters. Ask a student volunteer to choose the letter that matches the first one in the written message. When the child chooses the *H,* invite him to spread some glue on the back of the die-cut letter and glue it in place on the banner.

Continue matching the other letters until little ones have spelled the entire message. Then encourage two children at a time to use red and blue bingo markers to further decorate the banner. There—red, white, and blue and festive, too!

HAPPY BIRTHDAY, USA!

Star-Spangled Vests

Wondering what to wear to this preschool parade? Your students will be well dressed in these painted vests! To make one, open a brown paper grocery bag and set it upside down on a newspaper-covered table. Paint the bottom of the bag and all four sides with white tempera paint. When the paint is dry, cut up the center of one wide side, making a V-neck and a neck opening in the bag bottom as shown. Then cut an arm hole in each narrow side of the bag. Next, use red and blue tempera paint to add stripes to the vest wherever you like. Use a star-shaped sponge to add even more pizzazz! When all the paint is dry, have all your youngsters slip on their vests and model them for the class.

Special Sparklers

Since you can't have any real Fourth of July fireworks at your parade, make these glittery versions of handheld sparklers instead! To prepare, cut two four-inch circles of waxed paper for each child. To make one sparkler, squeeze several lines of glue onto each of the two circles to create a starburst. Sprinkle multicolored glitter over the glues lines; then shake off the excess. Allow the glue to dry completely. Place the two glittered circles back-to-back with one end of a drinking straw between them; then staple the circles together around the edges and over the straw to hold it in place. Ta-da—a shiny sparkler!

Drum Patterns

Marching bands are a big part of a parade, so your little ones are going to need some instruments. How about some drums? In advance, ask parents to donate large cardboard canisters, such as those that hold oatmeal or powdered baby formula. You may wish to cut tall oatmeal canisters in half to more closely approximate the shape of a drum. To make a drum, glue a cut-to-fit strip of black construction paper around a canister. Invite a child to decorate the canister with scraps of red, white, and blue construction paper and patriotic stickers. Cut two slits on opposite sides of the canister lid and thread a long length of ribbon through the slits to make a neck strap.

Once the drums are ready, tap into your preschoolers' listening and patterning skills for a fun copycat activity! Tap out a pattern on a tabletop (or on your own drum) and ask youngsters to copy it. For example, you might tap a pattern of *long, long, short, short* for your students to copy. Keep going as long as your drum players like. And as they get better at imitating your rhythms, invite each of them to take a turn as leader of the band!

A Song for Marching Along

Teach youngsters this tune and invite them to march around your room as they sing. Then have them sing the song as they march on parade day!

(sung to the tune of "Battle Hymn of the Republic")

We are [marching, marching, marching] in the big parade today!
We are [marching, marching, marching] in the big parade today!
We are [marching, marching, marching] in the big parade today!
We love the USA!

If desired, sing additional verses, substituting the words waving, waving, waving *and* drumming, drumming, drumming *for the underlined words.*

Red, White, and Blue Snacks

Both preschoolers and parents are likely to be hungry after the parade, so make some snacks and get in some counting practice, too! Visit your local candy store and purchase some M&Ms candies in blue and red. Buy a large bag of miniature marshmallows, too. To make one snack, have a child count out five red M&Ms, five blue M&Ms, and five marshmallows onto a square of plastic wrap. Gather the plastic wrap around the candies and tie the bundle with a length of star garland. Have each child make a snack for herself and one for each of her expected visitors. (Make several extra snacks to have on hand.) On the day of the parade, serve the snacks with red punch or that summertime favorite—lemonade!

The Big Day

At last! When the day of your big parade arrives, help little ones dress in their "Star-Spangled Vests" (page 82). Have them put on the drums made in "Drum Patterns" (page 83) and carry their "Special Sparklers" (page 82). Ask two children to carry the "Birthday Banner" (page 81) at the front of the group. Then get your youngsters marching and singing along a predetermined parade route through your school or center. You may wish to have them sing "A Song for Marching Along" (page 83) all through the parade, or have them march to the recorded music you chose for "Marching Mania" (page 80), stopping the tape periodically so youngsters can sing for the crowd. Marching, drumming, waving, singing…don't you just love a parade?

PRESCHOOL

PASSPORT

©The Education Center, Inc. • *THE MAILBOX*® • Preschool • June/July 2002

Glue
photo
here.

Name _____

Age _____

Birthday _____

Passport Pages
Use with "Have Passport, Will Travel" on page 88.

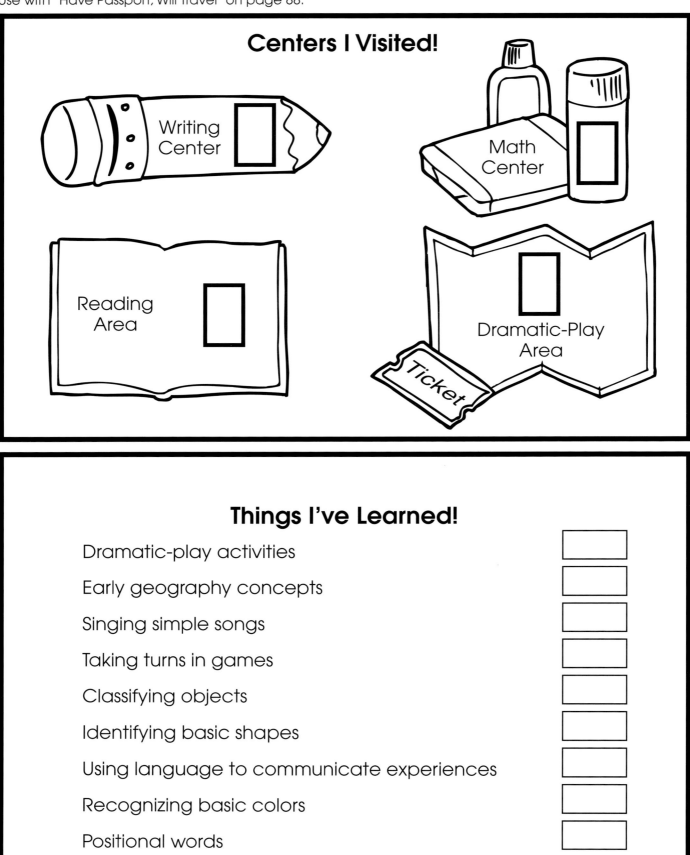

Centers I Visited!

Writing Center

Math Center

Reading Area

Dramatic-Play Area

Ticket

Things I've Learned!

Dramatic-play activities

Early geography concepts

Singing simple songs

Taking turns in games

Classifying objects

Identifying basic shapes

Using language to communicate experiences

Recognizing basic colors

Positional words

©The Education Center, Inc. • THE MAILBOX® • Preschool • June/July 2002

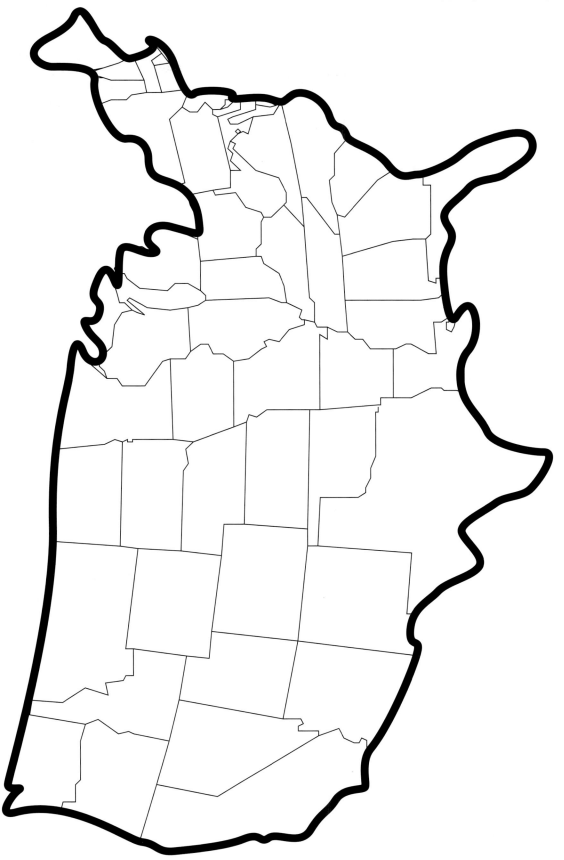

Wish You Were Here!

Looking for a way to transform the lazy days of summer into the *learning* days of summer? This cross-curricular vacation unit is just the ticket! From map explorations to exotic locations, this collection of ideas makes the perfect getaway!

ideas by Sue Fleischmann—Preschool, Holy Cross School, Menomonee Falls, WI

Have Passport, Will Travel

In order to visit all the sites and attractions in this unit, a pretend passport is a must! To make a preschool passport, photocopy pages 85 and 86; then cut out the passport pages. Stack the pages in order and staple them along the left side. Help the child write his personal information on the first page; then glue a photograph to the page where indicated. After each little traveler has been outfitted with a passport, use it with "Let's Take a Trip!" on page 89, as a tracking sheet for the center activities on page 92, and as an assessment sheet for the various skills covered in this unit. **assessment**

I'm Going on Vacation!

Going on vacation makes most people want to sing for joy! So teach youngsters this tune and get ready to do some traveling! **singing simple songs**

(sung to the tune of "Sing a Song of Sixpence")

I'm getting out my suitcase
And packing it with clothes.
I'm getting all dressed up,
From my head down to my toes.
I'm getting out my ticket
And putting on my hat.
I'm going on vacation!
Now, what do you think of that?

Travel Talk

Have your youngsters taken a trip recently? If so, they'll most likely want to tell the class all about it! Set up this display and encourage your traveling tots to talk about their vacations. In advance, visit a local hotel, visitor's center, or American Automotive Association to collect a supply of maps and brochures for various tourist attractions. Display the brochures on the board. Use the maps to create a bulletin board border. After a child has told the class about a vacation that he has taken, have him dictate a sentence or two about the trip. Write his response on a sun-shaped cutout; then add the cutout to the display. *language development: communicating experiences*

Josephine Sheldon—Preschool, The Child's Place
Somers, CT

Let's Take a Trip!

After discussing youngsters' travel experiences, prepare little imaginations to take flight with this circle-time idea. In advance, gather souvenirs and pictures of different places your youngsters will "visit." Store the items for each destination in a separate suitcase or backpack. Set up a class supply of chairs to resemble rows of airplane seats; then provide each child with a play airline ticket and her passport. (See "Have Passport, Will Travel" on page 88.) As students board the plane, take their tickets and stamp their passports with fun stamps or stickers.

After a brief "flight," have students exit the plane and sit in your circle-time area. Use the items in the suitcase to begin a discussion about the chosen vacation spot. Afterward, set the different suitcases in your dramatic-play area and invite youngsters to use the props to act out a trip to an exotic location. *early geography, dramatic play*

89

Baggage Check

Do you have any carry-on luggage? Youngsters will answer "Yes!" with this action poem. To prepare, make a class supply of suitcase cutouts in the following colors: blue, red, black, and brown. Provide each child with a cutout; then have him listen for his color and perform the appropriate action as directed in the poem below. *positional words, color recognition*

If your suitcase is blue,
Put it beside your shoe.
If your suitcase is red,
Put it on your head.
If your suitcase is black,
Put it behind your back.
If your suitcase is brown,
Hold it upside down!

Let's Unpack!

What's more fun than packing a suitcase? Unpacking it! Gather two small suitcases and then set up this small-group game. In one suitcase, place several items necessary for a warm-weather vacation, such as an empty bottle of suntan lotion, sunglasses, a beach towel, shorts, and a T-shirt. In the other suitcase, place several items needed for a cold-weather vacation, such as a wool hat, gloves, a scarf, a sweater, and a child's coat. Collect a variety of postcards from tropical and wintry vacation spots and place them in a stack near the suitcases.

To play the game, the first child draws a postcard from the stack. He looks at the picture to decide which suitcase is needed for that destination. Then he takes an item from the appropriate suitcase. The next child continues the game in this manner, and the game proceeds until all of the items have been unpacked. When the game is over, invite students to sort the items by season and then repack the suitcases. *taking turns, classification*

Barbara Carr
Fountain Valley, CA

90

Mapping It Out

If you've ever been a tourist, you know the importance of a map! Use this activity to help your youngsters become familiar with this handy tool. To begin, have students examine a variety of maps. Point out your state on a U.S. map; then have each child create a mock map of the United States.

To make a map, use the pattern on page 87 to make a United States cutout. Place the cutout in a box. Then pour a spoonful of red tempera paint onto it. Drop a marble in the box. Gently tilt the box repeatedly so that the marble rolls through the paint, creating a maplike design on the cutout. Repeat the marble-painting with blue paint; then remove the cutout from the box. When the paint is dry, help a child locate the area of your state on the cutout and glue a small photograph of herself to that area. Display each child's mock map on a bulletin board titled "You Are Here." ***early geography***

Shutterbugs and Shapes

In addition to having a map, every tourist needs a camera! This crafty camera is perfect for the preschool traveler. It never needs film, *and* it makes a great lesson on shapes! Read through the directions below. Gather the needed materials. Have each child make a camera and then start clicking away! ***shape identification, dramatic play***

Materials needed to make one camera:
4¹/₂" x 6" piece of black construction paper
4" x 3" piece of gray construction paper
2¹/₂" square piece of black construction paper
2" foil circle
1¹/₂"-long yellow construction paper oval
glue
scissors

Have a child identify the different shapes; then help her glue them together to resemble the camera shown. Cut a small rectangle in the camera to create a viewfinder; then laminate the camera for durability.

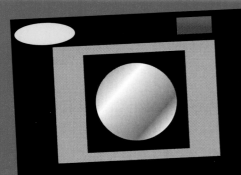

Vacation Hot Spots

Set up the following centers in your classroom and they're bound to become major tourist attractions for your preschoolers!

Dramatic-play area: Set up a preschool travel agency. Place a small desk in the area. Then add maps, travel brochures, pretend tickets, and a toy telephone. Place a sign in front of the area and you're ready for business!

Tiny Tot Travel

Writing center: Ask your local airport for donations of unused luggage tags. Set the tags at the center along with several pieces of luggage. Invite each child to write her name on a tag and then attach the tag to a piece of luggage.

Karla

Math center: Visit your local hotels and request donations of soap bars, shampoo bottles, and lotion bottles. If desired, empty and clean the bottles before placing them in the center. Have students sort the soaps and bottles in a variety of ways.

Toot & Puddle
by Holly Hobbie

The Bears' Vacation
by Stan and Jan Berenstain

Curious George Goes to the Beach
by Margaret Rey

The Bag I'm Taking to Grandma's
by Shirley Neitzel

Reading area: Fill a plastic wading pool with pillows; then cover the pillows with a blue sheet to resemble pool water. Add a few child-size lawn chairs around the pool. Place a variety of vacation-themed picture books in a cooler and set it in the area. Invite each child to pore over a good book as he lounges in or around the pool. For literature suggestions, see the list to the left.

CENTER UNITS

Crazy About Cookies

Oatmeal, chocolate chip, gingerbread too! These cookie-based centers were baked just for you!

ideas contributed by Roxanne LaBell Dearman and Suzanne Moore

Investigating Ingredients

What's in a cookie? Your youngsters will find out when you invite them to examine and compare the different ingredients of two favorite cookies—oatmeal raisin and chocolate chip. To prepare for this center, place the dry ingredients from each type of cookie in separate resealable plastic bags. Then place an oatmeal raisin cookie and a chocolate chip cookie each in a separate resealable plastic bag. Seal the bags closed with duct tape; then set plastic magnifying glasses near the area. Have each child use the glasses to examine the dry ingredients and then have her match each cookie with its ingredients.

Gingerbread Blocks

Your blocks area will be a sweet treat when you add a supply of candy cutouts! In advance, make several copies of the candy patterns on page 99. Color, laminate, and then cut out each pattern. Next, use clear ConTact paper to attach each pattern to a different block. Invite each child to use the blocks to build a pretend gingerbread house. As an extension, place a craft foam or stuffed gingerbread man in the area and encourage the child to dramatize a story. Run, run as fast as you can!

Bubble Bakery

Use this idea and invite your youngsters to make batches and batches of bubble cookies. Place a supply of plastic spatulas and a cookie sheet near the table. Squirt a generous amount of mild bubble bath into the water. Then use an egg beater to create a blizzard of bubbles. To make a bubble cookie, a child uses the spatula to skim bubbles out of the table and then places them on the cookie sheet. Bubble cookie, anyone?

Ada Goren
Winston-Salem, NC

Literacy Center

Who Me? Yes, You!

At this literacy center, little ones will quickly learn each other's names and the classic rhyme "Who Took the Cookies From the Cookie Jar?" To prepare for this center, copy the cookie patterns (see page 100) for each child. Color each pattern and then cut it out. Next, write a different child's name on the front of each cookie and glue the child's photograph to the back. Laminate the cookies for durability; then place them in a plastic cookie jar.

To use this center, a child begins chanting, "Who took the cookies from the cookie jar?" She then pulls a cookie out of the jar, identifies the child on the cookie, and then continues reciting the rhyme using the child's name. She recites, "Couldn't be. Then who?" She pulls another cookie out of the jar and then continues the activity in the same manner.

Play Dough Center

Rolling Out the Dough

Little hands will enjoy squishing, kneading, and rolling out some pretend cookie dough. In advance, follow the recipe shown to make a batch of dough. Place it in your play dough center along with a supply of rolling pins, cookie cutters, and cookie sheets. As each child makes a batch of pretend cookies, be sure to remind him that the dough is not for tasting. Afterward, reward your little baker for his work by treating him to a real cookie that he can eat!

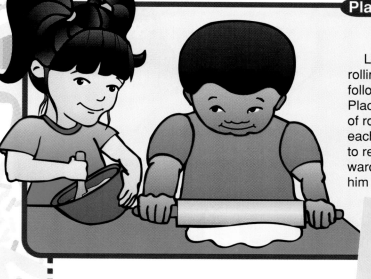

Pretend Cookie Dough

Ingredients:
3 c. flour
1 c. salt
1 c. water
1 tbsp. vegetable oil

Combine the flour and salt in a bowl. Stir in the water and vegetable oil. Mix thoroughly. Knead the dough until smooth. Store in an airtight container.

Sand Prints

Here's a simple sand table idea that youngsters will love. Wet the sand in your table to molding consistency. Then place plastic cookie cutters and cookie stamps at the table. Invite each child to use the cutters and stamps to make imprints in the sand. This idea will make quite an impression on youngsters!

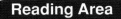

Reading Area

A Sweet Seat

Sweeten up your reading area with this chocolate sandwich-cookie cushion! To make one, you will need two 22" x 22" sheets of black felt, fabric glue, and a 22" x 22" sheet of foam (available at your local fabric shop). Cut the felt and foam into 22-inch circles. Next, use a craft stick to spread fabric glue over one side of the foam. Be sure the glue covers the entire surface and extends to the edges of the foam. Place a felt circle on the foam and rub the surface so the glue will adhere. Flip the cushion over and repeat the procedure with the remaining piece of felt. Allow the glue to dry overnight; then place the cushion in your reading area. Add a collection of cookie books and invite your youngsters to have a seat on this sweet treat!

A Cookie Book Collection

If You Give a Mouse a Cookie
Written by Laura Joffe Numeroff
Illustrated by Felicia Bond

The Doorbell Rang
By Pat Hutchins

Cookie Count: A Tasty Pop-Up
By Robert Sabuda

Who Took the Cookies From the Cookie Jar?
Written by Bonnie Lass and Philemon Sturges
Illustrated by Ashley Wolff

Sam's Cookie
Written by Barbro Lindgren
Illustrated by Eva Eriksson

A Cow, a Bee, a Cookie, and Me
Written by Meredith Hooper
Illustrated by Alison Bartlett

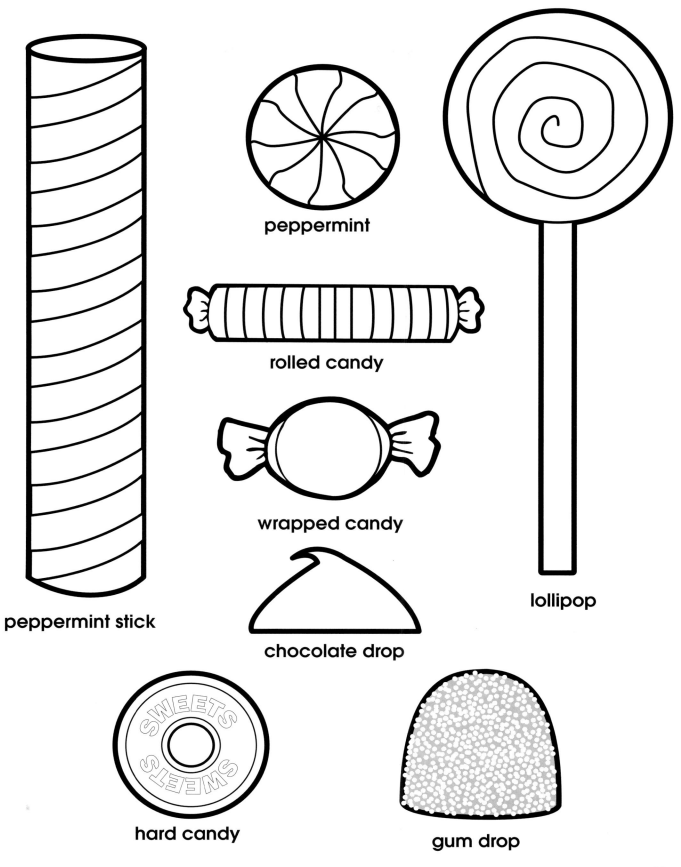

peppermint

peppermint stick

rolled candy

wrapped candy

chocolate drop

lollipop

hard candy

gum drop

Cookie Patterns
Use with "Who Me? Yes, You!" on page 95.

©The Education Center, Inc. • *THE MAILBOX®* • *Preschool* • Aug/Sept 2001

A Cornucopia of Centers

Welcome the Thanksgiving holiday with this fabulous feast of center ideas!

ideas by Angie Kutzer

Dramatic-Play Center
Turkey With All the Trimmings!

Set up this dramatic-play center and invite youngsters to try their hands at stuffing a pretend turkey. In advance, use a craft knife to cut off the handle of a gallon-sized plastic milk jug. (See illustration.) Cover any sharp edges with masking tape. Mix a small amount of liquid dish detergent with brown tempera paint and then paint the entire jug with the mixture. When the paint is dry, cut out a pair of craft foam turkey legs and then hot-glue them to the jug. Next, create pretend stuffing by mixing together small pom-poms and sponge pieces. Place the stuffing in a bowl with a large spoon and set it near the turkey. Invite each child to use the spoon to fill the turkey with stuffing. Mmm! This turkey *almost* looks good enough to eat!

Sensory Center
Turkeys in the Straw

Why wait for Easter eggs? Go on this turkey hunt instead! Ahead of time, collect an assortment of small turkey figures, such as magnets, candles, plastic cupcake decorations, or novelty erasers. Fill your sand table with crinkled yellow and brown paper strips. Hide the turkeys in the filler and let the hunt begin! To incorporate math skills, give each student a numeral card and have her find the corresponding number of turkeys. For a more competitive edge, give two students one minute to find as many turkeys as they can; then help them count and compare their totals. Gobble, gobble, gobble!

Art Center
Fabulous Feathers

Shoo youngsters on over to the art center to create these dashing gobblers. To prepare, set out a supply of washable markers, paper towels, and several spray bottles filled with water. Each student will also need a coffee filter; brown, yellow, and red paper scraps; two wiggle eyes; scissors; and glue.

To make a turkey, color a coffee filter with the markers and then spray the filter to allow the colors to run together. Sandwich the filter between paper towels to blot any excess water. While the filter dries, cut out an oval-shaped body from brown paper. Use the yellow and red paper to make a beak and wattle. Then glue them onto the body. Glue the body to the filter feathers as shown. Add two small sticky dots for eyes; then use a black marker to draw pupils. Let these colorful birds strut their stuff on a hallway bulletin board for all to admire.

Gross-Motor Center
Horn of Plenty

Use cornucopias and gourds to help little ones practice coordination skills. Tape several cornucopias to the floor and ask parents to send in an assortment of round mini gourds that will roll. Tape a line on the floor a short distance away from each cornucopia. Have youngsters visit the center and try to roll the gourds into the openings. (If your cornucopias have ribbed openings that won't lie flush with the floor, suspend the cornucopias between two chairs and have youngsters toss the gourds instead.) Now that's *plenty* of fun!

Play Dough Center
That's So Corny!

Little ones love corn on the cob! So stock your play dough center with several ears of dried Indian corn. Invite youngsters to use the corn to roll out balls of dough. As they do, they'll notice a corny design appear in the flattened dough. Impressive!

Match Me!

Introduce your little ones to the traditional symbols of Thanksgiving with this file folder game. To prepare, photocopy page 104 onto white paper. Color the pictures; then hold a black sheet of paper under the page and cut out the pictures through both thicknesses. Glue the black images to the inside of a file folder. Laminate the file folder (opened) and the pictures for durability. Store the picture pieces in a plastic zippered bag attached to the back of the folder. To play, a child matches each piece to its shadow.

Math Center
Pumpkin Patterns

Roll out some patterning fun using pumpkins! Prepare a batch of pumpkin-pie-scented play dough using the recipe below. Then use large and small pumpkin-shaped cookie cutters to trace simple patterns onto separate sentence strips. If desired, leave room on each strip for youngsters to continue the pattern. Laminate the strips; then place the strips, the dough, and the cutters in the center.

To complete the activity, a child cuts large and small pumpkins from the play dough, then lays them on a strip to create the programmed pattern. A "scent-sational" way to celebrate the holiday!

Pumpkin Play Dough
Ingredients:
2 c. flour
1 c. salt
2 c. water
3 tsp. pumpkin pie spice
orange food coloring or paste
2 tbsp. vegetable oil
4 tsp. cream of tartar

Combine ingredients in a large pot. Cook on low heat. Stir until a dough forms and pulls away from the sides of the pot. Remove the dough and cool.

Hooray for Hats!

Warm up your classroom with this well-knitted collection of hat-themed centers.

ideas contributed by LeeAnn Collins and Carol Plaut

Games Center

Find the Snowball

Even without snow, your youngsters will have a ball playing this sensory guessing game! Place several knitted caps and a small Styrofoam ball at a table. Invite a pair of children to the area. To use the center, one child closes her eyes while the other child hides the ball in one of the hats. The first child opens her eyes and then tries to find the ball by feeling each of the caps. After she finds it, the children switch roles and play again.

Fine Motor

In Stitches

This center provides little fingers with fine-motor practice and tactile stimulation. To prepare, duplicate and cut out the large hat pattern on page 105. Trace the pattern onto a piece of tagboard and then cut on the resulting outline. Punch holes around the edge of the tagboard shape to create a hat-shaped lacing card. Then tie a length of ribbon through one of the holes. For easier lacing, wrap the end of the ribbon with tape. Make several cards in a variety of colors and with a variety of laces, such as satin, raffia, and velvet. As your little ones lace up, encourage them to discuss the different textures of the ribbons. Ooh, this one is soft!

Hats in the Snow

To prepare for this center, ask parents to donate old, white baby socks. Cut off the toe of each sock right below the heel. Roll the cut edge of the toe to create a miniature hat; then use craft glue to attach a small white pom-pom to the top of the hat. Fill your sensory table with pretend snow (white Styrofoam packing pieces) and then hide the hats in the snow for your students to find.

For added fine-motor fun, create a milk jug snowman for each hat in the table. To make one snowman, remove the label from a small, clean plastic milk bottle. Next, remove the lid and hot-glue a small Styrofoam ball over the bottle opening. When the glue is dry, use paint pens or permanent markers to draw snowman features on the ball. Wrap a brown pipe cleaner around the neck of the bottle to create two arms. Then twist a two-inch length of pipe cleaner around the end of each arm. Finally, glue a felt scarf around the snowman's neck. Set the snowmen near the table; then invite students to find the hats and place them on their frosty friends.

Flannelboard

Hats Off to Graphing!

Youngsters will quickly warm up to graphing with this flannelboard idea! To prepare, gather a collection of old baby socks in a variety of colors. Then follow the directions in "Hats in the Snow" to create a supply of miniature hats. Next, use masking tape to create a graphing grid on your flannelboard. Place the hats in a container or a wool cap and set them near the board. To use the center, a child sorts the hats by color, places each set in a row or column on the graph, and then counts the number of hats in each row. No doubt about it, this graphing activity tops them all!

Sandy Caps

With wet sand and a bucket, you can make great sand castles. But did you know you can also make great sand *hats?* Invite your youngsters to create some sandy headgear with this sand table idea. To begin, wet the sand in the table to a molding consistency. Place a supply of small sand buckets or plastic bowls at the table; then add an assortment of craft items such as large pom-poms and lengths of rickrack, ribbons, or lace. If you have a supply of old knitted caps, cut off the pom-poms and place them at the table. Invite each child to use a bucket or bowl to mold the sand into a hat shape. Then have the child decorate the sand hat with the craft items. "Sandsational!"

How Much Is That Hat?

Knit together writing and language skills by setting up a hat shop in your dramatic-play area. In advance, collect a variety of hats and a supply of shopping bags. Set the hats on a shelf and then place a cash register at a table in the area. Next, place a small notepad and a pencil near the register for your youngsters to use to write receipts. Invite students to visit the center in pairs. Have one child be the customer and the other be the store clerk. Direct the customer to tell the clerk which hat she would like to purchase. Then have the clerk find the hat that she described and place it in a shopping bag. After the clerk has collected the money and given a receipt to the customer, encourage the children to switch roles. Thank you! Please come again!

P Is for Pom-Pom

If you have youngsters who are ready for beginning letter sounds, invite them to put on their thinking caps and head over to this literacy center. In advance, cut out one magazine picture for each letter you wish to reinforce. Glue each picture to a copy of the large hat pattern on page 105. Laminate the hats and then cut out each one. Next, create a pom-pom for each hat by programming a clean plastic milk jug lid with the corresponding letter. To make the center self-checking, also write the letter on the back of the hat. To use the center, a child identifies the picture on a hat, finds the corresponding letter on a "pom-pom," and then places it on top of the hat.

Buttons and a Hat to Match!

Here's a cool way to reinforce number recognition and counting. In advance, create ten milk jug snowmen and ten miniature hats. (See "Hats in the Snow" on page 107.) Use a fabric marker to label each hat with a different number from 1 to 10; then use a permanent marker to program each snowman with a different set of buttons from one to ten. Invite each child to count the number of buttons on a snowman, find the hat with the corresponding number, and then place the hat on the snowman's head. Afterward, encourage older preschoolers to place the snowmen in numerical order. What frosty fun!

The Hat
by Jan Brett

Sadie

Top Hat Stories

The Hat
by Jan Brett

A Hat for Minerva Louise
by Janet Morgan Stoeke

Caps for Sale
by Esphyr Slobodkina

Hats Hats Hats
by Ann Morris

Old Hat New Hat
by Stan and Jan Berenstain

Check It Out

Set up this library system in your reading area and invite youngsters to borrow a book for a night. To begin, stock the area with a variety of books about hats. (For literature suggestions see "Top Hat Stories.") Then use the small hat pattern on page 105 to make a hat cutout for each book. Label each hat with a different title and then laminate the hats. Attach a piece of hook Velcro to the back of each hat; then place the hats inside the corresponding books.

Next, use the patterns on page 110 to make a personalized, laminated child cutout for each student. Place a piece of loop Velcro on the head of each cutout and then display the cutouts on the wall of your reading area. To check out a book, a student removes the hat from the book of her choice and then places it on the head of her cutout. When the child returns the book, she removes the hat and places it back inside the book.

Child Patterns
Use with "Check It Out" on page 109.

©The Education Center, Inc. • *THE MAILBOX* • *Preschool* • Dec/Jan 2001–2

Lobster Pattern
Use with "Catch of the
Day" on page 114.

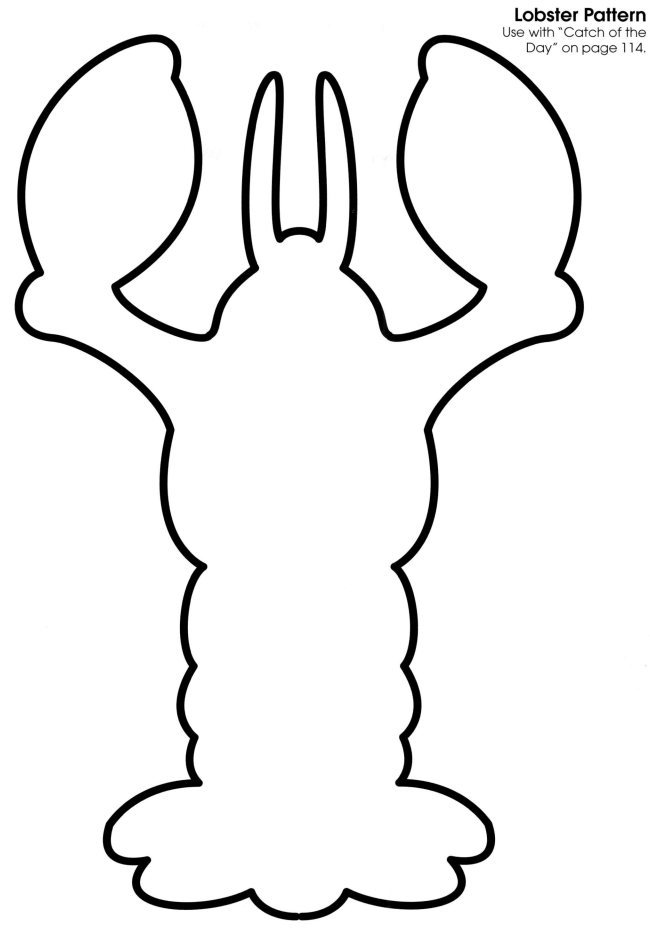

To Market, to Market

Shopping for new center ideas? Stock your learning centers with grocery-related activities that feed the need for preschool learning fun!

by Angie Kutzer

Attention, All Shoppers!

Enlist co-workers, relatives, friends, and students' parents to collect enough materials for the ideas in this unit. Make sure to request that the food containers be emptied and cleaned before being sent in.

— food boxes, bags, and cans
— milk or juice cartons (a supply that is the same size, quart or larger)
— paper grocery bags
— boxes of cereal rings (such as Cheerios, Froot Loops, or Apple Jacks) to fill your sensory table and for snacking
— grocery store ads
— coupon sections from newspapers
— discarded food and household magazines (such as *Cooking Light, Good Housekeeping,* and *Woman's Day*)
— novelty toys to use as prizes (optional)

food boxes
bags
cans
milk cartons
juice cartons

TACO CHIPS

COLORFUL WAFERS

CHOCO Pudding

CHOCO Pudding

TACO CHIPS

Literacy Center
Shopping Lists

With a little preparation, you can help your students load up on literacy skills. In advance, cut off the front panels of several food packages and put them in a pile. Make shopping lists by cutting out the brand names from the leftover packaging and gluing groups of them onto different sheets of paper as shown. Staple each list onto a paper grocery bag. To complete the activity, instruct a child to read a list and fill the bag with the correct items. If desired, have a partner check the child's work by unloading the bag. Now the center is ready for the next shoppers.

Bag It!

Math is in the bag with this nonstandard-measurement activity. Stock the math center with a supply of milk or juice cartons that are the same size (quart or larger). You'll also need to include a paper grocery bag and a canvas grocery bag. Have each shopper who visits the center estimate how many cartons the paper bag will hold. Then instruct her to count as she fills the paper bag. Now encourage the child to predict which bag will hold more: the paper or the canvas. Direct her to fill the canvas bag and compare the results. What a bagful of learning!

Pam Crane

Which do you prefer?

chocolate chip	peanut butter
Hunter	Evan
Torie	Jill
Cassidy	
Ross	

Discovery Center

Taste Tests

Conduct a few taste tests during your grocery store unit to give your little consumers practice with graphing. Make a simple two-column graph and laminate it. Use a washable marker to program the graph as shown. Provide taste samples for each student and then have him record his preference on the graph. Discuss the results during a later group time. Try a new test each day!

Possible taste tests:
Coke vs. Pepsi
name brand vs. generic brand
chocolate chip cookie vs.
    peanut butter cookie
fresh fruit vs. dehydrated fruit
tomato soup vs. chicken noodle soup

Water Table
Catch of the Day

Ask a child what he likes to see at the grocery store, and the lobster tank is sure to be on his list. Use a copy of the lobster pattern on page 111 to make a supply of craft foam cutouts. Use different colors of foam or use a permanent marker to program pairs of lobsters with matching letters, shapes, or numbers. Put the lobsters in your water table along with several pairs of tongs. Invite youngsters to use the tongs to catch all the lobsters and then find matching pairs or sort them. Get your fresh seafood right here!

Blocks Center
Dazzling Displays

Your youngsters will exercise their problem-solving skills as they pretend to be store stockers in this building activity. Put a large supply of cans, plastic bottles, and boxes in your blocks center. Each day, give the students in the center a cardboard base that's different in shape or size. Encourage the stockers to work together to create a product display that uses as many of the empty food packages as possible. "Tower-ific!"

Fine-Motor Center
Snip, Snip, Snip!

Scissor skills get checked out at this fun center. Have youngsters look through a variety of grocery advertisements, coupon sections of newspapers, and magazines that contain grocery coupons. As each child finds products that her family uses, encourage her to cut out the correlating coupons and take them home. Or have students cut out all the coupons they find and then set them out for parents to pick from. Preschoolers get cutting practice and parents get to save money. Now *that's* a bargain!

Art Center

That's My Name

Take advantage of all the environmental print coming into your room to reinforce letter and name recognition. To prepare, cut apart paper grocery bags so that each child can have the front or back panel of one. Direct the child to look at a supply of food packages (and the leftover ads from "Snip, Snip, Snip!" on page 114) to find the letters in her name. Have her cut out the letters, arrange them to spell her name, and glue them onto her paper. Then encourage her to add pictures of foods she likes to eat to make a collage. Display the finished projects on a board titled "We Are What We Eat!" Yummy!

Sensory Table

Cereal Surprises

Turn your sensory table into one big cereal bowl to provide your youngsters with an opportunity to explore. Fill the table with several boxes of cereal rings, such as Froot Loops, Cheerios, or Apple Jacks. Provide scoops, large spoons, measuring cups, and yarn lengths for youngsters to use to work on measurement and patterning concepts. For added fun, hide novelty toys in the cereal for students to find. Be sure to have some "untouched" cereal nearby for kids who want to crunch and munch!

BIRTHDAY BASH!

Everybody has one every year. What is it? It's a birthday! Nothing excites a preschooler more than a birthday party. With these fun-filled, birthday-themed centers, learning opportunities are simply the icing on the cake!

ideas contributed by LeeAnn Collins—Director,
Sunshine House Preschool, Lansing, MI

Math Center

CANDLE COUNTING

What makes a birthday cake so special? The candles, the candles! Set up this candle-counting center and help light up youngsters' math skills. Use the patterns on page 121 to make five birthday cakes and 15 candles. Color the cakes and candles; then label each cake with a different number from 1 to 5. After laminating the cakes and candles, cut them out and attach a strip of magnetic tape to the back of each one. Set the cakes and candles near a magnetic board. Then invite each child to place the cakes on the board and add the corresponding number of candles to each cake. Now close your eyes and make a wish!

Dramatic Play

COME TO MY PARTY!

Hang a birthday banner and streamers in your house-keeping area. Add a fake cake, and little ones won't be able to resist the urge to plan a pretend party! To pre-pare for this center, hot-glue birthday-candle holders into a white Styrofoam block to create a pretend birth-day cake. Place the cake in the area along with a box containing the following party items: a plastic tablecloth, party hats, paper plates, paper cups, plastic utensils, birthday candles, and empty gift-wrapped boxes. Invite youngsters to visit the area and use the items in the box to set up and host a pretend birthday party. Let's see. Set the table. Put candles on the cake. Stack the gifts. Sing "Happy Birthday." A host's work is never done!

SPECIAL DELIVERY!

Here's a simple center idea that reinforces prereading skills to the letter! In advance, die-cut the beginning letters of students' names. Cut out only one of each letter, even if more than one child has a name beginning with that letter. Glue each letter onto a white paper lunch bag; then decorate the bag with birthday-themed stickers. Next, make a class supply of the invitations on page 122. Program each invitation with a different child's name and then have her color it. Set the bags and invitations at the center. Then invite students to read the name on each invitation and place it in the bag with the same beginning letter. For added math reinforcement, encourage students to count the sorted invitations and compare the number in each bag.

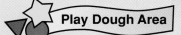
Play Dough Area

CAN'T GET ENOUGH OF THOSE CAKES!

Big cakes. Little cakes. Layered cakes. Cupcakes! Little ones will be making all kinds of cakes at this play dough center. Place miniature pie tins, muffin tins, round cookie cutters, and birthday candles in the area. Then invite each child to use the tins and cookie cutters to make a variety of cakes. What should your little baker do after he completes a cake? Add candles and sing "Happy Birthday," of course!

Art Center

BIRTHDAY PLACEMATS

Birthdays are special days. So have each child make a special birthday placemat to use on her day. To prepare, use decorative-edged scissors to cut the edges on a 12" x 18" sheet of craft foam. Next, use a paint pen to write "It's My Birthday!" in the center of the placemat. Then add the child's name and birthdate. When the paint is dry, invite the child to add stickers, glue on craft foam candles, and then add gold glitter glue flames. For an extra special touch, punch two holes in the top of the mat, thread a length of wire-edged ribbon through the holes, and then tie a bow. Little ones will be so excited about using these pretty placemats, you might have to celebrate just a little bit early!

Shake, Shake, Shake

Shaking a birthday present is *almost* as much fun as opening it! So set up this discovery center and invite students shake to their hearts' content. To prepare, gather pairs of clear containers, such as GLADWARE disposable food storage containers. Fill each pair with items such as rice, beans, or pennies. Secure the lids with duct tape if desired. Then gift wrap each container so that a small portion of the bottom is exposed, revealing the contents inside. To use the center, a child shakes the "gifts" and then pairs them up according to sound. To check his work, the child peeks under the bottom of each pair to see whether the contents match.

Games Area

Cake Match

Looking for a simple game that packs in a lot of learning? This idea takes the cake! To prepare, photocopy the cake patterns on page 121 twice to make five pairs of cakes. Color the cakes. Laminate them and then cut out each one. Place the cakes in your games area and invite students to use them to play a game of Memory.

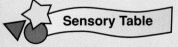

Sensory Table

Birthday Bows

This sensory table idea combines gift-wrapping fun and one-to-one correspon-dence skills. Wrap several small boxes with birthday wrapping paper and place them near your sensory table. Fill the table with different-colored crinkle paper; then hide a bow for each box in the paper. Invite each child to find the bows and then place one on each box. That's a wrap!

FRESHLY PAINTED CAKES

Bring out the little cake decorator in each child with this idea. From painting paper, cut out a class supply of birthday cakes similar to the one shown. Place the cakes at your painting center; then invite each child to paint a design on the cake. If desired, have students use sponge shapes and silk flowers to print designs on their cakes. When the paint is dry, help the child glue candle cutouts to the cake to represent her age. Want to show off your preschoolers' paintings? Label each child's cake with her name and then display it on a board titled "How Old Are You Now?"

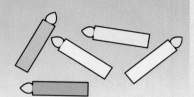

Blocks Area

BLOCKS, BOXES, AND BOWS

Add a birthday twist to your blocks area by gift wrapping several blocks and then placing a variety of bows in the center. Invite each child to stack the gift-wrapped blocks and then add a bow on top. Or have students arrange the blocks to resemble a box and then top off the structure with a large birthday bow.

**Writing Center**

CREATE A CARD

Cards are the hallmark of a birthday! So set up this center and encourage your youngsters to get writing! To begin, photocopy the card pattern on page 123 to make a class supply. Then fold each pattern on the line to create a blank greeting card. Place the cards in your writing area and invite each child to create a birthday card, thank-you note, or party invitation. If desired, cut out phrases from discarded greeting cards, such as *happy birthday, you're invited,* and *thank you.* Add the phrases to the center to help guide students as they write.

"A-Weigh" We Go!

Science process skills will be celebrated at this science center. To prepare, place a balance scale in the area and then add birthday items such as the following: a supply of birthday candles, a party hat, a blower, a paper cup, and a small paper plate. To use the center, a child places an item on one side of the scale and estimates the number of candles it will take to balance the scale. Then she counts out the number of candles needed to balance the scale and compares that number to her prediction. The child continues the activity in this manner until she has weighed each item at the center.

Puzzle Area

Wrapping Paper Puzzles

Party plates and sheets of wrapping paper can make inexpensive yet interesting puzzles! Gather a variety of paper plates and sheets of wrapping paper. Laminate the sheets of paper. Then cut each sheet and plate into large interlocking pieces. Place each set of pieces inside a resealable plastic bag. Then invite each child to assemble the birthday party puzzles. Happy learning to you!

Motor Skills Area

Tilt! Tilt!

On your next trip to the grocery store, visit the bakery counter and request a donation of an unused cake box with a clear top. Now you've got the key ingredient in this motor skills center! Have a child place a construction paper cake cutout inside the box. Then help him spread a thick layer of paint over the top half of the cutout. Drop a marble inside the box and close it. Then have the child tilt the box forward and backward so the marble rolls through the paint and creates a frostinglike design on the cake. Remove the cake from the box. Then, when the paint is dry, have the child glue candle cutouts to the top of the cake. Exercising motor skills is a piece of cake with this activity!

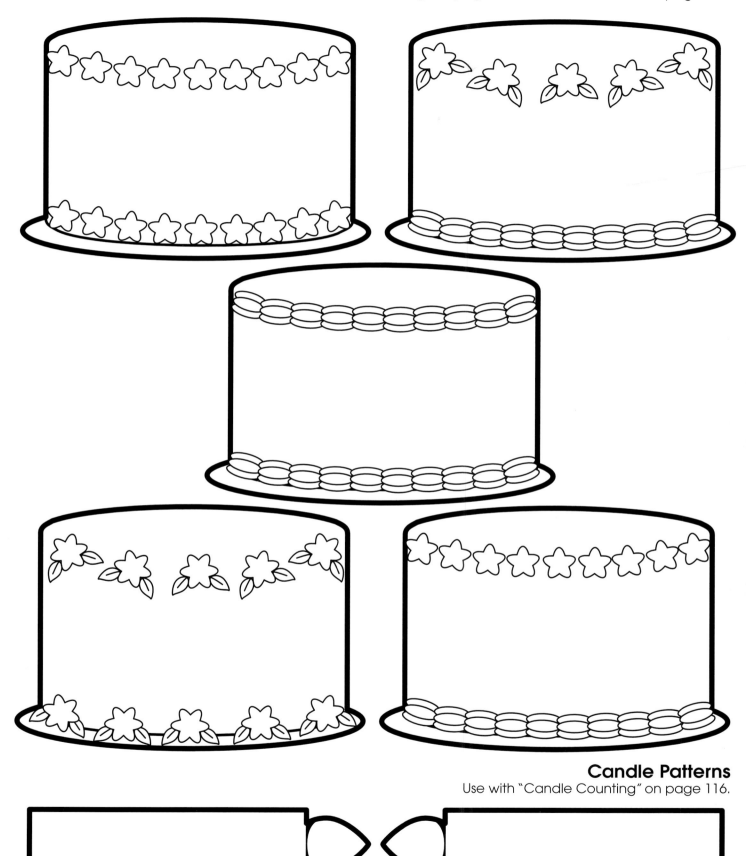

Candle Patterns
Use with "Candle Counting" on page 116.

Invitation Patterns
Use with "Special Delivery!" on page 117.

You're invited to a birthday party!

©The Education Center, Inc. • *THE MAILBOX*® • *Preschool* • April/May 2002

You're invited to a birthday party!

©The Education Center, Inc. • *THE MAILBOX*® • *Preschool* • April/May 2002

©The Education Center, Inc. • *THE MAILBOX®* • *Preschool* • April/May 2002

Sand and Surf Centers

You just might hear the roar of the ocean when you set up centers that make learning as exciting as a day at the beach!

ideas contributed by LeeAnn Collins—Director
Sunshine House Preschool, Lansing, MI

Discovery Center
A Little Bit of Beach in a Bag

How do you bring a bit of beach right into your classroom? It's easy! Gather a few seashells, some resealable plastic bags, and sand. Partially fill each bag with sand; then add a few seashells to each bag. Seal the bags with clear packaging tape and then place them at your discovery center. Have each child tilt the bags back and forth, and observe the movement of the sand and shells. For added sensory discovery, encourage youngsters to listen carefully to the sound of the moving sand. Hey, that sounds a lot like the ocean!

Sarah Booth—PreK, Messiah Nursery School
South Williamsport, PA

crab

Literacy Center
S Is for Sand

Sand pails aren't just for building sand castles! Fill one with magnetic letters to help build youngsters' literacy skills! In advance, photocopy the cards on page 129. Color the cards. Laminate them and cut them out. Next, place a self-adhesive magnetic strip on the back of each card. Set the cards near a magnetic board and the pail filled with letters. To use the center, a child places a card on the board, finds the matching magnetic letters, and then places them under the card to spell the word.

Flannelboard Center
Five Little Sand Castles

To prepare for this center, record yourself reciting the poem below and then place the recording near your flannelboard. Make five felt sand castle cutouts; then place the sand castles on the flannelboard. To use the center, a child begins playing the recording and removing the castles according to the poem. When students are familiar with this activity, encourage them to recite the poem without the recording.

Five little sand castles built by the shore.
Along came a wave and whoosh!
There were four.

Four little sand castles built just for me.
Along came a wave and whoosh!
There were three.

Three little sand castles built just for you.
Along came a wave and whoosh!
There were two.

Two little sand castles built in the sun.
Along came a wave and whoosh!
There was one.

One little sand castle built just for fun.
Along came a wave and whoosh!
There were none.

Art Center
Sturdy Sand Castles

Having your sand castle washed away sure can be a disappointment! With this craft idea, your youngsters can create sand castles that are here to stay! To make a castle, provide a child with paper towel tubes cut into a variety of lengths. Help the child use a paintbrush to cover each tube with glue. (To keep the glue off little fingers, clip a spring-type clothespin to the tube and have the child hold the tube by the clothespin.) Next, roll the tube in a shallow pan of sand until it is covered. Set the tubes aside to dry. Afterward, help the child create a sand castle by gluing the sides of the tubes together with craft glue. Next, pour Elmer's glue onto a small plastic plate so that the bottom of the plate is covered. Set the castle on the plate. Sprinkle sand over the glue; then pour off any excess sand. For a finishing touch, invite the child to glue a construction paper flag to the top of one of the tubes. Ah, a sand castle fit for a queen!

Play Dough Area
Calling All Sand Fans!

Invite your little ones to dig in to some grainy fun by placing a batch of sand dough in your play dough area. To make a batch of sandy dough, follow the recipe shown. Place the dough in an airtight container and set it near a bucket of small shells. Invite each child to roll out the dough and then press the shells into it to make impressions. Or have students use the shells and dough to create some sensational sand castles.

Sandy Play Dough
Ingredients:
1 c. flour
$\frac{1}{2}$ c. salt
1 tbsp. cream of tartar
1 c. water
$\frac{1}{4}$ c. sand
brown food coloring paste

Mix all of the ingredients together in a medium-sized pot. Stir constantly over medium heat until the mixture is slightly lumpy. Turn out onto a piece of foil and let cool; then knead until smooth.

Jill Simon—Three- and Four-Year-Olds
Poland Boardman Child Care Center
Poland, OH

Fine-Motor Center
Weaving for Wee Ones

Beach chairs are great for relaxing at the shore. But did you know they also make wonderful weaving tools? Invite your preschoolers to participate in some weaving fun with this center idea. In advance, gather a couple of beach chairs similar to the one shown. Tie lengths of ribbon to each chair; then have your youngsters weave the ribbons through the chairs. Over, under, over, under…

Sand Pails and Shovels

To prepare for this math center, make ten copies of the pail and shovel patterns on page 130. Color the patterns and then program each pail with a different number from 1 to 10. Program each shovel with a different set of stickers from 1 to 10. Laminate the pails and shovels; then use a craft knife to cut a three-inch slit across the top of each pail. Place the shovels and pails in the center. To complete the activity, a child reads the numeral on each pail and finds the shovel with the matching set of stickers. Then he places the shovel inside the pail by slipping it through the slit. To reinforce other preschool skills, program the pails and shovels with other pairs for youngsters to match.

Seashore Snack

Set up this snack center and invite your tots to take a dip—in some edible sand! Read through the recipe shown and then gather the needed ingredients and supplies. Have each child follow the steps to create a fun fruit dip that will remind her of the beach!

Ingredients needed to make one snack:
2 tbsp. instant vanilla pudding mix
1/4 c. milk
crumbled vanilla wafers
3–4 apple slices
Supplies:
5 oz. paper cup for each child
tablespoon
1/4 c. measuring cup
plastic spoon for each child

Place pudding mix and milk in a paper cup and then mix thoroughly with the plastic spoon. Top the pudding with vanilla wafer crumbs. Dip apple slices in the mixture and eat!

Perimeter and Area for Preschoolers?

It's true! You can introduce your youngsters to the concepts of perimeter and area in a perfectly preschool way! Place a variety of beach towels in your blocks area. Invite each child to lay out a towel and then place blocks around the outside edges of the towel (perimeter). Or have her use the blocks to cover the entire towel (area). Encourage the child to count the number of blocks needed to cover the perimeter or area of the towel. Then have her remove the blocks and try the activity again with a different towel.

Pail and Shovel Patterns

Use with "Sand Pails and Shovels" on page 127.

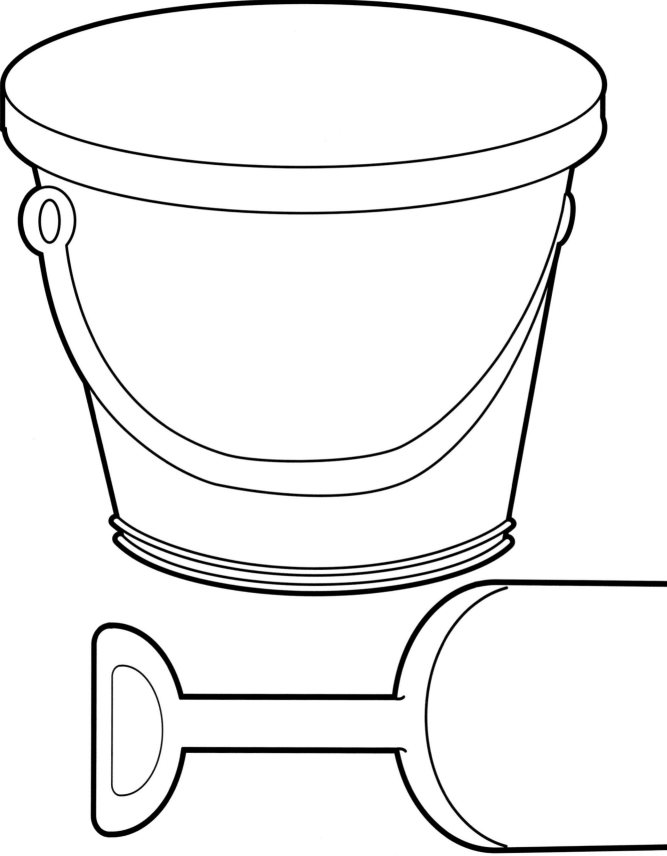

©The Education Center, Inc. • *THE MAILBOX® • Preschool* • June/July 2002

Zoom! Zoom! Zoom! I'm Off to the Moon!

Written and illustrated by Dan Yaccarino

Rocket into reading with this rhyming space adventure! Then prepare for a liftoff into lunar learning with these extension ideas! To order this book, visit our Web site: www.themailbox.com.

by Ada Goren

Pack for the Moon

After reading the story, draw your preschoolers' attention to the first page and the next-to-last page. In each illustration, the young boy has a suitcase in one hand. What do your little ones think might be inside? What might your students pack if *they* were going on a trip to the moon? Invite them to answer by completing this activity. Give each child an open suitcase shape cut from a 12" x 18" sheet of construction paper. Provide a supply of magazines, scissors, and glue. Encourage each child to cut or tear pictures from magazines to show what he thinks might be good to pack for a trip to the moon. Have him glue his pictures onto his suitcase. When each child has finished, help him fold his suitcase "closed" and label the outside with his name. During a group time, invite each child to share what he has packed. If desired, give each student a moon sticker for the outside of his suitcase so that it will resemble the suitcase at the end of the story. *critical thinking, fine-motor skills, language*

A "Space-y" Snack

You don't have to be a rocket scientist to construct this cheese-and-crackers snack! Precut American cheese slices as shown; then give each child the three triangles resulting from one slice. Have the child place two saltine crackers on a paper plate as shown. Then have her place the three cheese triangles as shown to complete her rocket. Three…two…one…eat! *following directions, shape recognition*

A Countdown Fingerplay

This lively fingerplay will have your preschoolers practicing both math and movement. After your students "blast off" in the last line, invite them to zoom all around your room—making rocket sound effects, of course! *oral language, movement, math*

Come on, everybody! Let's go to the moon!	*Motion "come on" with one hand.*
Hurry! Hurry! We're leaving soon!	*Pretend to tap watch.*
Put up your hand and let's all count.	*Hold up five fingers.*
We're going to lift off and zoom about!	*Sweep other hand upward from hip.*
Ready? Five…four…three…two…one…	*Show each number of fingers.*
Blast off!	*Jump up and raise both hands in the air.*

Preschool Astronauts on Display

Point out Dan Yaccarino's colorful illustrations of space to your young readers. Then encourage your students to make a similar space background for a bulletin board. Place blue bulletin board paper on a newspaper-covered floor. Set out paper plates of red, orange, and yellow tempera paint. Invite a few children at a time to dip their fingertips into the paint and make colorful dots all over the blue paper. After everyone has had a turn, let the paint dry; then use the paper to cover a bulletin board.

Next, duplicate the space suit pattern on page 134 onto orange paper for each child. Cut out each pattern, including the dotted area inside the helmet; then place a photo of the child so that her face shows through the opening. Mount each paper astronaut on the board, along with a speech bubble. Ask each child to recall the part of the story that she'd most enjoy if she were the one traveling to the moon. Write her response on her speech bubble and then add the title shown. *story recall, art*

133

NUTS TO YOU!

WRITTEN & ILLUSTRATED BY LOIS EHLERT

Nuts
to
You!

Lois Ehlert

Your youngsters will be nuts about this tale of a mischievous squirrel! So invite them to scamper on over to hear it; then follow up with these extensions. To order this book, visit our Web site: www.themailbox.com.

by Ada Goren

FOR SAFETY, PLEASE CHECK WITH PARENTS FOR STUDENT NUT ALLERGIES BEFORE BEGINNING THIS UNIT.

Nuts
to
A. J.!

NUTS TO WHO?

The cutout pages of this class book echo Ehlert's cover design and will also help your little ones learn to recognize one another's names. To begin, snap a photo of each child as he holds up a peanut. Next, take your class outdoors and give each child a sheet of white construction paper and a peeled brown crayon. Have him do a bark rubbing to cover his entire piece of paper.

To make each page, use a craft knife to cut a round hole in each child's paper, leaving the circle attached on the right side (as shown). Then tape the child's photo behind the cutout circle. Finally, write "Nuts to [child's name]!" below the flap. Stack the pages, add a cover that reads "Nuts to Us!", and bind the book along the left side. As a child reads the book, he tries to decipher each name, then opens the flap to reveal a classmate's picture.

A POCKET FULL OF NUTS

The narrator of this story decides to keep nuts in her pockets—just in case she needs to lure the squirrel away from trouble again! Keep some paper nuts in *your* pockets to make the most of transition times! First, make a class supply of peanut cutouts. Label each one with a child's name; then stash the peanuts in your pocket. When you have an extra moment to fill, pull out a paper peanut and say, "Nuts to you, [child's name]!" Then invite the named child to choose a squirrel action for the whole class to perform, such as "Eat with your paws" or "Dig for buried nuts." What cute little squirrels!

Sally   Corey

136

A Treat Fit for a Squirrel

The squirrel in this story isn't exactly shy—he sits up and begs for a treat! Invite your preschoolers to prepare a treat for the real squirrels who live in their backyards. Give each child a paper lunch bag and set out the following ingredients: peanuts (in the shell), sunflower seeds, and plain popped popcorn. Have each child count ten peanuts into her bag; then have her measure and pour a half-cup of sunflower seeds and a cup of popcorn into the bag. Write a parent note similar to the one shown; then staple a copy of it to each bag. Invite each child to take the treat home and put it out for a squirrel friend. As the squirrels eat, your little ones will get a treat too—observing real squirrels!

A Nutty Center

Dig into sorting skills with this center idea! To prepare, make a few copies of the sorting sheet on page 135. Color the sheets as desired; then laminate them for durability. Place the sorting sheets in a center, along with a bowl of peanuts, walnuts, and pecans in their shells. Invite each youngster at this center to sort the nuts onto a sorting sheet.

When you're finished with this center, bring in some nutcrackers and crack open the nuts for tasting. Take a vote to find out which type of nut your little squirrels like best!

Squirrel Scamper

Combine movement and math in this game where preschoolers pretend to be squirrels on the hunt for nuts. Before you begin, hide a supply of unshelled peanuts in your classroom. Give each child a small paper bag for collecting her peanuts. Then give a starting signal and invite students to scamper like squirrels, looking for the nuts. After a few minutes, give a stop signal. Have each child count her peanuts. The child with the most peanuts is the winner! What's the prize? The winner gets to pass out a nutty snack for everyone—Nutter Butter cookies, of course!

YO! YES?

Looking for a unique way to teach youngsters about feelings and friendship? If you answered, "Oh, yes!", then check out Chris Raschka's *Yo! Yes?* With just a few simple words, this picture book perfectly captures the range of emotions in a budding friendship between two boys. After sharing the story, use these follow-up activities to help your youngsters explore feelings, friendship, and fun! To order this book, check out our Web site at www.themailbox.com.

ideas by Roxanne LaBell Dearman

READING BODY LANGUAGE

Before beginning the story, invite your youngsters to do a different type of reading—reading body language. Show each illustration to your youngsters and have them examine the characters and discuss how they might be feeling. Invite students to predict what the story is about; then read the book. Afterward, discuss youngsters' predictions.

SIMON SAYS

Now that your little ones have *read* some body language, invite them to *express* some body language with this adaptation of Simon Says. Before playing the game, discuss different words that describe feelings, such as angry, sad, scared, and happy. Have students demonstrate facial expressions and body language that reflect each feeling; then begin playing Simon Says. Cue students to show a particular emotion with directions such as "Simon says, 'I'm happy.' " When your youngsters are familiar with the game, invite different children to take turns giving cues.

HOW DO YOU SAY HI?

Greetings and giggles will fill the air when you have youngsters act out the following rhyme. After reciting the last line, encourage each child to turn to a classmate and give him a warm greeting. Hello, friend!

Hey! Hi! Howdy! Yo!
There are many ways to say hello!
Wave your hand. Nod your head.
Smile big or wink instead.
Blow a kiss. Tip your hat.
Shake your hands. Give a pat.
Of all the ways to say hello,
Here's the way I like to go….

GREETINGS!

Oh, there are so many ways to say hello. Find out which method each child prefers with this display activity. To begin, have students brainstorm different greetings and list their responses on a chart. If desired, review the poem from "How Do You Say Hi?" to help students think of ideas. Next, ask each child to choose his favorite way to say hello. Write his response in a speech bubble and then photograph the child acting out his greeting. Display each child's photo and speech bubble near your classroom door. Add a copy of the poem to the display, and visitors to your classroom are sure to feel a warm welcome!

PALS AT PLAY

The final pages of *Yo! Yes?* show the two boys running hand in hand and jumping into the air. Review these pages with your students and discuss some activities the two new friends might do together. Then have each child illustrate what she thinks the boys may do. Encourage the child to dictate another phrase the boys might exclaim; then write her response on her paper. Wow!

Mouse Mess

In this lively rhyming story, a mischievous mouse makes a mess in a family's kitchen. Make the most of the mess by using the following story extensions to sweep in some preschool learning fun! To order this book, visit our Web site: www.themailbox.com.

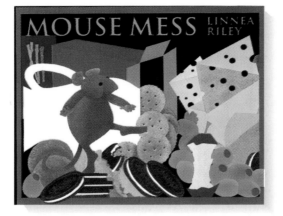

ideas by Rosemary Kesse—PreK
Little People Playtime, Hampshire, IL

A Feast for the Eyes

The bright, bold illustrations in this book make it perfect for an observation and prediction activity. Before reading the story to your class, show students each page and have them carefully examine the illustrations. Invite your youngsters to identify various food items on the different pages and make predictions about the story. Then, after the initial reading, discuss the mouse's mischievous adventure and compare it with your youngsters' predictions. *observation, prediction*

Acting It Out

"Crackle-sweep, he rakes corn flakes and jumps into the pile he makes." With such descriptive text, *Mouse Mess* can easily be acted out by your preschoolers. When students are familiar with the story, invite one child to stand in front of the class and play the role of the mouse. As you read the book, have the child dramatize the story for the class. If necessary, encourage the child to look at the illustrations to help him think of actions to perform. *literature experience, role-playing*

What a Mess!

That mouse sure does leave a mess to clean up! Invite your youngsters to tidy up the mess with this classification activity. In advance, collect clean, empty food containers, such as corn flakes boxes, cracker boxes, milk cartons, and plastic peanut butter jars. If possible, have the same brand for each type of container. Scatter the containers in a large open area and then invite a small group of children to the area. Remind your youngsters of the story; then invite them to work together to sort the containers and clean up the mess. With this activity, little ones will be cleaning up, classifying, *and* cooperating. How neat! *classification*

Cereal in the Reading Center

Set up this center and invite your youngsters to curl up with a good book—in a pretend bowl of cereal! To prepare, have youngsters help tear brown paper bags or bulletin board paper into corn flake shapes. Place the shapes in a small wading pool and set the pool in your reading area. Hide a few books in the flakes; then place a plastic rake in the pool. Invite each child to visit the area, use the rake to uncover a book, and then curl up in the "bowl" and read! *fine motor, literature experience*

Sand Castles, Just Like the Mouse Makes!

The mischievous mouse in the story uses brown sugar to create sand castles. After hearing the story, your youngsters just might want to make some castles of their own. To prepare, decorate a plastic container to resemble the brown sugar container in the story. Next, wet the sand in your sand table to a molding consistency. Then fill the plastic container with some of the sand. Place the container in the table; then add plastic forks, spoons, and measuring cups to the area. Invite your youngsters to scoop out the "brown sugar" and use the supplies to make castles. *creative thinking*

141

The Very Quiet Cricket

Written & Illustrated by Eric Carle

Youngsters will be chirping with delight when you share this tale of a young cricket who finally finds his song. And they'll jump at the chance to try these fun extension activities, too! To order this book, visit our Web site: www.themailbox.com.

by Ada Goren

Eric Carle · The Very Quiet Cricket

What Next?

When you preview this book, you'll find the charming sound effect of a cricket's chirp when you turn to the last page of the story. But when you share the book with your preschoolers, pause before turning to that last page. Ask the children to predict what will happen when the very quiet cricket attempts to "talk" to the female cricket. Will he make a sound? What will it be? After listening to all predictions, turn the page and let everyone enjoy the beautiful cricket song! Then read the factual information about crickets that Eric Carle includes on the book's dedication page.

He Keeps Growing and Growing...

After sharing the book a few times (or maybe a few dozen, depending on how much your preschoolers love it!), ask youngsters to pay attention as you flip the pages of the book from front to back. What do they notice about the cricket on each page? Guide them to notice the cricket's size on each spread of pages. Do they believe his growth has anything to do with his ability to make a sound? Ask a student volunteer to name something he can do now that he couldn't do when he was smaller. Write his accomplishment on a sheet of chart paper. Continue with other students' accomplishments until everyone has had a turn to add to the list. Then label the chart "Things We Can Chirp About." Display it for classroom visitors to admire!

Things We Can Chirp About

I can button my jacket.
Elise
I can brush my teeth by myself.
Terrence
I can play on the computer.
David

Have your preschoolers got the acting bug? Then invite them to dramatize this story! Assign the parts of the very quiet cricket and the other insects who greet him throughout the story, including as many buzzing mosquitoes as you need to give each child a part. Encourage everyone to dress in costume—a set of pipe cleaner antennae! Narrate the story and have each actor return to a seat in the audience when his part is over. Ask the audience to participate throughout the play by having the children recite the repetitive lines beginning with "The little cricket wanted to answer" and ending with "Not a sound." Use the book's chirping sound effect to bring the play to its exciting conclusion. Bravo!

Hi, Hello, and How Do You Do?

Each insect who meets the very quiet cricket uses a different greeting. Go back through the book with your little ones and list all the different ways the bugs say hello. Then ask youngsters to add to the list any other greetings they can think of. Keep the finished list handy for use with the next activity.

Artistic Insects on Display

Conclude your study of this Eric Carle book with a project that imitates his beautiful illustrations. To begin, cut out insect body-part tracers from tagboard. Next, invite each youngster to fingerpaint on white copy paper. Use colors that are seen in the insects in the story, such as blues, yellows, browns, and greens. Help each child trace insect head and body shapes onto his dry painting and cut the shapes out. Have him glue the cutouts onto a sheet of copy paper and use crayons to add legs and antennae. If the child would like to add wings to his insect, have him rub peeled crayons over a paper towel. Then trace a wing pattern onto the paper towel and cut it out. Have the child glue the wings in place. Finally, draw a speech bubble next to his insect. Have him choose a greeting (see "Hi, Hello, and How Do You Do?"); then write it in the speech bubble.

To create a display, cut larger shapes from some of the fingerpainted paper and put them together to create the very quiet cricket in the center of the board. Then mount the children's insect creations around it.

The Napping House

by Audrey Wood

Little ones will be wide awake when you read this cumulative tale about a house full of snoozing, snoring, slumbering friends. After sharing the story, tuck in some learning with the following story extensions. To order this book, visit our Web site: www.themailbox.com.

ideas contributed by Sue Fleischmann—Preschool
Holy Cross School
Menomonee Falls, WI

Snoring, Take Two!

After reading the story to your class, youngsters will most likely say, "Read it again!" So use this listening activity to make a second reading just dreamy! Instruct students to listen carefully for the word *sleeping* and then make snoring sounds each time the word is mentioned in the story. Begin reading the book and get ready to catch some Zzz's! *listening, story participation*

Positions, Everyone! Positions!

When a wakeful flea bites a mouse, the characters in *The Napping House* are tossed over the bed, under the covers, beside each other, and everywhere else in between. What a perfect opportunity to teach a lesson on positional words! In advance, photocopy the patterns on page 146. Color the patterns. Cut them out and then attach a piece of self-adhesive felt to the back of each one. Place the bed in the middle of your flannelboard; then give each character to a different child. Begin singing the song shown and have the child with the granny pattern place it on the board as directed in the song. Continue the activity in this manner, using other characters and positional words in the song. *positional words, listening*

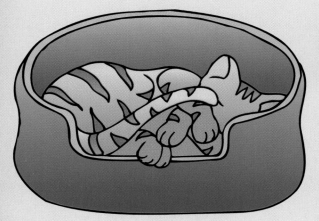

(sung to the tune of "The Farmer in the Dell")

The [granny] is [on] the bed.
The [granny] is [on] the bed.
Heigh-ho, the napping house!
The [granny] is [on] the bed.

Build Me a Story

Language skills will start stacking up with this idea for encouraging youngsters to tell *The Napping House* over and over again. To prepare, photocopy the patterns on page 146. Color the patterns. Laminate them and then cut out each one. Next, tape each pattern to a block from your blocks area. Invite students to stack and then unstack the blocks in sequence as they retell the story. *language development, story retelling, sequencing*

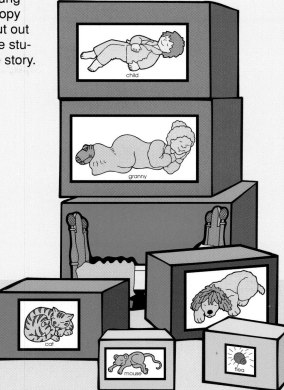

Who's That Napping in the House?

Create a pretend napping house for this group game by draping a large blanket or sheet over a pair of chairs. Have your youngsters sit facing the house. Direct one child to close her eyes. Then quietly select another child from the group to crawl under the blanket and lie in the napping house with only his feet exposed. Signal the first child to open her eyes by having the class chant, "Someone's napping in the house, sleeping soundly like a mouse." Then invite the child to guess which student is snoozing under the sheet. *thinking, language development*

The Story Unfolds

A class book that youngsters will flip over is the perfect way to encourage independent reading and story retelling. To make a flip book for *The Napping House,* duplicate and cut out the patterns on page 146. Color the patterns and then glue each one onto a 4" x 6" index card. Sequence the cards in a vertical row. Add a blank card to the bottom of the row and glue a construction paper roof to the top card. Next, tape the cards together as shown. Flip the cards over and then cover the exposed adhesive with additional pieces of tape. Fold the cards accordion-style. Then glue construction paper windows and a door to the card that is now on the top. Write "The Napping House" on the roof, and the book is complete.

To begin reading the book, flip over the top card to reveal the bed. Continue unfolding the stack of cards until all of the characters have been revealed and the story has been told. *literacy, story retelling*

145

Patterns

Use with "Positions, Everyone! Positions!" on page 144 and
Build Me a Story" and "The Story Unfolds" on page 145.

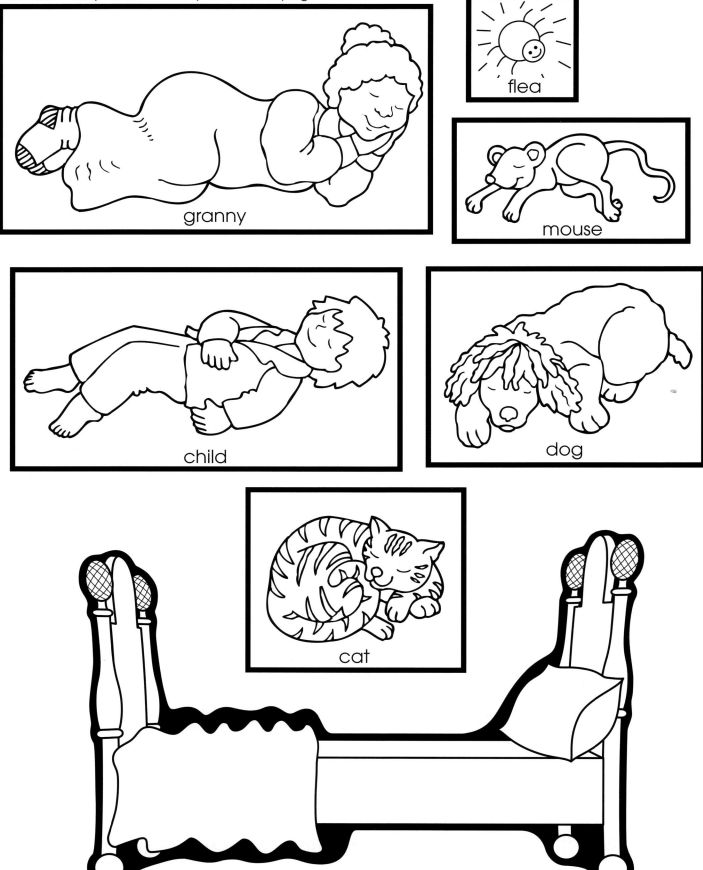

granny

flea

mouse

child

dog

cat

©The Education Center, Inc. • THE MAILBOX® • Preschool • April/May 2002

CONCEPT FEATURES

The Ins and Outs of In and Out

Invite your little preschoolers to wiggle their way through these appealing activities that reinforce the concepts of *in* and *out*.

ideas contributed by Lucia Kemp Henry

Where Is Wormie?

What's the best way to introduce this in-and-out study? In song, of course! To prepare for this singing activity, cut a worm shape out of green felt and then glue on a pair of wiggle eyes. Gather several objects large enough to hold the worm, such as a child's purse, a lunchbox, and a seasonal-shaped container.

To begin the activity, gather students together and introduce the felt worm as Wormie. Place the worm inside one of the containers and have students join you in singing the call-and-response song shown. After singing, invite a child to take the worm out of the container. Direct him to place it in a different container and then sing the song again, replacing the underlined word with the name of the new container.

(sung to the tune of "Where Is Thumbkin?")

Teacher: Where is Wormie?
Students: Where is Wormie?
Teacher: There he is!
Students: There he is!
Teacher: Wormie's *in* the [apple].
Students: Wormie's *in* the [apple].
Teacher: Take him *out*.
Students: Take him *out*.

Watch It Wiggle

Worms just might wiggle as much as your preschoolers, so grab your youngsters' attention with this wiggly fingerplay. In advance, purchase a class supply of Gummy Worm candy. Have each child wash her hands; then provide her with a worm. Next, invite her to use the worm as she acts out the following fingerplay. Where should the Gummy Worm candies go when the fingerplay is over? *In* youngsters' mouths to be eaten! Yum!

Here is an apple with a hole so small.	*Make fist with a small opening.*
In goes the worm. I can't see it at all!	*Put Gummy Worm in the hole.*
Out comes the worm.	*Pull the worm out.*
Then in it goes once more.	*Put the worm in the hole.*
Out, in, out!	*Move the worm out, in, and out of fist.*
As it eats the apple core!	*Make fist with large opening.*

Go In and Out of the Apple

Invite students to act like worms in apples with this movement activity. To prepare, cut the top and bottom flaps off a large appliance box. Next, cut out two large apple shapes from bulletin board paper. Then tape them to opposite sides of the box. Cut out two tagboard stems and glue each one onto an apple cutout.

To begin the activity, have students stand in a circle and place the box in the middle. As you sing the song below, invite one student at a time to crawl in and out of the apple box.

(sung to the tune of "The Bear Went Over the Mountain")

Go in and out of the apple.
Go in and out of the apple.
Go in and out of the apple,
Just like a little worm!

Worms on the Move

Set up this discovery center and watch those worms wiggle in and wiggle out! To prepare, cut out a tagboard worm shape for each child. Have the child color the worm as desired and then glue on a pair of wiggle eyes. When the glue is dry, help each child accordion-fold his worm as shown. Next, stock a center with items that the worm can crawl into, such as cardboard tubes, paper cups, and plastic PVC pipes. Invite each child to visit the area with his worm and place it in and out of the items. For added discovery, also stock the area with objects that the worm will not fit into and encourage the child to find which items will accommodate the worm. "In-credible!" "Out-standing!"

Over, Under

Put a new spin on spiders with this web–themed study of over and under. Your youngsters will catch on as quickly as spiders weave their webs!

ideas by Lucia Kemp Henry

Spider Song

Start your over-under study with a song and a demonstration! In advance, follow the directions in "A Spider and a Web" (below) to make a model web and spider. Have one child hold the web as you sing the song and move the spider. When students are familiar with this activity, place the web and spider in a center for youngsters to use independently.

There Is a Little Spider
(sung to the tune of "Go in and out the Window")

There is a little spider.
There is a little spider.
There is a little spider
Who builds a good strong web.

The spider hurries over.
The spider hurries over.
The spider hurries over
Her good strong spiderweb.

The spider scurries under.
The spider scurries under.
The spider scurries under
Her good strong spiderweb.

A Spider and a Web

You don't need eight legs to create this model web! But, you will need four 12-inch pipe cleaners and white string. Twist the pipe cleaners at midpoints to join them; then separate them into a spoke arrangement as shown. Tie one end of the string near the middle of the pipe cleaners. Then weave a circular web design with the string, wrapping the string around each spoke as you cross it. (See illustration above.) When the web is complete, cut the string and tie it to the end of a pipe cleaner. For added durability, bend the ends of each pipe cleaner around the string to keep the web from unraveling.

To make a spider, glue two wiggle eyes to an iridescent pom-pom. When the glue is dry, flip the pom-pom over and glue on a 12-inch piece of string and four craft crinkle strips. Use the completed spider and the web to act out the song "There Is a Little Spider." Little ones will want to sing the song and use the props *over* and *over* and *over!*

Easy Weaving

Introduce your wee ones to weaving with this crafty web that reinforces *over* and *under*. To make one, you will need the following: four three-inch lengths of pipe cleaners, an iridescent pom-pom, wiggle eyes, a large black paper plate, and white yarn. Twist the pipe cleaners together in the middle; then hot-glue them to the pom-pom as shown. Flip the pom-pom over and then glue on a pair of wiggle eyes. Next, cut one-inch slits around the edges of the black paper plate.

Have a child weave white yarn around the plate, anchoring the yarn in the slits. Encourage the child to say "over" and "under" as he moves the yarn over and under the plate. When the web is complete, help the child attach the pom-pom spider to the web by bending the tips of the pipe cleaners around the yarn. To display the webs, staple the plates to a bulletin board with a black background; then add a title.

Web Sights

Over, under, over, under. Encourage students to use these positional words as they interact with pretend spiderwebs in your blocks area. To make one web, cut off the front of a clean gallon-sized milk jug as shown. Cover any sharp edges with masking tape; then use Slick paint to draw a web design on the jug front. Place several webs in the blocks area along with a few pom-pom spiders. (To make a spider, see "Easy Weaving.") Invite each child to build a structure with the blocks and webs. Then have him use the words *over* and *under* as he moves a spider through his completed structure. "Look! The spider is crawling under the web!"

Spiders All Over Me!

Little fingers will be wiggling and little voices will be giggling with this fingerplay that reinforces body parts as well as *over* and *under*.

(sung to the tune of "The Caissons Go Rolling Along")

Over here.	*Hold one hand over the other. Wiggle fingers on top hand.*
Under there.	*Move top hand under the other and wiggle fingers again.*
There are spiders everywhere!	*Both hands out, wiggling fingers.*
And the spiders are crawling on me!	*Wiggle fingers all over body.*
On my arms.	*Hands on opposite arms, wiggling fingers.*
On my eyes.	*Wiggle fingers on eyes.*
Now they're running down my thighs!	*Wiggle fingers moving down thighs.*
Oh, the spiders are crawling on me!	*Wiggle fingers all over body.*
Underneath my chin	*Wiggle fingers under chin.*
And on my arm again.	*Hands on opposite arms, wiggling fingers.*
Over and under all my toes!	*Wiggle fingers over and under toes.*
Now they're in my hair!	*Wiggle fingers in hair.*
There are spiders everywhere!	*Both hands out, wiggling fingers.*
Oh, the spiders are crawling on me!	*Wiggle fingers all over body.*

On and Off

On Dasher, on Dancer, on Prancer, on Vixen… When it comes to the concepts of *on* and *off*, there's no better expert than a reindeer! Let Santa's hoofed helpers demonstrate on and off to your youngsters, and learning spatial concepts will be as exciting as a sleigh ride!

ideas by Lucia Kemp Henry

A Reindeer of My Own

Before taking off with this unit, have each child craft her own reindeer manipulative to use with the following activities. To make one, use the pattern on page 154 to make a brown tagboard reindeer cutout. Add a little more color to the reindeer by rubbing the side of an unwrapped brown crayon over the cutout. Next, punch a hole in the reindeer's head and then thread a brown pipe cleaner half through the hole. Twist the pipe cleaner to create a pair of antlers. Then glue on a pom-pom tail, sequin nose, wiggle eye, and a tagboard triangle ear. Finally, clip two spring-type clothespins to the body to give the reindeer a pair of sturdy legs. Perfect for jumping on and off high rooftops!

Reindeer on Rooftops

The great thing about having a tin roof is being able to hear the reindeer's hooves as they land! Provide each child with a pie tin to use as a rooftop. Then invite him to position his reindeer on and off the roof as directed in the following song.

(sung to the tune of "Up on the Housetop")

Who's **on** the rooftop?
Can you hear?
Sounds just like a small reindeer!
Oh, but the reindeer just can't stay.
He jumps **off** and flies away!

Off and **on**!
Can't stay long.
Off and **on**!
Can't stay long. Oh!
Up **on** the rooftop,
Hey! Hey! Hey!
He jumps **off** and flies away!

Santa Says

This seasonal adaptation of Simon Says also reinforces body parts. Have each child and his reindeer come to your circle-time area. Don a Santa hat and give a direction such as "Santa says, 'Put your reindeer *on* your head.'" Then give a similar direction instructing students to take the reindeer *off*. Continue the game by giving additional on and off directions with other body parts. When students are familiar with the activity, invite a child to play the role of Santa and lead the class in another round of Santa Says. Ho! Ho! Ho!

Housing Developments

Your youngsters' reindeer will leap for joy when you add these paper bag houses to your blocks area! To make one house, photocopy the door and window patterns on page 154. Cut out the patterns, color them, and then glue them onto a paper lunch bag. Stuff the bottom third of the bag with newspaper; then staple the bag closed. Fold a 9" x 6" piece of construction paper in half; then glue it to the bag, as shown, to create a roof. For added sparkle, glue a row of sequins to the roof to resemble holiday lights. Create a neighborhood of paper bag houses in your blocks area. Then invite each child to visit the center with his reindeer. As the child moves his four-legged friend through the rooftops, encourage him to use the words *on* and *off* to tell where his reindeer is wandering.

Reindeer Games

Use masking tape to mark a triangular roof shape on the floor of your circle-time area. Then invite your youngsters to participate in this lively movement activity! To begin, use face paint to color the tip of each child's nose red or black. Or use a red or black sticky dot. Have students stand around the rooftop shape; then instruct your little reindeer to take flight by giving a direction such as "Red-nosed reindeer jump on the roof!" Give a similar command to have the group jump off the roof. For added movement fun, have your little reindeer move onto the roof by performing additional actions such as hopping, skipping, crawling, and tiptoeing. "Black-nosed reindeer tiptoe on the roof!"

153

Same and Different

NEAT
B[...]
B[...]
GUES
WHO
TRUE
LOVE
MY
GUY
R U
SHY?
NEAT
HEY
THERE
TRUE
LOVE
EZ 2
LOVE
GUESS
WHO?
BE
TRUE
COOL
FOOL
TRUE
LOVE
R U
SHY?
EZ 2
LOVE
NEAT

Gather up some valentines; then use these lovely ideas to help your youngsters sort out the concepts of same and different.

ideas contributed by
Lucia Kemp Henry

It's Great to Be Different!

An inexpensive box of valentine cards is all you need to get your same-and-different study started. To prepare for this group activity, find four or five matching cards and one that is different. Place each card in its envelope. During your group time, pass each envelope to a child and direct him to stand in front of the class. Invite the standing students to open their envelopes and hold up the valentines for the class to see. Sing the song shown and then have your youngsters identify the valentine that is different. Afterward, place the cards back inside the envelopes, shuffle them, and repeat the activity with a different set of children.

(sung to the tune of "Mary Had a Little Lamb")

Can you find the valentine,
Valentine, valentine?
Can you find the valentine
That's **different** from the rest?

Value-Packed Valentine Ideas

Use your supply of valentines to set up these extension activities.

Provide each child with a valentine. Have students sort themselves into groups according to valentines that are the **same.**

Place pairs of valentines in a stack to create a deck of cards. Use the deck to play Go Fish with a small group of students.

Prepare a set of valentines for flannelboard use. Display two **different** cards on the board and have youngsters discuss the differences.

A Truly Different Valentine

Hearts will be doing flip-flops with this craft. To make one, die-cut four red construction paper hearts and four paper hearts from different patterned paper, such as wrapping paper, magazine pages, wallpaper samples, and stationery. Help a child glue each patterned heart onto a red paper heart. Then have her glue the hearts together as shown to create a double-sided strip—similar hearts on one side and different hearts on the other side. Punch a hole in the top of the strip, thread a length of yarn through the hole, and then hang the craft in your classroom. As these crafts spin, your youngsters will be surrounded by a "heart-y" display of same and different!

Conversation Starters

Conversation hearts are a surefire way to get your youngsters talking about same and different. Photocopy the heart patterns on page 155 in a variety of pastel colors. Laminate the hearts and then cut out each one. Place the hearts in a container decorated with conversation heart stickers; then invite youngsters to sort the hearts by color or by words. As your little ones work, encourage them to discuss the similarities and differences in the hearts.

A Perfect Match!

Valentine's Day just wouldn't be the same without a little matchmaking! So play this adaptation of Memory, and invite a small group of students to make some heart-to-heart matches. In advance, use the heart patterns on page 155 to make pairs of conversation hearts. Enlarge the patterns if desired. Have students stand in a circle with their hands behind their backs; then secretly place a heart in each child's hands. If you have an uneven number of students, keep one of the hearts and join the game.

To play the game, a child shows his heart to the group and then asks another child, "Are you my valentine?" The named child shows his heart. If it matches, he says yes, and the two children sit down together. If not, the child says no, and both students put their hearts behind their backs again. Call on another child and continue the activity until each child has found his valentine.

NEAT
GUESS WHO?
TRUE LOVE
NEAT
HEY THERE
TRUE LOVE
EZ 2 LOVE
GUESS WHO?
BE TRUE
COOL FOOL
TRUE LOVE
NEAT
HEY THERE
TRUE LOVE

Up and Down

Little ones will be all aflutter with butterfly-themed ideas that help teach the concepts of up and down.

ideas by Lucia Kemp Henry

Butterflies in Motion

What makes this activity about up and down so appealing to preschoolers? A catchy song and a crafty butterfly that moves like the real thing! Have each child create his own model butterfly by using a glue stick to attach a pair of tissue paper wings to a craft stick as shown. Then gather your students together with their butterflies. Have each child use his thumb and index finger to hold one end of the craft stick. Demonstrate how to gently move the butterfly up and down so the tissue paper wings flutter. After students have practiced flying their butterflies, sing the song below and direct each child to move his butterfly as directed in the song. *fine-motor skills, positional words, singing simple songs*

(sung to the tune of "London Bridge")

Butterflies fly **up** and **down,**
Up and **down,**
Up and **down.**
Butterflies fly **up** and **down!**
See them flutter.

They flap their wings
And **up** they go!
Up they go!
Up they go!
They flap their wings
And **up** they go!
See them flutter.

Gently, softly,
Down they come.
Down they come.
Down they come.
Gently, softly,
Down they come.
See them flutter.

Pulling Strings

How do you get these crafty butterflies to fly? It's easy! Just pull some strings! Have each child decorate a tagboard butterfly shape. Then punch a hole in the top of the shape and tie a 24-inch length of string through the hole. Next, use a pencil to poke a hole in the bottom of a six-ounce paper cup. Thread the string through the hole as shown and then tie a small bead to the end of the string. Gently pull and release the string to move the butterfly up and down. Have the child use her butterfly craft to act out the song in "Butterflies in Motion" or to play the game described in "Simon Says, 'Going Up!'" *positional words, fine-motor skills*

Simon Says, "Going Up!"

Reinforce a variety of preschool skills with this adaptation of Simon Says. Provide each child with the butterfly craft described in "Pulling Strings." Have students practice moving the butterflies up and down. Then give students simple directions such as "Simon says, 'Move your butterflies *up*.' " Gradually increase the level of difficulty by adding to the directions. For example, you might say, "Simon says, '*Slowly* move your butterflies *up*'" or "Simon says, 'Move your butterflies *down a little*.'" When students are familiar with the activity, invite a child to stand in front of the class and take a turn leading a round of Simon Says. *fine-motor skills, positional words, following directions, vocabulary*

Butterfly, I Spy

Get ready for some camouflage fun with this activity about up and down, which also sharpens visual discrimination skills. To begin, prepare a felt scene on your flannelboard similar to the one shown. Then cut out a supply of butterflies from white, green, and blue felt. During your group time, turn the flannelboard away from students' view and place the white butterflies on the cloud. Turn the board back around and invite students to participate in the call-and-response rhyme below. After reciting the rhyme, invite a child to remove the camouflaged butterflies from the board. Continue the activity in a similar manner, hiding the blue butterflies *down* in the water, and the green butterflies *down* in the grass and then *up* in the tree. *visual discrimination, positional words, language development*

Teacher: Do you spy some butterflies?
Students: Yes, we do with our sharp little eyes.
Teacher: Where can all those butterflies be?
Students: [Up] in the [clouds]! It's easy to see!

159

Patterns
Use with "Delicious Cargo" on page 161.

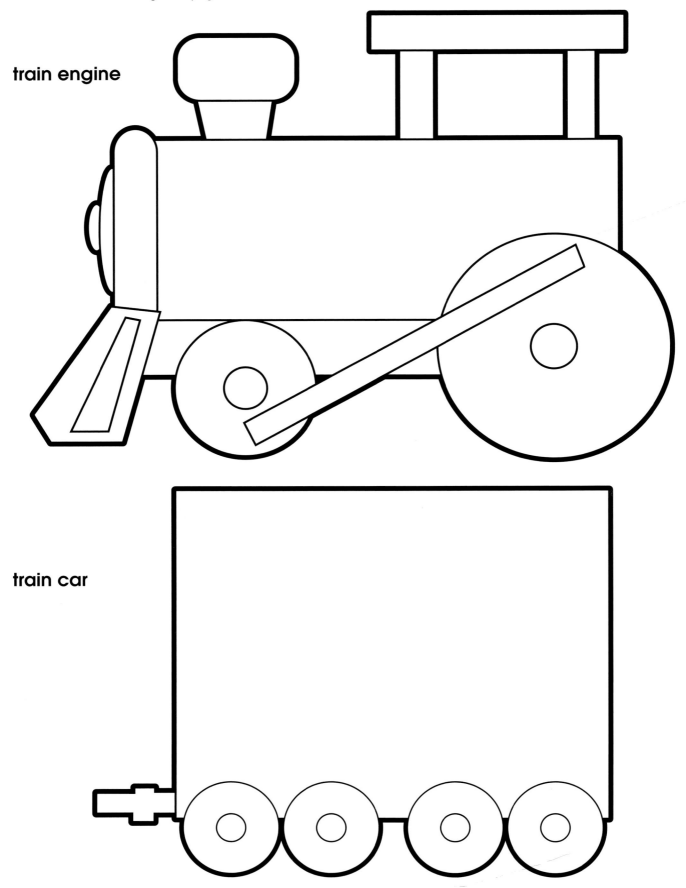

train engine

train car

©The Education Center, Inc. • THE MAILBOX® • Preschool • June/July 2002

Song Features

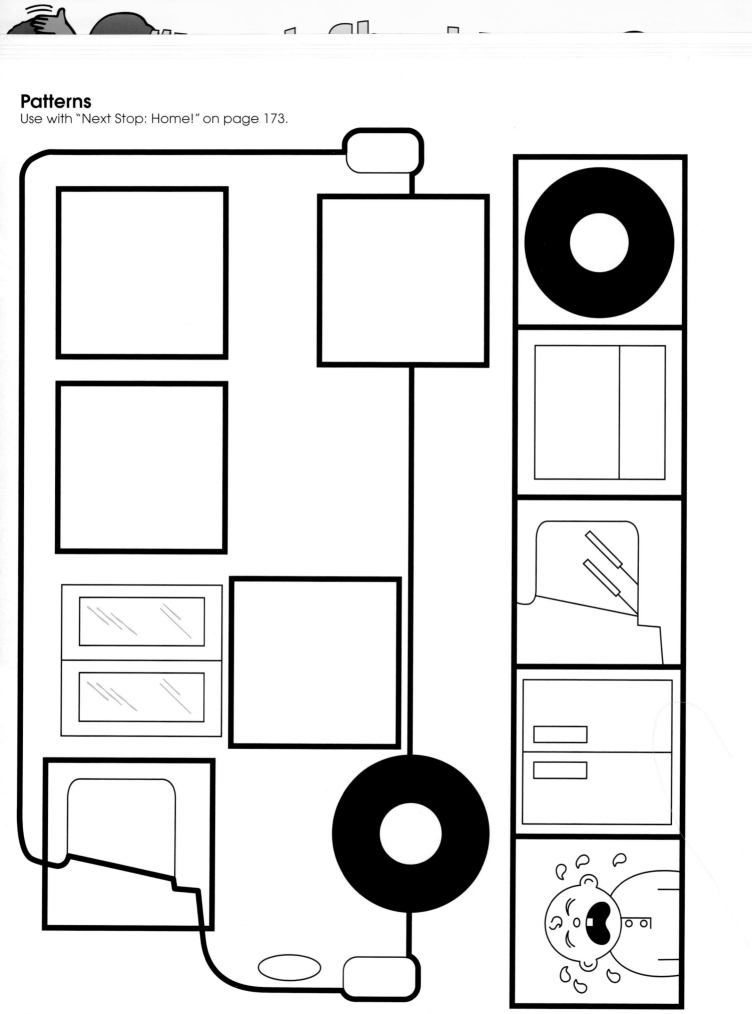

©The Education Center, Inc. • *THE MAILBOX*® • *Preschool* • June/July 2002

ONCE UPON A STORY....

Once Upon a Story...

The Mitten

This printing project is the perfect follow-up to Jan Brett's *The Mitten.* In advance, purchase a roll of rubber shelf liner. Cut out a pair of construction paper mittens for each child; then cut the lining into pieces slightly larger than the mittens, one piece for each child. To make a mitten print, tape a lining piece to a newspaper-covered table. Have a child paint a design onto the lining. Then have him press a mitten cutout onto the lining so that the paint transfers onto the paper. Set the mitten aside to dry; then reapply the paint on the lining before printing the second mitten.

Cari Lynn Rotenberger—Three-Year-Olds
First Congregational Church Preschool and Kindergarten
Winter Park, FL

Goldilocks and the Three Bears

Use a toy xylophone to add a little musical interest to your favorite version of *Goldilocks and the Three Bears.* While reading the story, play the lowest note on the instrument each time the papa bear is mentioned, a middle note each time the mama bear is mentioned, and the highest note each time the baby bear is mentioned. After several musical readings, play each of the three notes in turn and invite students to identify the corresponding bear. Ah, this story extension is just right!

Carolyn Argo—Three-Year-Olds
Prince of Peace Catholic School
Hoover, AL

See the corresponding book notes on page 183.

Kente Colors

Invite youngsters to make African hats in the beautiful shades described in Debbi Chocolate's *Kente Colors*. To prepare, cut four-inch-wide strips across a brown paper grocery bag. Cut open each resulting loop to form a length of brown paper; then cut the lengths to fit around a child's head. Provide strips of colored tape (cut to length) for youngsters to attach to their papers to make stripes. Or provide bright colors of paint and invite children to paint stripes across the papers. After the stripes are applied, fit each child's strip of paper around his head and staple the ends together to make a hat.

Maryetta Montgomery—Three- and Four-Year-Olds
Kingdom Kid Learning Center
Houston, TX

Koala Lou

"Koala Lou, I DO love you!" After reading Mem Fox's sweet story about a mother koala bear and her baby, invite each child to make a cute koala craft that clings! To make one, paint a child's hand with gray paint; then have her press her hand onto a piece of light-colored tagboard. Next, have the child wrap her fingers around her thumb to create a fist. Paint the fingers and palm of her fist; then have the child press her fist over the handprint to create the koala's head. (See illustration.) When the paint is dry, have the child add a black thumbprint nose, black fingerprint eyes, and gray fingerprint ears. Label the bear with the child's name and then cut it out. Hot-glue a spring-type clothespin to the back of the koala as shown; then use the clothespin to attach the koala to various items around your classroom. Or twist lengths of green bulletin board paper to create vines. Hang the vines in your room and attach the koalas to them. These clothespin koalas cling—just like the real thing!

Nancy M. Lotzer
Farmers Branch, TX

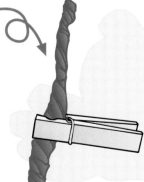

Seth

179

Once Upon a Story...

In the Tall, Tall Grass

Youngsters will go buggy when you share *In the Tall, Tall Grass* by Denise Fleming! After reading the book, have little ones craft their own lawns full of creepy-crawlies. Cut sheets of green paper in half lengthwise; then give a half sheet to each child, along with a pair of scissors. Have him snip from one long edge toward the other to fringe the paper and make it resemble grass. Then help him glue the uncut edge to a whole sheet of green construction paper. Next, give him some bug stickers to "hide" among the blades of green grass. Is that a grasshopper I see in there?

Stacy Tremblay—Preschool
Plymouth Elementary School
Plymouth, NH

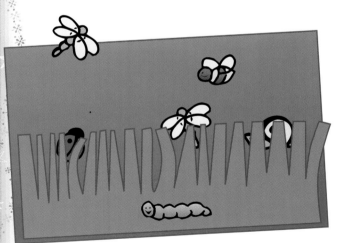

Are You My Mother?

Focus on baby animals with this follow-up to P. D. Eastman's *Are You My Mother?* After sharing the story, bring out a set of baby-and-mother animal pairs for youngsters to match. Have pairs or small groups use the toy animals to act out different versions of the story, with various baby animals searching for their mothers. Make the toy animals and the book available for youngsters to use during their free time—you'll be amazed at the ways they embellish the story!

Nola Surmanek—Two-Year-Olds
First United Methodist Child Enrichment Center
Hyattsville, MD

See the corresponding book notes on page 184.

The Very Lonely Firefly

Have your very busy preschoolers make this craft to enhance a reading of *The Very Lonely Firefly* by Eric Carle. To make a firefly, paint a wooden doll-head clothespin with black tempera paint, leaving the bottom inch unpainted. (If desired, mask the bottom of the clothespin with tape.) When the black paint is dry, paint the bottom of the clothespin with fluorescent yellow tempera paint and allow that to dry, too. Next, push a 4" x 11" piece of iridescent cellophane into the clothespin opening to make the firefly's wings; then wind a small rubber band around the clothespin just under the cellophane to hold the wings in place. Twist half a pipe cleaner around the head of the clothespin and bend the ends up to create antennae. Finally, add glitter-glue eyes to the firefly's head. Hang the finished fireflies around your room. Wow! That lonely firefly would find *lots* of company in this room!

Crystal Siemans
Child Care Contacts Resource and Referral
Milledgeville, GA

Little Blue and Little Yellow

Here's a cool way to reinforce the color-mixing lesson found in Leo Lionni's *Little Blue and Little Yellow.* In advance, tint two small bowls of water with food coloring—one blue and one yellow. Pour each container of colored water into a separate small, round balloon. Then freeze the balloons overnight. After reading the story to your students, cut the balloons open and remove the two balls of colored ice. Place your chilly versions of Little Blue and Little Yellow into a clear bowl. Have youngsters observe as the ice begins to melt and green water results. Revisit this science project throughout the day and discuss both the changes in color and in the state of matter. Science and literature—what a great mix!

Safety note: Balloons are a choking hazard for young children. Be sure to discard the used balloons immediately.

Jana Murphy—Preschool
American Lutheran Preschool
Prescott, AZ

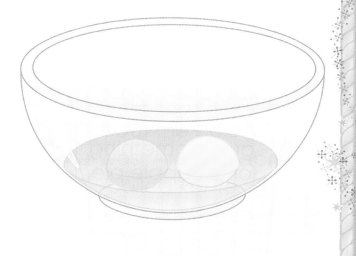

Book Notes

After reading each of the books mentioned below and on pages 180 and 181, send home copies of the corresponding note.

In the Tall, Tall Grass
by Denise Fleming

has beautiful pictures. Let's go to the library and find more books by the same author and illustrator.

©2002 The Education Center, Inc.

Our story today was

Little Blue and Little Yellow
by Leo Lionni.

When Little Blue and Little Yellow hug, they turn green! We won't turn green, but let's hug, anyway!

©2002 The Education Center, Inc.

"Here I am, Mother!" That's what a baby bird says in P. D. Eastman's book

Are You My Mother?

I'll hide and say, "Here I am!" Then you can come and find me!

©2002 The Education Center, Inc.

In Eric Carle's book **The Very Lonely Firefly,** something very special happens at the end.

Ask me to tell you what happens!

©2002 The Education Center, Inc.

IT'S CIRCLE TIME

It's Circle Time

Gingerbread Men on the Loose

Introduce your new preschoolers to your classroom centers with a treasure hunt involving that storybook favorite, the Gingerbread Man. To prepare the hunt, cut several small gingerbread men from construction paper. Write a clue on each cutout and place each one in an area of your classroom you'd like to introduce to your new students. At circle time, read aloud your favorite version of *The Gingerbread Man*. Then act surprised as you find the first note at the back of the book. It might read, "Look in the housekeeping area under the sink." Send a pair of children to that center, where they'll find the next note directing children's attention to another center. End your treasure hunt with a final clue that leads to a hidden stash of *real* gingerbread men for everyone to enjoy!

JaneLee Dozier—Four- and Five-Year-Olds
Goodpasture Christian School, Madison, TN

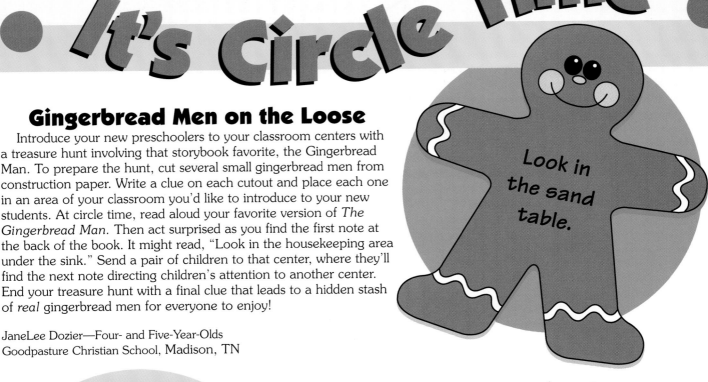

Look in the sand table.

Sensory Counting Box

Review numbers during circle time with this super sensory idea. Create a counting box by filling a small plastic tub with a sensory material, such as rice, sand, or dried beans. Each day, bury a specific number of thematic mini erasers in the tub. Write the corresponding numeral and draw a matching set of dots on a small dry-erase board. Place the board near the tub. Ask a volunteer to identify the numeral on the board; then have her find the corresponding number of erasers. After completing the activity at circle time, hide the erasers again and make the box and board available at your sensory center during free play.

Tami Bertini—Early Childhood Special Education
Bondurant-Farrar Community Schools
Bondurant, IA

Space Walk

If you're planning a space theme for the beginning of the year (see pages 6–13), this group activity will be astronaut-appropriate! Spread out a playground parachute and have little ones sit around it and hold its edge. Toss some inflatable beach balls or globes onto the parachute to serve as moons and planets. Then have a child take a turn walking, crawling, dancing, or hopping around the bouncing heavenly bodies as the remaining children shake the parachute to the beat of some lively music.

Lori Alisa Burrow—Preschool, Our Town Playschool, Yuba City, CA

Where's That Worm?

Combine rhyme and numbers in this seasonal group activity. To prepare, cut ten apple shapes from red construction paper. Label each apple with a numeral from 1 to 10. Tape a craft stick handle to each apple. Then tape a two-inch-long piece of green pipe cleaner (a worm) to the back of one apple.

At circle time, have ten children stand in front of the class and give each one an apple cutout. Have students recite the following poem; then have a child try to find the worm by naming a numbered apple. Direct the child holding that apple to answer yes or no and show the back of it. Continue the activity until a child finds the worm. Then collect the apples, move the worm, and play the game again.

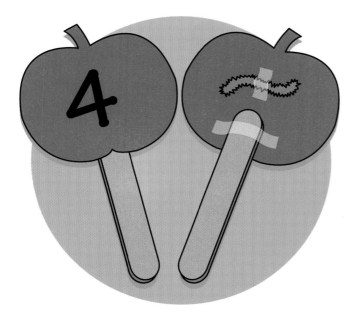

Ten red apples growing on a tree—
Five for you and five for me.
There's one little worm that you can't see.
Where, oh, where can that little worm be?

Julie Christensen
Littleton, CO

Whom Do You See?

Use these rhythmic chants to help your little ones learn one another's names at the start of school. Simply seat your youngsters in a circle and begin with the first chant. After a few days, when children are more confident about their classmates' names, try the second chant. In both cases, repeat the chant for each child as you go around the circle.

First chant:
[Justin, Justin], how are you? [Justin], can you tell me who is sitting next to you?

Second chant:
Teacher: [Nancy, Nancy], whom do you see?
Child: I see [Karen] sitting next to me.

Nancy Mattson, Chula Vista Presbyterian Preschool, Chula Vista, CA

Pass the Gourd!

This lively language activity is lots of fun! To begin, show your youngsters a gourd and say a few words to describe it. Encourage your little ones to add their own descriptions. Then pass the gourd to a child in the circle. Play a lively musical selection and direct the child to begin passing the gourd around the circle. Periodically stop the music and have the child holding the gourd describe it. Continue the activity in this manner until each child has had a chance to practice his expressive language. "This gourd is bumpy!"

Scurrying Squirrels

Your little ones will go nuts over this autumn adaptation of "Doggy, Doggy, Where's Your Bone?" In advance, make a squirrel headband by gluing two construction paper ears to a tagboard strip. To begin the activity, choose one child to be the squirrel and have him wear the headband. Direct him to leave the circle and cover his eyes. While his eyes are covered, secretly give another child an unshelled nut to hide in her lap. Signal the squirrel to turn around by having the class chant, "Little squirrel, little squirrel, want a treat? Find the nut for you to eat!" Then have the squirrel find the nut by asking each child, "Do you have a treat?" After he finds the nut, play the game again with a different squirrel.

Pizza Supreme

This matching activity will have mouths watering! To prepare, use bulletin board paper to make a large pretend pizza with toppings similar to the one shown. Next, cut out an additional set of paper toppings to match the toppings on the pizza. Laminate the toppings and then place them in a container. During circle time, have each child pick a topping from the container and then place it on the matching topping on the pizza. Mama mia!

Crystal Hampton—Two- and Three-Year-Olds
Kare Nursery
Arcadia, CA

Up to Bat

Little ones will go batty over this color-recognition idea! In advance, cut out a class supply of construction paper bats in different colors. Tape each bat onto a jumbo craft stick. To begin the activity, provide each child with a bat. Sing the first line of the song below. Have each child with a bat of the mentioned color hold it up and sing the response. Continue to sing the song and have those students respond. After singing the last line of the song, have the students "fly" away their bats. Then sing the song again using a different color word.

Teacher: Where is [blue] bat? Where is [blue] bat?
Students: Here I am! Here I am!
Teacher: How are you this morning?
Students: Very well, I thank you!
Teacher: Fly away! Fly away!

Boo!

To prepare for this group game, make a class supply of the monster mat on page 196. If desired, color the monsters as shown and then laminate the mats for durability. Provide each child with a mat and five Keebler RAINBOW Vanilla Wafers in a random assortment of colors. To play the game, pull a wafer out of the box and identify the color. If a child has a wafer in that color, she places it on one of the circles on the mat. If she has more than one wafer in that color, she chooses *one* to place on the mat. Continue calling out colors in this manner. When a child has placed all of her wafers on her mat, she says "Boo!" to signal that her mat is complete. She identifies the colors of her wafers and then *everyone* eats up!

adapted from an idea by
Roxanne Dearman
North Carolina School for the Deaf
Charlotte, NC

It's Circle Time

What's Missing?

Whether you're celebrating Kwanzaa, Hanukkah, or Christmas, this circle-time idea fits the bill! In advance, gather several small items related to the holiday of your choice. For example, use a dreidel, a box wrapped in Hanukkah paper, a Hanukkah card, and a piece of chocolate gelt. Show each item to your youngsters and then place them inside a box. Next, remove all but one of the items from the box. Can your little ones identify which one is missing?

I Spy

Prepare for a wild and wooly group time by inviting each child to wear her winter coat to your circle. Then begin playing I Spy by reciting a rhyme similar to the one shown. Have students carefully observe each other's coats to find the one in question.

I spy a coat
As warm as can be.
This special coat [has snowflakes].
Look carefully and you'll see!

LeeAnn Collins, Sunshine House Preschool, Lansing, MI

Ho! Ho! Ho!

Here's a fun audio discrimination activity that will get youngsters in the mood for the holidays. Have one child sit in a chair with his back to the class. Then choose another child to play the role of Santa and sneak up behind the seated child. Direct "Santa" to say "Ho! Ho! Ho!" and then quietly return to her seat. Have the seated child turn around and try to identify the mystery Santa. Who said "Ho! Ho! Ho!"?

Those Mischievous Elves!

Hiding Santa's belt is one of the elves' favorite tricks! Invite your youngsters to help find the missing belt with this color-identification idea. In advance, make several copies of the elf pattern below. Color each elf's clothes a different color. Cut out the elves and then place a piece of self-adhesive felt on the back of each one. Next, cut out a strip of black felt to represent Santa's belt. Before beginning the activity, place the elves on your flannelboard and then hide the belt behind one of them. To find the belt, have students name an elf by color; then remove the elf from the board to see if the belt is behind it. Continue searching in this manner until the missing garment is found.

Amy Grant—Preschool, Lakeview Head Start, Lakeview, OH

Elf Pattern
Use with "Those Mischievous Elves!" above.

It's Circle Time

Pin the Legs on the Octopus

This octopus adaptation of Pin the Tail on the Donkey is eight times as much fun! To prepare, cut out a large octopus body from poster board. Then cut out eight poster board octopus legs. Tape the octopus body on a wall in your classroom; then place loops of masking tape on the back of each leg. Provide eight children each with an octopus leg. Now, get ready to play a rousing game of Pin the Legs on the Octopus!

Patricia Merrick—PreK
T. G. Connors Elementary
Hoboken, NJ

Story Starters

Even with so-so sewing skills, you can create a bookbag that will capture youngsters' attention at storytime. First, visit your local fabric store to find inexpensive fabric with prints that correlate with a children's book. Use the fabric to make a simple tote bag. Or, if you have a parent who sews, enlist her help in making the bag. Place the corresponding book inside the bag; then add other related items if desired. Before reading the book at circle time, have students examine the fabric on the bag and predict what the book is about. Show the remaining items in the bag for added clues. Then reveal the book and begin reading.

Billie Kloote—Three- to Five-Year-Olds
Raggedy Ann Preschool
South Bend, IN

Bouncing Body Parts

Reinforce body part identification with this creative-thinking and movement activity! Encourage youngsters to imagine that they have swallowed a bouncy rubber ball. Name a body part and have students pretend that the rubber ball has traveled to that part. Direct each child to move that part of his body as if the ball were bouncing in it. Continue the activity in this manner, directing students to bounce other parts of their bodies, such as their shoulders, elbows, hands, and feet. For added fun, play a lively musical selection and have students bounce away!

Jennifer Barton
Elizabeth Green School
Newington, CT

Milk, Anyone?

June is National Dairy Month. Help youngsters celebrate with a circle-time activity that focuses on a favorite dairy product—milk! In advance, gather ten clean, plastic milk bottles. Set the bottles on a table in front of your class. As you begin saying the chant below, direct the named child to remove one milk bottle from the table. After saying the last line, have students count the remaining bottles. Then begin the activity again and have a different child remove another bottle of milk. Continue the countdown until all of the bottles have been removed.

Ten bottles of milk on the wall.
Ten bottles of milk.
[Child's name] walked by and took one down,
How many bottles of milk on the wall?

adapted from an idea by
Yolanda Rodriguez—Three-Year-Olds
Princeton Avenue Preschool
Moorpark, CA

ABC Octopus

Need a helping hand at circle time? Use this idea and you'll have eight hands to help with letter recognition! Cut out an octopus shape from felt; then use fabric paint to add features. Next, obtain a set of foam alphabet letters. Attach a piece of self-adhesive Velcro to the back of each letter and to each arm of the octopus. Place the letters in a container near the octopus. During your group time, have eight children each choose a different letter to place on the octopus. Then have the class identify the letters. For more literacy fun, encourage your youngsters to name words that begin with the letters, make the letter sounds, or find the letters in their names.

Tami Bertini—Early Childhood Special Education
Bondurant-Farrar Community Schools
Bondurant, IA

©The Education Center, Inc. • THE MAILBOX® • Preschool • Oct/Nov 2001

Note to the teacher: Use with "Boo!" on page 189.

Songs & Such

SONGS & SUCH

Apple, Apple, Apple!

Give any apple unit some crunch with this lively song!

(sung to the tune of "Dreidel, Dreidel, Dreidel")

I picked a little apple.
I picked it from a tree.
It was red and shiny,
And juicy as can be!
Oh, apple, apple, apple.
I picked it from a tree.
Oh, apple, apple, apple.
It sure tastes good to me!
CRUNCH!

Lori A. Cohen
Buffalo, NY

I Am Special

Find out what makes each of your youngsters special with this song and activity. To begin, have youngsters sing the chorus of the song below. Then invite a child to tell what makes her feel special. Sing the second verse of the song using the child's name and her response. Repeat the activity until each child has had a turn to share a unique quality.

(sung to the tune of "Where Is Thumbkin?")

Chorus:
I am special. I am special.
I'm a star! I'm a star!
There's no one quite like me.
There's no one quite like me.
Near or far.
Near or far.

[Cassie] is special.
[Cassie] is special.
She/He [helps her mother].
She/He [helps her mother].
There's no one like [Cassie].
There's no one like [Cassie].
Near or far.
Near or far.

LeeAnn Collins—Director
Sunshine House
Lansing, MI

Feelings

Lead your little ones in singing this tune about feelings. After singing the last line, make the appropriate face and invite each child to make a face that also reflects the feeling mentioned in the song.

(sung to the tune of "For He's a Jolly Good Fellow")

When I feel very [happy],
When I feel very [happy],
When I feel very [happy],
My face will look like this.

Sing additional verses, replacing the underlined word with other feeling words, such as *sad, angry, frightened,* and *sleepy.*

LeeAnn Collins, Lansing, MI

This Friend Is My Friend

Use this simple song to introduce your youngsters to each other and to the meaning of friendship.

(sung to the tune of "This Land Is Your Land")

This friend is your friend.
This friend is my friend,
When we are working,
When we are playing.
And when I need help,
He's/She's there to help me.
[Child's name] is a friend to you and me!

Lucia Kemp Henry
Fallon, NV

PreK, Hooray!

Hip, hip, hooray! Little ones will sing this class song proudly!

(sung to the tune of "You Are My Sunshine")

We are the PreK,
[Your name]'s PreK.
We learn so many things each day.
We laugh and play here.
Let's give a big cheer.
Hip, hip, hooray
For our PreK!

Beverly Russo—PreK
St. Margaret's-McTernan School
Waterbury, CT

SONGS & SUCH

Helpful Firefighters

(sung to the tune of "She'll Be Coming Round the Mountain")

Oh, firefighters wear big rubber boots.   *Stomp feet two times.*
Oh, firefighters wear big rubber boots.   *Stomp feet two times.*
Oh, when fire causes trouble,
They'll be right there on the double!
Oh, firefighters wear big rubber boots.   *Stomp feet two times.*

Oh, firefighters drive a great big truck.   *Say, "Vroom! Vroom!"*
Oh, firefighters drive a great big truck.   *Say, "Vroom! Vroom!"*
Oh, when fire causes trouble,
They'll be right there on the double!
Oh, firefighters drive a great big truck.   *Say, "Vroom! Vroom!"*

Oh, firefighters spray a fire hose.   *Say, "Woosh! Woosh!"*
Oh, firefighters spray a fire hose.   *Say, "Woosh! Woosh!"*
Oh, when fire causes trouble,
They'll be right there on the double!
Oh, firefighters spray a fire hose.   *Say, "Woosh! Woosh!*

Oh, firefighters put the fire out.   *Say, "All done!"*
Oh, firefighters put the fire out.   *Say, "All done!"*
Oh, when fire causes trouble,
They'll be right there on the double!
Oh, firefighters put the fire out.   *Say, "All done!"*

Lucia Kemp Henry

Tossing Leaves

Here's a lively song that little ones will fall for! If desired, scatter a supply of construction paper leaves on the floor and invite youngsters to toss the leaves as they sing. Hooray!

(sung to the tune of "The Ants Go Marching")

I like to toss the leaves up high.
Hooray! Hooray!
I like to toss the leaves up high.
Hooray! Hooray!
I toss them up
And they come down,
Yellow, orange, red, and brown!
Oh, I like to toss the leaves,
Toss the leaves
Way up high
In the sky!

Diana Shepard—Preschool, First Presbyterian Preschool
Wilmington, NC

In Case of Fire...

Use this catchy tune to teach youngsters the three numbers to call if there is a fire. 9-1-1!

(sung to the tune of "Head, Shoulders, Knees, and Toes")

When you see a fire, call 9-1-1!
When you see a fire, call 9-1-1!
9-1-1!
The fire truck will come!
When you see a fire, call 9-1-1!

I'm a Little Scarecrow

(sung to the tune of "I'm a Little Teapot")

I'm a little scarecrow
Stuffed with hay.
Here I stand in a field all day.
When I see the crows,
I like to shout,
"Hey! You crows, you better get out!"

Abby Carney—Three-Year-Olds
Kid's Connection
S. Hamilton, MA

Kelly Williams, Jacksboro, TX

Here Turkey, Turkey

(sung to the tune of "My Dreidel")

I saw a little turkey
Standing by a tree.
It gobbled and it wobbled,
Then ran away from me!

Oh, turkey, turkey, turkey,
Please come out and play!
I promise not to eat you
On Thanksgiving Day!

SONGS & SUCH

Ring-a-ling-a-ling

If it's Christmas and you know it, sing this song!

(sung to the tune of "If You're Happy and You Know It")

If it's Christmas and you know it, [ring a bell]!
If it's Christmas and you know it, [ring a bell]!
If it's Christmas and you know it,
Then your face will surely show it!
If it's Christmas and you know it, [ring a bell]!

Sing additional verses, replacing the underlined phrase with
trim a tree, wrap a gift, and *say "Ho! Ho! Ho!"* in turn.

Ada Goren
Winston-Salem, NC

Think Snow!

Get youngsters thinking about winter fun with a song that also reinforces days of the week. There's a different activity for each day. Cool!

(sung to the tune of "Here We Go Round the Mulberry Bush")

What shall we do in wintertime,
In wintertime, in wintertime?
What shall we do in wintertime
On [Monday] when it's snowing?

We'll build a snowman round and fat,
Round and fat, round and fat!
We'll build a snowman round and fat
On [Monday] when it's snowing!

Sing the song again, using different days of the week and activities such as the following:
Tuesday, take a sled ride down a hill
Wednesday, find some food to feed the birds
Thursday, skate around a frozen pond
Friday, pack some snowballs round and tight
Saturday, make some angels in the snow
Sunday, build a snow fort in the yard

Cele McCloskey and Brenda Peters
Head Start of York County, York, PA

Happy New Year!

Get ready to ring in a new year with this lively tune. Are you ready? 10...9...8...

(sung to the tune of "Head, Shoulders, Knees, and Toes")

There's a new year on the way,
On the way!
There's a new year on the way,
On the way!
Let's celebrate the year and give a cheer! *(Say, "Hooray!")*
There's a new year on the way,
On the way!

A Melody for Martin Luther King Jr.

Martin Luther King Jr. Day is January 21. Have your youngsters honor Dr. King with the following song.

(sung to the tune of "Mary Had a Little Lamb")

Dr. Martin Luther King
Dr. King, Dr. King!
Dr. Martin Luther King—
He was a loving man.

He loved all children everywhere,
Everywhere, everywhere!
He loved all children everywhere.
He was a loving man.

He had a dream for you and me,
You and me, you and me.
He had a dream for you and me
That we will live in peace.

Happy birthday, Dr. King,
Dr. King, Dr. King!
Happy birthday, Dr. King!
We will remember you.

Audrey Slater—PreK
The Betty Shabbaz School, Brooklyn, NY

SONGS & SUCH

Valentine Time

It's February! Time to bring out the valentines! Provide each child with a heart cutout or valentine card. Sing the song below and encourage your little sweethearts to position their valentines as directed.

(sung to the tune of "The Farmer in the Dell")

The valentines are here.
The valentines are there.
Hi-ho, the valentines are here and everywhere.
The valentines are up.
The valentines are down.
Hi-ho, the valentines are all around the town.
The valentines are in.
The valentines are out.
Hi-ho, the valentines are scattered all about.
The valentines are low.
The valentines are high.
Hi-ho, the valentines wave and say good-bye!

Jennifer M. Koch
Morningside College Child Care Center
Sioux City, IA

Rise and Shine, Little Groundhog!

On Groundhog Day (February 2) have each child make a paper bag groundhog puppet to act out this simple song.

(sung to the tune of "Are You Sleeping?")

Little groundhog,
Little groundhog,
Sleeping all
Winter long.
Come out of your burrow.
Do you see your shadow?
Is spring near?
Is spring near?

adapted from a song by
LeeAnn Collins—Director
Sunshine House Preschool
Lansing, MI

See the Leprechaun?

If you can't catch a crafty leprechaun, make one! Use green paint to color a wooden craft spoon. When the paint is dry, glue on a construction paper head, hat, and feet. Wrap a piece of green pipe cleaner around the middle of the spoon to create two arms. Then use this lucky little fellow as you sing the following song. As you sing the last line, have students identify the body part on which the leprechaun is standing. Finding a leprechaun is so much fun, your youngsters will want a repeat performance. So move the little fellow to a new body part and sing the song again!

(sung to the tune of "Do You Know the Muffin Man?")

Do you see the leprechaun,
The leprechaun, the leprechaun?
Do you see the leprechaun?
He's standing on my [hand]!

Lucia Kemp Henry
Fallon, NV

I'm a Little Bunny

Easter brings about bunches of bunnies. So teach youngsters the following tune and invite them to get hopping!

(sung to the tune of "I'm a Little Teapot")

I'm a little bunny.	*Point to self.*
See me hop.	*Hop up and down.*
Watch my ears go flippity-flop.	*Flip-flop hands like ears.*
My tail is soft as cotton. Look and see!	*Pretend to wag tail.*
My nose wiggles, so wiggle with me!	*Wiggle nose.*

Jill Coakley—Three-Year-Olds
Generations Childcare
Rochester, NY

Over in the Garden

Help your preschoolers prepare for some springtime planting with this song. Ready, set, grow!

(sung to the tune of "Over in the Meadow")

Over in the garden with a rake and a hoe,
I'll plant some little seeds in a nice, straight row.
"Grow," I will say. "Please grow all day long."
And the little seeds will grow into plants big and strong.

Lucia Kemp Henry
Fallon, NV

Zoo Tune

Get little ones in the mood for the zoo with this lively song!

(sung to the tune of "My Bonnie Lies Over the Ocean")

I came to the zoo to see lions,
Elephants, tigers, and bears.
I came to the zoo to see zebras.
I love all the animals there!

Lions, tigers,
Elephants, zebras, and bears,
And bears!
Lions, tigers,
Elephants, zebras, and bears!

LeeAnn Collins—Director
Sunshine House Preschool
Lansing, MI

Three Little Tulips

It's true! This tulip tune reinforces colors, numbers, *and* measurement! Before teaching the song to your students, cut out three tulip shapes from white, pink, and red construction paper. Give one tulip to each of three children and have the youngsters stand in front of the class. As they sing the song below, direct one child to raise his tulip above the others. After singing, invite the class to identify the color of the tallest tulip; then repeat the activity with three different children.

(sung to the tune of "Six Little Ducks")

Three little tulips I once grew,
A white one, a pink one, a red one too.
One little tulip grew, grew, grew.
It grew taller than the other two,
The other two, the other two.
It grew taller than the other two!

Arlea Kittredge
Arlea's Playhouse
Bowling Green, KY

Spring, Spring, Spring!

Sometimes you just can't say it enough—spring is here! So invite your youngsters to serenade the season with this simple song.

(sung to the tune of "Three Blind Mice")

Spring, spring, spring.
I love spring!
I love the way the flowers grow.
Tulips! Daffodils!
All in a row.
Oh, so pretty!
I want you to know
That I love spring!
I love spring!

Arlea Kittredge

SONGS & SUCH

Bubbles, Bubbles, Bubbles!

The next time you and your youngsters are blowing bubbles, sing this simple song to add to the fun!

(sung to the tune of "Twinkle, Twinkle, Little Star")

Bubbles, bubbles way up high!
Bubbles, bubbles in the sky.
Bubbles, bubbles way down low.
Bubbles, bubbles on my toes.
Bubbles, bubbles in the air.
Bubbles, bubbles everywhere!

Sherene Palmer
WMCAP HeadStart
McConnelsville, OH

Let's Give a Cheer for Summer!

(sung to the tune of "Daisy, Daisy")

Summer! Summer!
Oh, I'm so glad it's here!
I love summer!
It makes me want to cheer!
What a warm and sunny season!
There isn't a better reason
For me to say,
"Hip, hip, hooray!
What a wonderful time of year!"

Here's the Scoop!

Ah! Ice cream! Need we say more?

(sung to the tune of "Camptown Races")

I eat it on a summer day.
Ice cream! Ice cream!
I eat it any kind of way.
I love to eat ice cream!
Scoop it in a bowl!
Scoop it in a cup!
Add some sprinkles to an ice-cream cone,
And I'll eat the ice cream up!

Lucia Kemp Henry
Fallon, NV

Setting the Stage
With Learning Centers

Setting the Stage

Cinnamon Letters

This activity for your writing center will smell as good as it looks! Supply youngsters with cinnamon sticks and sheets of sandpaper cut into the shapes of various letters. Have little ones trace the lines and curves of the sandpaper letters with the cinnamon sticks. Once your preschoolers get the hang of writing with the cinnamon sticks, provide uncut sheets of sandpaper and invite them to write letters (or make drawings) freehand.

Karen M. Pyne—Five- and Six-Year-Olds
Tower Hill School
Randolph, MA

Fine-Motor Area

Mr. Pumpkin Head

He's not just a jack-o'-lantern—he's Mr. Pumpkin Head! Try this twist on pumpkin carving this fall season. Place a small to medium-sized pumpkin in your fine-motor area. Poke some holes where the eyes, nose, mouth, and other features (such as a hat or ears) should be. Then provide the pieces from a Mr. Potato Head game and invite youngsters to change Mr. Pumpkin Head's appearance daily!

Sheri Dressler—PreK
Woodland School
Carpentersville, IL

Dramatic-Play Area

Fire! Fire!

Are you and your students studying fire safety? Give your young firefighters a fire to put out right in your dramatic-play area! Stack two appliance boxes and tape them together. Cut out a door and windows from the resulting two-story house. Then tape red, yellow, and orange paper "flames" onto the house so that they appear to be coming out of the door and windows. Add some fire-fighting props, such as fire hats, rain boots, and a hose made from sewn-together tube socks. Be sure to place a phone in this center (outside the house, of course!), with "911" posted nearby so your preschoolers can practice dialing for help.

Carol Hargett—PreK
Kinderhaus III
Fairborn, OH

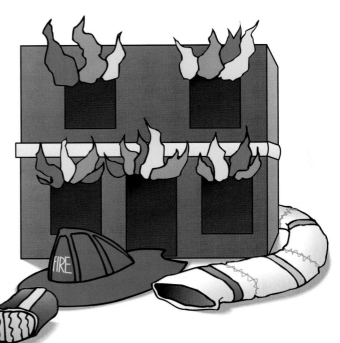

With Learning Centers

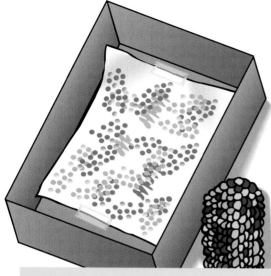

Art Center

Corn on a Roll

Preschoolers will fall for this seasonal painting technique! To prepare, purchase some ornamental corn and break the cobs in half. Then tape a sheet of paper into the bottom of a shallow box. Dip a cob half into fall-colored tempera paint; then place it in the box. Have a child tilt the box to make the corn roll around, creating an interesting design. Repeat the painting with more fall colors for some striking seasonal artwork!

Nola Surmanek—Two-Year-Olds
First United Methodist Child Enrichment Center
Hyattsville, MD

Sensory Table

An Autumn Environment

Bring some of the outdoors *in* when you add some seasonal materials to your sensory table. Partially fill the table with dry leaves, dry grass, sticks, and short twigs. Also place some toy squirrels or chipmunks in the table and encourage youngsters to create cozy nests for the critters. Engage students in conversation about the smells and textures of the natural materials, and have them talk about how the leaves change as they crumble with use.

Wanda Petrevics—Four-Year-Olds
Anna Mae Burdi Center
Chesterfield, MI

Game Center

Halloween Tic-Tac-Toe

Your little boys and "ghouls" will love this holiday version of tic-tac-toe! To prepare, purchase or ask parents to donate some paper plates with a Halloween design, as well as two different types of Halloween candies (such as candy corn and mini pumpkins). Use a black permanent marker to draw tic-tac-toe grids on a plate. Then use one type of candy for *X*s and the other for *O*s. Provide fresh candy for each game and invite youngsters to eat it afterward. Or keep the candy to be used as playing pieces in a designated bag, and have a separate bowl of treats for snacking.

Sarah Booth—Four- and Five-Year-Olds
Messiah Nursery School
South Williamsport, PA

Setting the Stage

Sensory Table

Faux Snow

It's white, it's cold…but is it snow? No, but it's a delightful sensory experience for your preschoolers, especially if you live in an area that doesn't see snow in the winter. Squirt some shaving cream into your sensory table. Then add ice cubes and watch little fingers slip and slide through this cold creamy stuff! Encourage youngsters to stack up ice cubes to build snowmen, too.

Paulette Shupack—Preschool
Gregory Gardens Preschool
Pleasant Hill, CA

Painting Center

Texture Mittens

If you have some mittens that have lost their mates, don't throw them out! Recycle them for your painting center. Sew a patch of lace, dust mop, sponge, or another interesting textured material to the palm of a mitten. Invite youngsters to slip on a mitten, dip it into paint, and make prints on paper. When the painting is through, wash the mittens and hang them up to dry for more painting fun later!

Nancy Kaczvowski—PreK
ECFE/SR
Luverne, MN

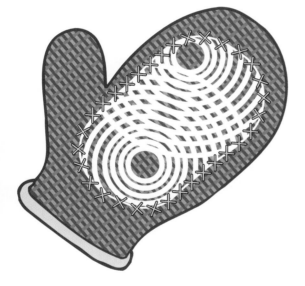

Dramatic-Play Area

Mmm…a Gingerbread House!

Making this house will be almost as much fun as playing inside it! To prepare, cut a large appliance box to form the house's roof, door, and windows. Cut six-inch-wide strips of brown kraft paper to match the lengths of your house's walls. Then cut or die-cut a large supply of candy canes, peppermint disks, candy hearts, gumdrops, and circles from construction paper. (Add a letter *m* to the circles so they resemble M&M's candies.) Give each child a brown paper strip and encourage her to form a simple pattern with the candy cutouts. Glue the cutouts in place; then glue the finished strips to the walls of the house. Finish the decoration by attaching strips of white bulletin board border to all the edges to resemble icing.

With Learning Centers

Water Table

Rainbow Ice

Is the ice melting outside? It'll be melting inside with this very colorful activity! To prepare, fill a bucket nearly full of water; then freeze it. Put the block of ice in your water table. Then prepare three containers of salted water: one red, one blue, and one yellow. Have your students use eyedroppers to drop the colored water onto the ice block. Have them observe how the salt water melts the ice, creating craters in the ice block. They'll also see how the colors of water blend to create new shades. Cool!

JoAnn Brukiewa—Three- and Four-Year-Olds
St. Clare School
Baltimore, MD

Fine-Motor Area

Scissors 'n' Scraps

Present your preschoolers with this idea for cutting practice. Cover a large box with holiday wrap and attach a bow so it resembles a gift. Use several staples to attach a long length of string to each corner of the box; then tie the loose end of each string to a pair of safety scissors. Fill the box with wrapping paper scraps and leftover lengths of ribbon. Merry cutting!

Elizabeth A. Cooper—PreK
Meadowbrook Elementary School
Fort Worth, TX

Game Center

Down the Chimney

Who can help your little ones improve coordination and develop gross-motor skills? Santa, of course! Simply cover a fairly tall cardboard box with chimney paper or rectangular bricks cut from red bulletin board paper. Set the box a few feet from a tape line. Have a child stand behind the line and toss a stuffed Santa toward the box, trying to make him go down the chimney. Ho! Ho! Ho!

Sylvia P. Ford—Two- and Three-Year-Olds
Dunedin, FL

Setting the Stage

Dramatic-Play Area

Flower Arranging

Creativity will be in bloom at your dramatic-play center when you add some oatmeal-canister vases! To make one, cover an oatmeal canister with Con-Tact paper. Snap the plastic lid on; then use a pencil to poke holes in the lid. Provide an assortment of artificial flowers and invite youngsters to insert the stems into the holes in the canister lid. Ta da—instant flower arrangements that are easy enough for little hands!

Mary Kay Vidmar—Preschool
St. Rose Catholic School, Wilmington, IL

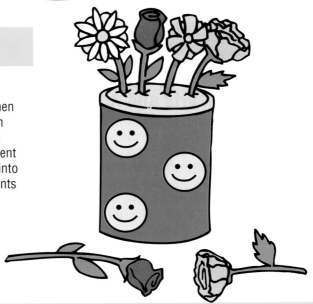

Reading Center

Reading's a Picnic!

Ahh…spring is here. Time to grab a picnic basket and some good books for your reading area! Bring the outdoors in by spreading a picnic blanket on the floor, tucking some books about spring into a picnic basket, and tossing in a few pairs of sunglasses. Then invite youngsters to settle in for some spring reading. Just leave the ants outside!

Lisa Leonardi
Norfolk, MA

Math Center

Ladybug Counting

Little ones will spread their wings and fly over to your math area for some number fun with ladybugs! Make a set of ten ladybug manipulatives to help your students practice counting and numeral recognition. To make one ladybug, cut two circles of the same size from red, laminated construction paper and a smaller circle from black, laminated construction paper. Cut one of the red circles in half to create two wings. Use a permanent marker to label the uncut red circle with a numeral from 1 to 10; then draw the corresponding number of dots on the wing set. Fasten all four pieces together with a metal brad as shown. Invite a child at this center to count the dots on a ladybug's wings and then spread the wings to see the corresponding numeral.

Kathy Myles—Three-Year-Olds, Hicksville Nursery School, Hicksville, NY

With Learning Centers

Sensory Table

Bugs in the Grass

Grasshoppers, beetles, and ants—oh my! They'll all be hiding in your sensory table when you set it up for a bug hunt your youngsters will love! Fill the table with green plastic grass; then hide an assortment of plastic insects in the grass. Provide magnifying glasses and let the hunt begin!

Jill Bivens—Four- and Five-Year-Olds
Two Rivers Head Start
Aurora, IL

Fine-Motor Center

Wild Cards

These animal lacing cards are "sew" wild! Use a photocopier to enlarge the patterns on page 220. Trace the zebra pattern onto white poster board and the tiger pattern onto orange poster board. Cut out the poster board shapes; then use a hole puncher to punch several holes as shown. Dip the ends of a long length of black yarn into school glue; then let the glue harden overnight. Thread the yarn through one hole and tie the end of the yarn to the sewing card. Then invite a child to lace the yarn through the holes to create stripes for the animal. Bet your students roar for more!

Diana Kraft—Preschool and Kindergarten
Growing Vines Playschool
Arusha, Tanzania

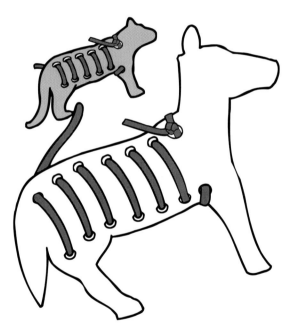

Science Center

Pollution Jar

If you take your youngsters on a walk to pick up trash as part of your Earth Day studies, add this fascinating science experiment that focuses on water pollution. Partially fill a large, clear, plastic jar with water. After discussing water pollution, have each child place a small piece of his gathered trash—such as a fast-food napkin, candy wrapper, or Popsicle stick—into the jar. Screw the lid on tightly and then secure it with duct tape. Set the jar in your science center for youngsters to observe. Ask what they think will happen to the water and to the trash. Then watch as the garbage breaks down over time and turns the clear water into a thick, brown liquid. Yuck!

Andrea Ludtke—Preschool, Preschool Project K.I.D.S., Burnsville, MN

Setting the Stage

Math Center

Sunshine Patterning

Here's a hot idea for helping youngsters understand sizes and simple patterns! Tape a large yellow construction paper circle onto a tabletop to represent the sun. Cut a supply of rectangles from yellow construction paper in two lengths. To use the center, a child arranges the rays around the circle in an alternating pattern of long and short.

Kimberly Curry—PreK Special Education
Cunningham Creek Elementary
Jacksonville, FL

Discovery Center

I Spy Bottle

This bottle full of tiny treasures will have youngsters looking again and again! To make one, gather a large variety of small items, such as coins, plastic insects, tiny dice, shaped confetti, jingle bells, pom-poms, novelty erasers, and small LEGO blocks. Put all the items in a clean 20-ounce or one-liter plastic bottle. Then fill the bottle to within two inches of the top with uncooked rice. Hot-glue the cap in place and shake the bottle well to mix everything together. Invite a child to look at the different items that show each time he rolls the bottle.

If desired, keep a duplicate of each tiny item in a separate bowl. Hold up one item at a time and ask a child to try to find its match in the bottle.

Linda Wittmann—Preschool
Belmont Community Center Preschool
Lincoln, NE

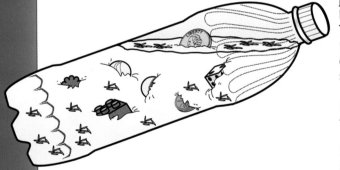

Painting Center

Cool Paint Trays

Help little ones explore color mixing with the help of some ice cube trays. Give each child an ice cube tray. Squirt two colors of tempera paint into a compartment of the tray; then invite the child to mix the paints with her brush and paint with the newfound color. Continue with other color combinations in other compartments of the tray.

Deborah Oesterling—PreK, Sterling Academy, Cary, NC

red paint   yellow paint   blue paint

With Learning Centers

Pirate's Treasure

Ahoy, matey! Send your petite pirates on a quest for buried treasure in your sand table! Bury various pieces of costume jewelry in the sand; then place a toy treasure chest (or box decorated to look like one) nearby. Encourage youngsters to use their hands and toy shovels to dig up the treasure and add it to the chest. At the end of center time, ask them to bury the loot again for other pirates to find!

Carol Breeding—Preschool, New Life Center Daycare, Des Moines, IA

Writing Center

Magic Paper

If you have preschoolers interested in writing letters and words, encourage them to use some magic paper—an overhead transparency! Write a simple word or a child's name on a sheet of white paper. Place the magic paper (the transparency) over the white paper. Give the child dry-erase markers and encourage her to trace the letters. Remove the magic paper and enjoy her look of delight as she sees she's written the word all by herself! An old sock slipped over the child's hand makes an excellent eraser, so she can reuse the marvelous magic paper to write another word!

Missy Glunt—Preschool
Child Advocates of Blair County CIRS
Roaring Spring, PA

Game Center

Build a Cone

This mouthwatering game will help preschoolers match colors. To prepare, draw an ice-cream cone at the bottom of a 12" x 18" sheet of construction paper. Cut three circles from construction paper—one red, one yellow, and one blue. Then cut four two-inch squares of black construction paper. Place a dot sticker on each of the squares—one red, one yellow, one blue, and one white. Draw a yellow sun on the white dot sticker.

To play the game, a child places the four black squares face-down on the tabletop. He turns over one square at a time and adds the matching color of ice cream to his cone. If he turns over the sun, his ice cream melts and he must start over.

Ann Bovenkamp—Preschool, Young Ideas Preschool, Newton, IA

©The Education Center, Inc. • THE MAILBOX® • Preschool • April/May 2002

CRAFTS FOR LITTLE HANDS

Crafts for Little Hands

Sand Bottles

Chances are your preschoolers had fun with sand at the beach or playground this past summer. Keep the sandy fun going when you make these beautiful bottles! To prepare, purchase a bag of playground sand at your local home improvement store. Pour the sand into bowls or sand pails; then stir a different color of powdered tempera paint into each container. Place a spoon in each container. Working with two or three children at a time, give each child a funnel and a small, clean, plastic bottle with the label removed. Invite a child to spoon as much sand of each color as he desires into his bottle (through the funnel), creating colorful layers. When the bottle is full, secure the top with hot glue and admire the finished product!

Ann Becker—Four- and Five-Year-Olds
Deerwood Center
Milwaukee, WI

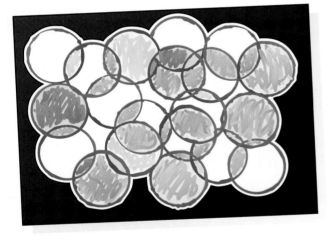

Paper Cup Printing

Focus on circles with this well-rounded painting project! First, set out a few different colors of tempera paint in shallow containers. Provide a supply of paper drinking cups and white construction paper. Have each youngster dip the rim of a paper cup into the paint color of her choice and then print it onto her paper. Have her continue with other colors, overlapping the circles as she desires. When the paint is dry, invite her to use crayons or markers to color in the areas created by the overlapping circles. Then help her cut around the perimeter of her design and glue it onto a sheet of black construction paper for a dazzling work of art!

Carrie Lacher
Friday Harbor, WA

Salty Squiggles

This art technique will produce an interesting texture—along with rainbows of color! Have a child squirt a glue design onto a piece of card stock. Then pour salt onto the glue to completely cover it. Shake off the excess salt; then repeat the pouring and shaking. Next, have the child carefully touch a small paintbrush dipped into watercolor to the salt-glue design. Watch as the color is immediately absorbed! Repeat the painting with other colors as desired. Then let the project dry overnight and shake off any remaining salt. As a variation, have a child run the glue over the traced letters of his name, a shape, or a number.

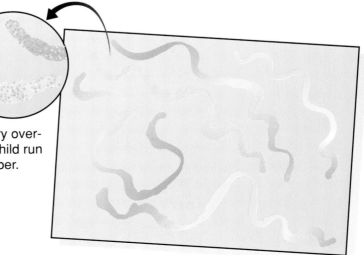

Terri Vrasich—Preschool
Noah's Ark Preschool
McHenry, IL

Acorn Artwork

Display these giant acorns around your classroom to welcome autumn! For each child, cut out a dark brown construction paper acorn, a light brown construction paper acorn cap, and two construction paper leaves in fall colors (see illustration). Have a child dip a small rectangular sponge into brown paint and make prints on her acorn cap. When the paint is dry, have her glue the cap, acorn, and leaves onto a sheet of yellow construction paper. Then have the child use a brown marker to add stems to the leaves. Now, watch out for squirrels!

Bonnie Cave
Duluth, GA

Stained Glass Windows

Looking for a craft to help youngsters learn about colors, color mixing, and shapes? Try this sticky version of stained glass! To make one stained glass window, use loops of tape to attach a square of clear Con-Tact paper to a tabletop (adhesive side up). Provide a child with several shapes cut from red, yellow, and blue cellophane. Have her stick the shapes onto the Con-Tact paper to make a collage, overlapping the shapes as desired. Seal her finished collage by covering it with a sheet of clear Con-Tact paper. To create a frame for the window, staple strips of construction paper (in the child's choice of colors) to the four edges. Then hang these see-through creations in a sunny window. Wow!

Sherry Gish—Two-Year-Olds
Highland Plaza United Methodist Preschool and Kindergarten
Hixson, TN

Blast Off!

Count down to creativity by having youngsters make these cool rockets! To prepare to make one, cut a 6½ inch half-circle from tagboard; then tape the half-circle into a cone shape. Use packaging or masking tape to attach the cone over the bottom of a Pringles potato chip canister as shown. Next, help a child cover the container and cone with aluminum foil. Then invite him to decorate his rocket with space-themed stickers and strips of red, white, and blue construction paper. To create engine fire for the rocket, have the child squirt some glue on the inside edge of the canister's open end; then direct him to insert pieces of red, orange, and yellow tissue paper into the opening. Hang these roaring rockets around your room for a stellar display!

Bonne Boodman—Three- and Four-Year-Olds
Congregation Mishkan Tefila Nursery School
Chestnut Hill, MA

223

Crafts for Little Hands

Moonlit Autumn Trees

"Who-ooo" wants to make these autumn tree sculptures? Your preschoolers will! To prepare, cut a small circle from yellow construction paper and a small, simple owl shape from brown construction paper for each child. To make one tree, lay four craft sticks on a piece of waxed paper; then paint the sticks with brown tempera paint. When the paint dries, turn them over and paint the other sides. Then use craft glue to assemble the sticks as shown. Glue the yellow moon to the back side of the treetop and glue the owl to the lowest branch. Then tear small pieces of red, yellow, and orange construction paper to make leaves. Glue the leaves on the tree branches where desired. Finish the sculpture by pushing a bit of play dough or clay into a film canister or small paper cup. Then anchor the tree trunk in place.

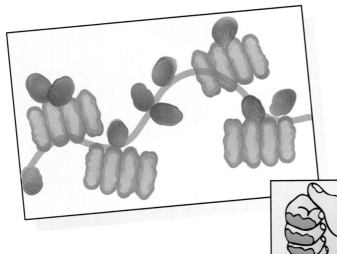

Pumpkins on the Vine

This "hand-some" painting project features a mighty fine vine! For each child, use a green marker to draw a curvy line across a sheet of white construction paper. Have a child make a fist and then dip her fingers into a shallow bowl of orange tempera paint as shown. Next, help her press the painted part of her fist onto the green line to make a pumpkin shape. Have her repeat this process to make a few more pumpkins along the vine. Then encourage her to finish the picture by using green paint to make thumbprints for pumpkin stems and leaves.

Sarah Booth—Four- and Five-Year-Olds
Messiah Nursery School, South Williamsport, PA

Dancing Spiders

Hang these dancing spiders from your classroom ceiling and watch the wiggling, jiggling, *and* giggling begin! For each child, cut from black or brown construction paper a five-inch circle, a three-inch circle, eight 1" x 6" strips, and one 1" x 2" strip. To make one spider, accordion-fold all the strips. Glue the short strip between the paper circles so that the smaller circle (the spider's head) appears to "pop out." Glue the eight remaining strips to the back side of the larger circle, four on each side, to serve as spider legs. Glue two wiggle eyes to the spider's face and draw a smile. Punch a hole in the top of the spider and thread a 15-inch length of string through the hole. Tie the string in place; then hang the spider from your ceiling. Watch out—it's wiggly!

Christy J. McClellan—Preschool
Song Woods School, Waynesboro, PA

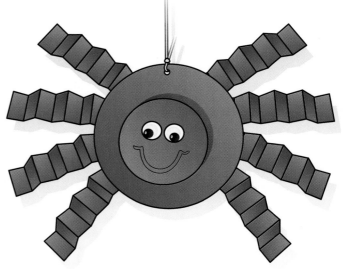

224

Fall T-Shirts

These seasonal T-shirts are lovely and leafy! In advance, ask each child's parents to send in a light-colored T-shirt. Then take your class on a walk and have each youngster collect two or three autumn leaves that are not too dry. Back in your classroom, spread a child's T-shirt flat on a tabletop; then slip a sheet of waxed paper or thin cardboard inside the shirt to prevent paint from bleeding through. Squirt some autumn-colored fabric paint into a clean Styrofoam tray. Then have a child use a paintbrush or her fingers to spread paint evenly and thinly over the vein side of a leaf. Have her lay the leaf carefully on the shirt front and then lay a paper towel over the leaf and press. Remove the paper towel and the leaf to observe the leafy impression. Continue with other colors and shapes of leaves as desired. Beautiful!

Cindy Bormann—Preschool
Small World Preschool, West Bend, IA

Batty Over Halloween

Here's a cute craft to tie into a Halloween celebration or a study of night-time. To begin, invite each child to paint at your easel, using yellow tempera paint on white paper. Cut a large circle from the painted paper. To make a bat picture, the child glues the circle to a sheet of purple construction paper. Then he glues on two precut, black construction paper bat shapes. Finally, he folds up the wings of each bat to give the project a more three-dimensional look. Flap, flap…swoosh!

Betsy Ruggiano—Three-Year-Olds
Featherbed Lane School
Clark, NJ

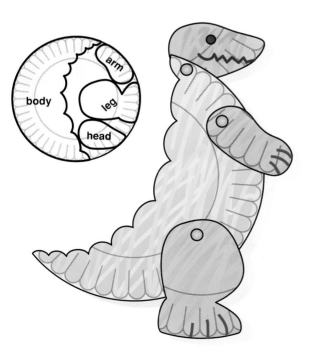

Dynamite Dinos

These paper-plate projects make for prehistoric preschool fun! In advance, use a black marker to draw the body parts of a dinosaur on a thin white paper plate as shown. To make a dinosaur, cut out the pieces. Help the child attach the head, arm, and leg to the dinosaur body with metal brads. Then have her use crayons or markers to decorate the dino as desired. Will your dinosaur be fierce or friendly?

Lisa Scaglione—Four- and Five-Year-Olds
Children's Village Preschool
Sherrill's Ford, NC

Crafts for Little Hands

Sensory Snowman

This frosty fellow will help teach your little ones about textures and colors. To prepare, cut a snowman shape for each child from white construction paper. Then cut the snowman's clothing from various materials. For example, you might cut mittens from sandpaper, a hat from felt, a nose from craft foam, and boots from ribbed packing material. Use sticky dots for eyes and a silky ribbon for a scarf. Invite each child to "dress" her snowman (using glue to attach the cutouts) as you prompt discussions about colors and textures. Simply "sense-ational"!

Barbara Bates—Two-Year-Olds and Four- and Five-Year-Olds
Brandywine YMCA
Coatesville, PA

Dandy Candy

'Tis the season for these pretty peppermints! To make one, have a child paint red and green alternating stripes on the rim of a small white paper plate. After the paint dries, help the child wrap the plate in a piece of clear plastic wrap or cellophane. Then twist the ends of the wrap and tie a length of red curling ribbon around each one.

Michelle LeMaster-Johnson—Four-Year-Olds
Windlake Elementary
Milwaukee, WI

Gingerbread Kid

This seasonal craft is full of fun and fine-motor practice! To prepare, trace around a large gingerbread boy or girl cookie cutter on brown craft paper two times. Cut out the shapes, stack them, and use a hole puncher to punch holes around the perimeter. Invite a child to decorate one of the shapes by sticking on white paper reinforcements for hair and sticky dots for buttons. Have him add sticky-dot eyes, tiny bows, pipe cleaner pieces, or any other decorations as desired. Restack the shapes and have the child use a long length of white yarn to lace the shapes together. To add a seasonal scent, slip a cotton ball sprinkled with cinnamon between the two shapes before the child laces the final holes.

Mickie Clements—Three-, Four-, and Five-Year-Olds
Young Ideas Preschool
Newton, IA

Winter Snow Scene

Use spools as tools to make this wintry picture! Glue brown paper tree trunks with green paper trees to a sheet of blue construction paper. Then dip one end of an empty thread spool into white tempera paint and press it onto the scene to make a snowflake. Use spools in various sizes to add as much snow as you like. Brrr!

Debbie Ellingworth, Wadena, MN

Puzzle-Piece Wreath

Got a jigsaw puzzle with some missing pieces? Then you've got the basis for these merry wreaths! For each wreath, cut an O-shape (three to four inches in diameter) from heavy cardboard. Staple a loop of ribbon to the cutout to be used for hanging the finished wreath. Then have a child glue on at least three layers of old puzzle pieces, covering the entire cutout. When the glue is dry, spray-paint the wreath green; then glue or wire a red bow to the bottom of the wreath. Have the child use red puffy paint or red glitter glue to add berries. Be sure to add the child's name and the date to the back of each wreath because parents will be hanging these crafty creations on their trees for years to come!

Kelly Nardi—PreK Special Education
Black Rock School
Thomaston, CT

Sweet-Smelling Gingerbread House

Construct a candy-covered gingerbread house without using a single baking pan or a drop of frosting! For each child, precut a simple house shape (similar to the one shown) from tan construction paper. Then provide a supply of scented stickers showing all kinds of candy and treats. Have the child peel and stick to make his house look and smell yummy!

Dana Smith
Baton Rouge, LA

227

Crafts for Little Hands

Valentine Boxes

Do you ask parents to send in boxes of baby wipes to use throughout the year? Specify that you'd like *red* boxes; then you'll be set to make these bright and cheerful containers for valentines! To make one, glue a child's photo to one long side of a red baby wipe box. Then use a black permanent marker to write her name in large letters on the opposite side of the box. Have her add valentine stickers all over the box. Then cut a small slit at the top of each short side. Cut a 30-inch length of ribbon, slip one end through each of the slits, and then knot the ends to hold the ribbon in place. After the valentine deliveries are made, youngsters can slip their boxes over one shoulder to carry them home.

Susan Glowski—Home Day Care
Suzy's Kids College
Dunkirk, NY

Piggy Bank Bottles

These pink porkers are precious! To make one, glue pink construction paper around a clean plastic soda bottle with a cap. Use tacky glue to attach four legs made from empty thread spools or egg-carton cups. Curl a pink pipe cleaner by twisting it around a pencil and then sliding it off. Poke a hole in the bottom of the soda bottle and stick one end of the curly tail inside, securing it with a bit of tacky glue. Cut two triangle ears from pink construction paper. Pinch each ear in the middle and glue it in place as shown. Glue on two button eyes. Finish the bank by cutting a slit through the paper and the bottle (a teacher's job). This little piggy is ready to save!

Cheri Anderson—PreK
First Presbyterian Church Day School, DeLand, FL

Hooray—A Bouquet!

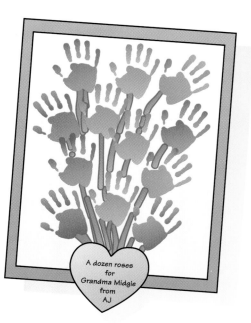

Even a preschooler can afford a dozen of these sweet roses! To make a Valentine's Day bouquet for someone special, have a child make 12 red or pink tempera paint handprints on a large sheet of white construction paper. Then have him dip one finger into green tempera paint and paint a green stem for each "rose." When the paint is dry, glue the bouquet painting to a sheet of green floral paper. Then write a note for the recipient on a heart-shaped cutout and glue it to the bottom of the painting. Happy Valentine's Day!

Lori L. Burt—Two- and Three-Year-Olds
Huffer Memorial Children's Center, Muncie, IN

228

Welcome, Wind!

March is the time for kite making, and these personalized kites are cool! Cut a 9" x 12" sheet of colorful construction paper into a nine-inch square. Turn the square on a tabletop to make a diamond shape. Paint a child's hand with white tempera paint; then have him make handprints on the paper as shown. Use a marker to print the child's name in the center. Next, have the child remove his shoes and socks. Paint the bottoms of his bare feet with white paint; then have him step onto another different-colored sheet of construction paper. Repeat this step twice to make a total of six footprints. When the paint is dry, cut around the footprints. Tape one end of a length of ribbon or crepe paper streamer to the back of the diamond; then tape the footprint cutouts to the ribbon to resemble bows. Now go fly a kite!

Donna Price—Infant–Preschool
Creative Kids Learning Center
Salt Lake City, UT

Rainbow Bracelets

These beautiful bracelets sport the colors of the rainbow! For each child, cut six one-inch-wide loops from paper towel or toilet paper tubes. Have each youngster paint one loop in each of the colors of the rainbow—red, orange, yellow, green, blue, and purple. When the paint is completely dry, ask the child to string the loops (in any order she wishes) onto a pipe cleaner. Wrap the pipe cleaner around her wrist and twist the ends together to secure the bracelet. What a colorful accessory!

Betty Silkunas
Lower Gwynedd Elementary
Ambler, PA

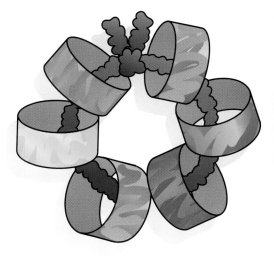

Leprechaun Wind Dancer

Deck the halls for St. Patrick's Day with these colorful wind dancers! Have each child glue a black construction paper band to a green leprechaun hat cutout. Then have her glue a yellow shamrock cutout to the band and print her name on the hat's brim. Give her six crepe paper streamer lengths—one in each color of the rainbow—to glue to the back of the hat cutout. Ahh…it's the look of the Irish!

Sarah Booth—Four- and Five-Year-Olds
Messiah Nursery School
South Williamsport, PA

Crafts for Little Hands

Wonderful Window Box

These spring flowers don't need any showers—just your preschoolers' imaginations! Give each child six to 12 craft sticks. Set out an assortment of craft materials, such as paper cupcake liners, pom-poms, cotton balls, tissue paper, and small gift bows. Invite each child to make flowers by gluing the materials of his choice onto one end of each craft stick. When the glue is dry on all his flowers, give the child an upside-down egg carton. Help him poke the free end of a craft stick into the bottom of an egg cup. Continue until all the flowers are in place. Tuck some green plastic grass between and around the craft stick stems. Ta-da—a window box!

Susan Pufall—Three-Year-Olds
Red Cliff Early Head Start
Bayfield, WI

I made this gift, Mom,
Just for you,
Because you're special
And I love you, too!
No need to water it,
For it can't grow.
It's just something
To let you know...
I'm thinking of you
On your special day!

Happy Mother's Day!
Love, Amy

Garden in a Jar

Encourage your little ones to "plant" these everlasting gardens to give to their moms on Mother's Day. In advance, collect a small plastic jar with a lid for each child. Help the child roll out a thick layer of green play dough. Then have her use the jar lid to cut out a circle of the play dough. Have her poke a few small artificial flowers into the dough to create a unique miniature garden. Allow the dough to harden completely before gluing it to the inside of the jar lid. Screw the jar over the flowers; then attach a pretty ribbon and a copy of the poem shown.

Dawn Anderson, Marietta, GA

Watercolor Orchids

If you're studying the rain forest or you just want a unique Mother's Day gift, these beautiful paintings are perfect! To make one, cut a sheet of white construction paper in half lengthwise. Drop a bit of green liquid watercolor paint onto one end of the paper. Have a child use a straw to blow the paint across the paper, creating long green "stems." Help him press a small circle-shaped sponge into a bright color of liquid watercolor and then dab "petals" onto the end of each stem. Oh my—orchids!

Tracy Karczewski—Three- and Four-Year-Olds
La Jolla Presbyterian Preschool
La Jolla, CA

230

Shake-a-Vase

Making tissue paper flowers for Mother's Day? These easy-to-make vases can hold them! In advance, collect a class supply of small Sunny Delight bottles with caps. Make sure the bottles are clean and dry; then remove the label from each one. To make a vase, mix one tablespoon of liquid tempera paint with one-half tablespoon of liquid dish detergent. Pour the mixture into the bottle; then replace the cap. Invite a child to shake the bottle vigorously until the entire inside of the bottle is covered with paint. Remove the cap and set the bottle aside to dry. Add a length of ribbon around the top. Arrange tissue paper flowers inside the bottle, and the craft is complete!

Jane Klein—Three- and Four-Year-Olds
St. Therese PreK
Succasunna, NJ

Pretty Rainbows

Spring rain means lots of rainbows, so color your room with these pretties. For each child, use a permanent marker to draw a rainbow onto a piece of clear Con-Tact covering. Peel off the backing and then have each child tear small pieces of colored tissue paper and stick them inside the rainbow. (If desired, provide a picture of a rainbow for youngsters to use as a reference.) Once the sticky side is covered, trim off the excess as shown. To complete the project, have each child write her name on cloud cutouts and glue the cutouts to each end. Hang the rainbows from the ceiling or tape them to the windows for a suncatcher effect. Just "bow-tiful!"

Lola M. Smith, Hilliard, OH

Mother's Day Magnet

These flower magnets make attractive gifts for Mother's Day! In advance, color some rotini pasta in a variety of floral colors. Break each colored pasta piece in half. For each child, cut a two-inch circle from white poster board or tagboard. Use a pencil to draw a small center circle. To assemble a magnet, cover the small inner circle with tacky glue; then sprinkle on some millet birdseed. Allow the glue to dry. Then spread tacky glue over the remainder of the cutout circle and arrange the pasta "petals" around the millet center. Glue on a tagboard stem and leaves; then add a length of self-adhesive magnetic tape to the back of the flower. Have each youngster take her magnet home, along with a Mother's Day message to post on the fridge!

adapted from an idea by Jane Walker—PreK
Hubbard Pre-K
Forsyth, GA

Crafts for Little Hands

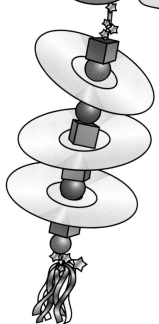

CD Sparkler

Looking for a use for those free compact discs that arrive in the mail? Make these shiny decorations for the Fourth of July! To make one, bend a small loop in one end of an 18-inch length of star garland. Through the loop, thread three lengths of thin, shiny ribbon in patriotic colors; then tie the ribbon into a knot to create a tassel. Next, thread red and blue beads onto the garland in an alternating pattern. Between a few of the beads, slip on a CD for extra shimmer and shine! To complete the project, bend the top of the garland into a loop for hanging.

Cindy Essen and Jan Solomonson—Four- and Five-Year-Olds
Trinity Preschool, Watertown, MN

Beach Props

Is there a beach in your classroom at this time of year? Enhance children's imaginary play by making simple sunglasses from craft foam! Use the sunglasses patterns on page 234 to make tagboard tracers. Then use the tracers to create craft foam glasses. Punch holes in the top corners of the glasses. Then twist a length of pipe cleaner through each hole to create an earpiece. Glue colored cellophane over the eyeholes to make the glasses more realistic. Invite each child to choose a pair of glasses and then decorate them with slick or puffy fabric paint. They'll look just "beach-y"!

Nancy Wolfgram—Four-Year-Olds
Kindercare Learning Center #1111, Lincoln, NE

Glittery Goldfish

Transform your classroom into a giant fishbowl when you suspend these giant goldfish from the ceiling! To prepare, make a large, simple goldfish pattern (about two feet long) from tagboard. For each child, staple two 2' x 2' sheets of newsprint together. Help the child trace the goldfish pattern onto the newsprint and cut it out through both thicknesses of paper. Have the child paint both cutouts with orange tempera paint and then sprinkle gold glitter over the wet paint. When the paint is dry, have her add a sticker-dot eye and three elbow-macaroni gills to each cutout. Then place the cutouts back-to-back and staple around the edges. If desired, leave an opening and stuff the fish lightly with tissue paper before stapling it shut. Your goldfish are ready to swim!

Eva Bareis—Preschool
Westside Preschool, Rapid City, SD

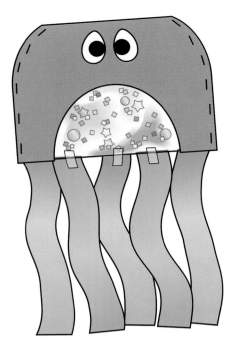

"Gel-lyfish"

This peekaboo project is perfect to enhance a study of ocean critters! For each child, fold a sheet of construction paper in half. Draw three curved lines as shown. Have the child cut along the lines and discard the scraps. Then ask her to draw two eyes above the center cutout. Next, help her squirt a bit of clear hair gel into a zippered plastic bag. Then have her sprinkle in some glitter and metallic confetti. Squeeze out any air and seal the plastic bag. Tape the bag inside the jellyfish cutout so that the seal is covered by the paper. Then staple around the edges of the paper. Finally, have the child tape a few lengths of crepe paper streamer to the bottom of the jellyfish to create tentacles.

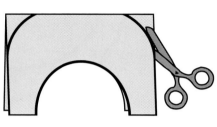

Karen Reed—Four- and Five-Year-Olds
Trailside Daycare, East Providence, RI

Patriotic Painting

Celebrate Independence Day with these star-spangled paintings! Have a child lay several plastic glow-in-the-dark stars (available at craft stores) on a sheet of red, white, or blue construction paper. Then have him dip an old toothbrush into liquid watercolor or diluted tempera paint in a different patriotic shade. Direct him to hold the toothbrush over the paper and run his thumb over the bristles to make the paint "spray" onto the paper and stars. Allow the paint to dry; then lift off the stars. Negative space—neat!

Lori Alisa Burrow
Our Town Playschool
Yuba City, CA

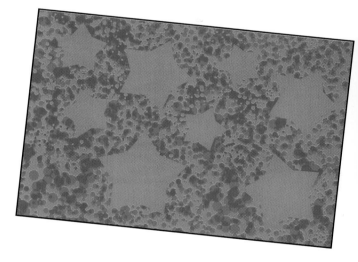

"Tutti-Fruity"

Encourage your young sculptors to make these fruit bowls that look good enough to eat! First, provide each child with a portion of Crayola Model Magic modeling compound. Help her flatten it to a thickness of about one-half inch. Have her use cookie cutters to cut out a large circle, a small circle, and a small heart shape. Have her use a plastic knife to cut each circle in half. Have her set her pieces on a paper plate to dry. When the shapes are dry, direct the child to paint the larger half circles orange, the smaller ones yellow, and the heart shape red. Then assist her in adding lines of white paint to make the half circles resemble orange and lemon wedges. Have her add white paint dots to the heart shape to make it resemble a strawberry. Then display all the finished pieces in a small paper or plastic bowl. Yum!

Christy J. McClellan—Preschool
Song Woods School
Waynesboro, PA

233

Sunglasses Patterns

Use with "Beach Props" on page 232.

©The Education Center, Inc. • THE MAILBOX® • Preschool • June/July 2002

Busy Hands

BUSY HANDS

Creative Learning Experiences for Little Hands

LAUNDRY FOR LEARNING

You might think of laundry as a humdrum chore, but with these ideas it's so much more!

by Ada Goren

Sock Toss

Ready to put away that clean laundry? Just toss it into a laundry basket! Set up a sock toss by positioning a laundry basket a few feet from a tape line on the floor. Gather several pairs of socks, and roll each pair into a ball. Have a youngster stand behind the tape line and attempt to toss the rolled socks into the laundry basket.

For more of a challenge, don't preroll the sock pairs. Have youngsters match the socks and roll them before tossing them into the basket.

Powder or Liquid?

Save a few empty laundry-detergent boxes and bottles for this sensory exploration. To prepare, color some play sand with blue or green powdered tempera paint to create look-alike laundry detergent. Pour the colored sand into the detergent boxes; then set the boxes inside an empty sensory tub. Provide various laundry scoops for youngsters to use as they scoop and pour. For a sensory contrast, fill a separate tub with pretend liquid detergent (colored water). Place the detergent bottles in the tub; then add plastic measuring cups. Invite your budding mathematicians to use the cups and bottles to practice measuring and pouring.

IN THE BAG

Help little ones get a feel for doing laundry with this sensory activity. Place a few laundry-related items—such as a clothespin, a laundry scoop, a dryer sheet, a sock, a plastic clothes hanger, and a washcloth—inside a cloth laundry bag. Encourage a youngster to reach into the bag, feel an item, and try to guess what it is. Have her pull the item out to confirm her guess. Then have her continue until she's emptied the bag. Replace the items for the next child to use.

FOLD 'EM AND STACK 'EM

Folding washcloths and hand towels will present your preschoolers with both cognitive and motor challenges. Set up a folding table with a supply of washcloths and hand towels. After a demonstration by you, have a child fold the cloths and towels and try to stack them. There—now your students are ready to help out with the laundry at home!

SORT IT ALL OUT

Before you can start the first load, you've got to sort the colors from the whites. So gather a supply of dress-up clothing, colored and white washcloths, and/or colored and white socks. Set up two laundry baskets and invite youngsters to sort the white items from those with color. Careful now—we don't want those white socks to turn pink!

CLIP, CLIP, CLIP

For some fine-motor fashion, invite little ones to create clothespin necklaces! In advance, cut 24-inch lengths of yarn and tie the ends of each length together to create a necklace. Also provide a large supply of colored plastic clothespins. Encourage a child to clip clothespins onto a yarn necklace to create her own design. Older preschoolers may try to create color patterns with the pins. After they've modeled their creations, have little ones remove the clothespins for the next young jewelers to use!

BUSY HANDS

Creative Learning Experiences for Little Hands

SMOOTH AND ROUGH

Help your preschoolers explore smooth and rough textures with these activities. It's tactile stimulation at its finest!

by Ada Goren

ROLLIN'

Do wheels work better on smooth surfaces or rough ones? Have your preschoolers experiment to find out! Give a child a toy car and invite him to try rolling it on the floor and then on the carpet. Also try a tabletop and a straw mat. What can your young scientists conclude?

ROUGH GOING IN THE WATER TABLE

Toss some mesh bath sponges into your water table. As little ones squeeze and rub the sponges, they'll feel the rough texture. For contrast, squirt a little mild shower gel onto each child's hands. Have her rub the gel into her hands and onto her arms to feel the smoothness. Then have her rub a sponge over her skin to feel the roughness. And what happens to the gel? Ooh—cool!

ROUGH IT UP

How do you turn a smooth sheet of tagboard into something rough? With a little glue and some stuff for sprinkling! Have each child spread white glue over a section of tagboard and then sprinkle on sand, glitter, or rice to change the texture of the surface. Invite him to continue covering the tagboard with other materials. When the glue has dried, have the child run his hand over the tagboard to feel the interesting, rough textures.

GLUE

GLIDING ALONG

Encourage your little ones to reflect on smoothness when they fingerpaint on a mirror. Place a mirrored vanity tray or another large mirror on a tabletop. (Be sure to provide supervision if the mirror is breakable.) Invite youngsters to fingerpaint with a mixture of tempera paint and a squirt of dishwashing liquid. Or use nonmenthol shaving cream for a smooth and creamy sensory delight!

SANDPAPER SHAPES

Making pictures isn't so rough—or is it? With these sandpaper shapes, it just might be! Cut a collection of basic shapes in different sizes from sheets of fine sandpaper. Stick a piece of magnetic tape to the back of each cutout. Then give a child a cookie sheet and encourage him to use the shapes to form a picture. Or, if you prefer, use the side of a metal filing cabinet as the canvas for this sandpaper shape art.

TEXTURE SORTING

Is it smooth or is it rough? Preschoolers will find out when they sort this stuff! Gather a variety of rough items, such as a stick, a rock, a piece of sandpaper, scraps of burlap or netting, and an emery board. Then gather some smooth items, such as a small glazed ceramic tile, a rubber ball, scraps of satin, and a CD. Have youngsters sort the items into two groups—smooth and rough. For added fun, provide a straw bag for the rough items and a satin pillowcase for the smooth ones.

RIBBON WEAVING

Bring out that satiny holiday ribbon and invite youngsters to create some smooth and shiny artwork. To prepare, make one or more weaving boards. To make one, punch five holes in each long side of a clean Styrofoam tray. Thread a length of yarn through a hole on one end and tie a knot to hold it in place. Thread the yarn through all the holes as shown; then tie a knot at the end. Cut some wide satin ribbon into 12-inch lengths.

Invite a child to weave pieces of ribbon under and over the yarn to make a design. When she's through, have her remove the ribbon so another child can use the weaving board.

BUSY HANDS

Creative Learning Experiences for Little Hands

SPOTS AND DOTS

What will youngsters learn with these exploration activities involving spots and dots? Lots and lots!

ideas contributed by Roxanne LaBell Dearman—PreK
North Carolina School for the Deaf, Charlotte, NC

SPOTS AND DOTS AFLOAT

Want to make a splash at your water table? Add some colorful dots that float! Use a hole puncher to cut out a supply of dots from craft foam. Place the dots in the water table. Add a variety of plastic strainers, spoons, and cups, and then get ready for a flood of exploration excitement!

I SEE SEQUINS!

Prepare your sand table for this idea by hiding large round sequins in the sand. Add a variety of clear plastic containers and scoops for students to use at the table. As your youngsters scoop up the sand, encourage them to spot the colorful dots.

CONFETTI FUN

Hooray! What's more fun than tossing confetti? Making confetti! Set up this confetti-cutting center to sharpen youngsters' fine-motor skills. In advance, place scraps of colorful paper near a cardboard box; then tie several hole punchers to the box. Invite each child to hold the paper over the box and use the hole puncher to make confetti dots.

BINGO!

Bingo markers make such perfect dots that they are a must in a spot and dot exploration! Place the markers in your art center along with a variety of construction paper circles. Invite each child to use the markers, the circles, and her imagination to create a spotted work of art.

POM-POMS AND PATTERNS

Big fuzzy dots are just the thing for fine-motor exploration. Fill a container with large pom-poms. Then set a pair of tongs and poster board strips near the container. Have students use the tongs to transfer the fuzzy dots to the poster board strips. Encourage your preschoolers to create patterns and count the number of dots that will fit on each strip.

DOTTY DOUGH

Bottle caps at your play dough center will have youngsters going dotty! Set a variety of plastic bottle caps in the area. Then invite students to use the caps to make dotty designs in the dough. Or have youngsters use the caps to cut out a supply of play dough dots.

DOT-TO-DOT

Place colorful sticky dots, paper, and crayons at a center and invite youngsters to go dotty! Have each child arrange sticky dots on a sheet of paper and then use a crayon to connect the dots. When she is finished, have her step back and look at the dotty design she created.

241

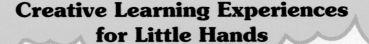

Creative Learning Experiences
for Little Hands

PICNIC PLAY

It's spring! Picnics are in season! So grab a blanket and basket, and set up a super spread of picnic-themed explorations!

ideas by Roxanne LaBell Dearman—PreK
North Carolina School for the Deaf, Charlotte, NC

BRING ON THE BEANS!

When it comes to picnic foods, baked beans are a standard! Invite your students to pack up some beans for a picnic with this sensory table idea. In advance, fill the table with dried beans; then place a variety of plastic food-storage containers and utensils in the table. If desired, also add paper plates for students to fold and use as funnels. Invite each child to use the utensils and plates to fill the containers. Have him seal the containers, and the beans are ready for packing!

PICNICKING WITH FRIENDS

Pack a picnic basket with all the needed supplies and then watch a variety of preschool skills unfold! In advance, place an equal number of fabric napkins and paper plates in a picnic basket. Add a tablecloth; then set the basket in a center. Invite each child to unpack the basket and spread out the tablecloth. Direct the child to match each napkin with a paper plate. Have him count the number of place settings and then invite the correct number of guests to join him. Once the picnic is over, have the child refold the tablecloth and napkins and pack the basket. Math skills, social skills, language development, spatial reasoning—there's a whole lot of learning packed into this picnic idea!

ANT TRACKS

They may be a little pesky, but no picnic would be complete without the ants! Gather a supply of plastic ants and a light-colored paper tablecloth. Tape the cloth to a table and then set shallow pans of paint on it. Add the ants to the area; then invite youngsters to dip the ants' feet into the paint and make tracks across the cloth. The ants go marching one by one. Hooray! Hooray!

ANTS AGAIN!

How well can your little picnickers spot those pesky ants? Find out with this exploration idea! Half-fill several clear plastic jars, each with a different dry ingredient such as rice, beans, or pasta. Next, hide a plastic ant in the contents of each jar; then hot-glue the lid onto the jar. Have students tilt and turn the jars until they spy those picnic pests! Gotcha!

HERE'S THE SCOOP!

Fill an ice chest with DUPLO bricks or small blocks. Add a plastic ice scoop and then set a variety of cups near the chest. Invite each child to scoop the play ice out of the chest and fill the cups. For added exploration and discovery, encourage the child to estimate how many scoops will fill each cup. Then have her count as she fills the cup with the ice. One, two, three!

SANDWICH STACKERS

Request parent donations of unused car wash sponges and kitchen sponges. (See the parent note on page 246.) Then set up this super sandwich-building center. Place the car wash sponges in a bread bag and place the kitchen sponges in plastic food-storage containers. If desired, sort the sponges into the containers by color; then write the name of a different sandwich ingredient on each container. For example, label yellow sponges *cheese,* pink sponges *ham,* and green sponges *lettuce.* To use the center, a child stacks the kitchen-sponge ingredients in between two car wash–sponge bread slices to create a pretend sandwich. Uh-oh! You're going to need a bigger picnic basket for *these* sandwiches!

Looking for more sandwich ideas? See "Sandwiches? Super!" on pages 71–78.

lettuce

ham

BUSY HANDS

Creative Learning Experiences for Little Hands

THE GREAT OUTDOORS—INDOORS!

Bring some of the outside inside and invite youngsters to get busy exploring nature!

ideas contributed by Roxanne LaBell Dearman—PreK
Western NC Early Intervention Program for Children Who Are Deaf or Hard of Hearing
Charlotte, NC

WATER POWER

Whether you use pinecones or dandelions, this water table exploration will make a splash with your students. In advance, gather a few pinecones or dandelions. (Check your local craft store for packaged pinecones.) Place the pinecones or dandelions in your water table; then set a couple of empty liquid dish detergent bottles near the table. Have each child explore the power of water by filling a bottle with it and then squirting the pinecones or dandelions to make them race across the table.

HEY, HEY, HAY!

Is it really hard to find a needle in a haystack? Your students will have fun finding out with this exploration idea! Fill your sensory table with a supply of hay. Or if you have students with hay allergies, use yellow crinkle paper to represent hay. Then place one or two large plastic safety needles near the table. Invite pairs of students to take turns hiding and then finding the needle in the hay. Hey! I found it!

Such Lush Trees!

Prepare for this activity by taking youngsters on a nature walk to collect fallen green leaves. Laminate the leaves to preserve them and then cut out each one. (If you collect only a few leaves on your walk, supplement your supply with laminated construction paper leaves.) Next, tape tree trunk cutouts to a wall at children's level. Above each trunk, tape a piece of clear Con-Tact paper adhesive side out (see illustration). Place the laminated leaves in a container near the tree trunks; then have students create lush green trees by attaching the leaves to the Con-Tact paper.

Sticks and Stones Make Great Homes

Gather some sticks and stones for use with this idea. Place a supply of plastic bugs near the sticks and stones. Then have your youngsters use the materials to construct homes for the plastic critters. For added fine-motor fun, set pairs of tweezers in the area and have students use them to place the bugs in, on, or under the stick-and-stone structures. Ah, there's no place like home!

Rock and Roll!

To prepare for this sound-exploration activity, collect a variety of rocks and pebbles. Place them at a center along with an assortment of containers with lids, such as clean margarine tubs, potato chip canisters, and peanut butter jars. Have each child place rocks and pebbles in the different containers and then shake them to experience the different sounds. Come on, everyone! Let's rock!

Seed Search

It sounds messy, but it's not! With this activity, youngsters will be searching through soil for seeds. First, purchase a few packets of large seeds, such as sunflower, corn, pumpkin, and green bean. Place one seed from each packet in a clear plastic jar, one seed per jar. Half-fill the jars with potting soil. Replace the caps. Seal the jars with duct tape and then gently shake them to hide the seeds in the soil. Next, reseal the seed packets and place them near the jars. To use the center, a child turns and tilts the jar to find the seed; then he finds the matching seed packet. Fascinating for youngsters and there's no mess to clean up!

SWEET CORN
Early Sunglow

SUNFLOWER
Daybreak

BEANS, Garden
Blue Bush

Dear Family,

    We are collecting unused car wash sponges and kitchen sponges for a super sandwich-building center. If you would like to donate a sponge, please send it in by _____ .

date

    Thanks for your support!

_____
teacher

©The Education Center, Inc. • *THE MAILBOX*® • *Preschool* • April/May 2002

Dear Family,

    We are collecting unused car wash sponges and kitchen sponges for a super sandwich-building center. If you would like to donate a sponge, please send it in by _____ .

date

    Thanks for your support!

_____
teacher

©The Education Center, Inc. • *THE MAILBOX*® • *Preschool* • April/May 2002

Bulletin Boards and Displays

BULLETIN BOARDS

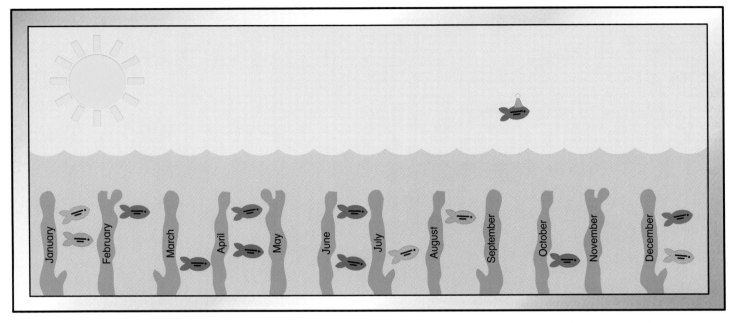

Make a splash with this creative birthday display. Label each of 12 paper seaweed shapes with a different month; then mount them in sequence onto an ocean scene. Have each child decorate a fish cutout labeled with his name and birthday. Use pushpins to display each fish beside the appropriate month. On the day of a child's birthday, display his fish so that it looks as if it is jumping out of the water. If desired, add a party hat cutout to the fish. Happy birthday!

Heather Campbell, Pennington, NJ

To make this inviting display, cover a bulletin board with a plastic tablecloth. Mount a line of ant cutouts across the cloth. Then add a personalized napkin for each child and the title. Have each of your youngsters cut out pictures of food and glue them onto a white paper plate. Mount each child's plate beside her napkin, and the display is complete!

Nancy O'Toole—Preschool
Ready, Set, Grow
Grand Rapids, MN

AND DISPLAYS

Brighten up your classroom with a bulletin board that shows sweet thoughts about new friends. Cut student-fingerpainted paper into circles; then glue a construction paper lollipop stick onto each one. Divide students into pairs. Have each child say something sweet about her partner; then write the sweet statement on her partner's lollipop stick. Mount the completed sweets on a display with a catchy title.

Lori Kent
Hood River, OR

Sweet Thoughts

Haley always shares.

BAA, BAA, BLACK SHEEP

Here's a great display for a nursery rhyme unit. Have students sponge-paint black circles onto a large sheet of white bulletin board paper. Cut the paper into the shape of a sheep's body. Add a face and legs; then display the sheep on a bulletin board. Have students stuff three plastic trash bags with newspaper. Tie the bags closed with string and then add them to the display. Title the board "Baa, Baa, Black Sheep" and then mount a copy of the nursery rhyme near the display.

adapted from an idea by Wendi Coker—Preschool, Wonderland School, Bellflower, CA

Make this red-hot display for Fire Prevention Week. Cut out a large house shape from bulletin board paper; then glue or paint orange flames onto the house. Provide each child with a red fire truck cutout. Help him use paper fasteners to attach wheels and a bell to the truck. Then have him glue on yellow strips of paper to create a ladder. Fire trucks to the rescue!

Ann Becker—Four- and Five-Year-Olds
Deerwood Center
Milwaukee, WI

Little ones will wise up to shapes with this owl display. Have each child glue two white circle eyes and an orange triangle beak onto a paper bag. Then have him cover the rest of the bag with yellow rectangle feathers. As a final touch, direct the child to glue on two black circles for pupils and two yellow paper wings. Display the owls on a tree made from crumpled bulletin board paper. Passersby are sure to say, " 'Whooo' made this nice display?"

Barbara Meyers
Fort Worth County Day School
Fort Worth, TX

AND DISPLAYS

Here's a unique way to create a class Christmas tree! Have each child paint a white snow scene on a green sheet of construction paper. Display the paintings in the shape of a Christmas tree; then add student-decorated star cutouts, presents, and light cutouts. Looks great and it doesn't need watering!

Sue Dupree—PreK
First Presbyterian Child Development
Gainesville, GA

Ms. Tadie's Reindeer

David   Karen   Scott   Misty   Derik   Shawn   Clay   Bonita

This row of reindeer will add some holiday charm to a hallway or your classroom! Paint each child's palm and fingers with brown tempera paint. Have the child press his hand onto a long sheet of bulletin board paper; then write his name under the resulting print. Have students make a row of handprints on the paper. When the prints are dry, invite each child to add construction paper eyes and a pom-pom nose to his print. Label the display to resemble the one shown, and you're ready for a sleigh ride!

Robin Tadie—Preschool, Audubon School, Colorado Springs, CO

What's the catch of the day? This lovely valentine display! Provide each child with a large red heart cutout and three small pink heart cutouts. Invite the child to glue the hearts together to create a fish; then have him use glitter glue pens and markers to decorate his fish. Display youngsters' fish on a bulletin board with cutout starfish and seaweed; then add a title similar to the one shown. You won't need to fish for compliments with this idea!

Maria Rotberg—Three-Year-Olds, Prince of Peace Educational Center, Howell, NJ

To set up this Presidents' Day display, use the patterns on page 256 to make tagboard tracers. Then use the tracers to make black paper cutouts for each child. Have the child paint red and blue stripes on a white sheet of paper. When the paint is dry, direct her to glue the cutouts to her paper. Mount each child's project on a wall or bulletin board to salute George Washington and Abraham Lincoln on Presidents' Day.

Valerie Cadden—PreK
Westchester Learning Center
Clearwater, FL

AND DISPLAYS

Create an eye-catching wall display with these fanciful flowers. Direct each child to lie down in a *T* shape on a piece of green bulletin board paper. Trace around the child's body and cut out the resulting shape. Have each child color a small paper plate to resemble her face. Glue the paper plate to the head of the child's green figure. Then invite her to cut out paper petals (or have them precut) and glue them around the plate's edge. Mount the finished flowers along a hallway and add construction paper grass, clouds, and other spring things. My, oh my, what a bloomin' bunch!

Silvy Mastalsz—Director, PreK
Herb's House
Elizabeth, NJ

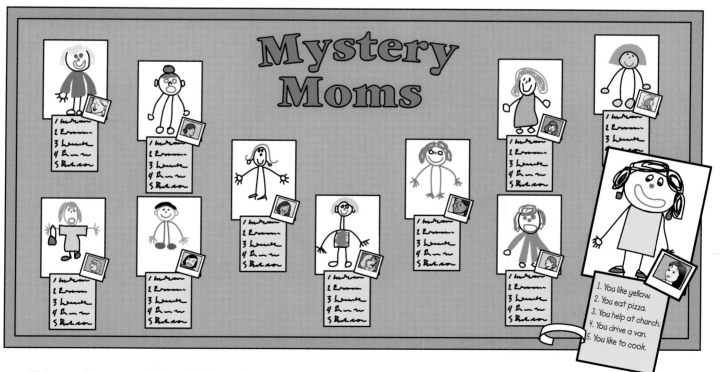

This guessing game will be a hit for Mother's Day! Have each child draw a picture of his mother. Then have him dictate five clues about his mom. Tape a strip of paper over each of the last four clues; then display the clues under the picture. Each day, reveal an additional clue, and encourage moms to pick out their pictures. On the last day, mount photos on the matching drawings to reveal the identities.

Anjali Gadre—PreK, Good Shepherd Christian Day Care, Somerville, NJ

Out-of-This-World Art!

Set up this display and compliments are sure to be launched your way! To begin, cut student-fingerpainted paper into planet shapes. Or, if you have access to a spin-art machine, have each child squeeze two or three different colors of liquid tempera onto a spinning sheet of paper. When the paint is dry, cut the paper into a circle to resemble a planet. Display the planets on a dark blue or black background. Then add die-cut stars, student-made rockets, and the title "Out-of-This-World Art!"

Kelly Noll
Family Growth Child Care
Reamstown, PA

Inching Our Way Toward Kindergarten

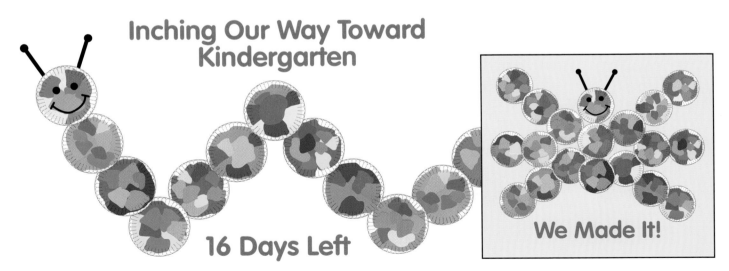

16 Days Left

We Made It!

The end-of-the-year countdown is so much more exciting with this changeable display! Have each child sponge-paint a white paper plate. Display the plates in the shape of a caterpillar; then add a title similar to the one shown. Each day, remove a different plate from the board and set it aside. Time the removal of plates so that the last caterpillar segment is removed the day before school ends. On the last day of school, reposition the plates in the shape of a butterfly and change the title to say "We Made It!"

Wendi Southwick—Three-Year-Olds, Novi Community Education Preschool, Novi, MI

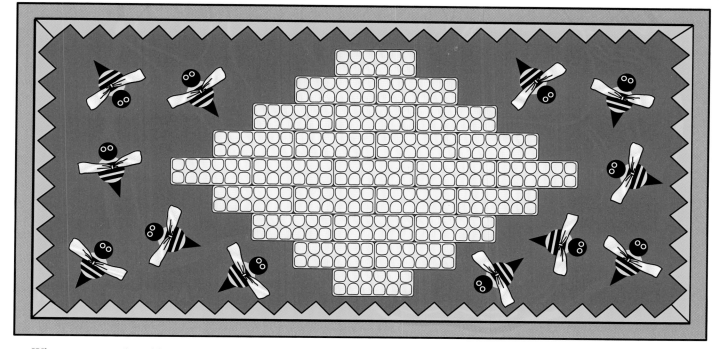

What can you make with 25 yellow egg cartons? A bulletin board beehive! Cut the bottom off of each egg carton and staple it to a bulletin board as shown. Have each child make a construction paper bee with hole reinforcers for eyes and plastic-wrap wings. Staple the bees around the hive, and this display is sure to cause quite a buzz!

Jill Glass—Preschool and Extended Kindergarten, Gaston Elementary, Gaston, IN

Welcome, Summer!

If you have a supply of summer-themed rubber stamps, have students use them to create a banner that welcomes the summer season. Place a sheet of bulletin board paper on a table. Then set the rubber stamps, ink pads, and markers near the paper. Help students use the materials to stamp out a super summer display.

Peggy Stratton—Four-Year-Olds
First Baptist Church Preschool
Okeechobee, FL

Explorations

Dusting for Prints
This fingerprint investigation is sure to make a mark on little ones' learning!

STEP 1
Give each child in a small group one sheet of paper and a pencil. Help each child trace a hand onto his paper.

STEP 2
Give an index card to each child. Have him repeatedly rub the card with one side of the pencil lead until a layer of graphite forms.

STEP 5
Have the child remove the tape and stick it onto the index finger of his hand outline. Repeat Steps 3–5 to make prints of the child's other fingers.

STEP 6
Give each child in the small group a plastic magnifying lens. Have him compare the fingerprints on the tape with the markings on his fingertips. Encourage youngsters to discuss their observations.

Science You Can Do *by Suzanne Moore*

To investigate fingerprints, you will need the following:
pencil for each child in a small group
sheet of white paper for each child
small index card for each child
transparent tape
plastic magnifying lenses

Instruct each child to roll the tip of his index finger in the graphite.

Provide each child with a strip of transparent tape. Help him put the tape on the tip of his index finger as shown. Then have him rub the tape so the graphite sticks to it and makes a print.

Did You Know?

- No two people have exactly the same fingerprint.
- Fingerprints are formed five months before birth.

What Now?

Have each child use a black washable ink pad to make a thumbprint on a small piece of paper. Then use a photocopier to enlarge the print. Cut out the enlarged print. Glue it onto a small index card and then label the card with the child's name. Place each child's card at a center and invite youngsters to examine and compare the enlarged prints.

Jeremy

Suna

259

Explorations

Pulling Power

Little ones will be attracted to this series of simple experiments involving magnets.

STEP 1

Give each child in a small group a magnet and a few paper clips. Allow the students to explore the magnets and clips. Then have students discuss their observations.

STEP 2

Have each child hold a paper clip in the palm of his hand. Then direct him to hold a magnet in his other hand and slowly lower it toward the clip. Instruct the child to observe the paper clip closely. When the magnet gets close enough to the clip, the clip will "jump" out of his hand and stick to the magnet!

STEP 5

Provide each child with a small paper cup. Have him place a paper clip inside the cup. Then direct him to touch the outside of the cup with the magnet and observe the movement of the clip.

STEP 6

Have each child cover the paper clip in his cup with a small amount of dry rice. Then have the child hold the magnet over the rice. The paper clip will jump up and stick to the magnet, leaving the rice inside the cup.

Science You Can Do
by Suzanne Moore

To explore magnets, you will need the following:
strong magnetic wand for each child in a small group
1" newspaper square for each child in a small group
paper clips
paper cup for each child in a small group
dry rice

STEP 3

Have students set the paper clips aside. Provide each child with a small newspaper square. Direct him to repeat Step 2 using the newspaper instead of a paper clip. Have the child compare the results. *(The newspaper will not jump or stick to the magnet.)*

STEP 4

Direct the child to place a paper clip in the palm of his hand and then cover it with the newspaper square. Have the child repeat Step 2 using the newspaper and the clip. The clip will jump to the magnet and carry the newspaper with it!

This Is Why

- Only objects containing iron are attracted to magnets.
- Paper clips are made of a metal that contains iron.
- The magnetic force can act through some surfaces, such as the newspaper square, the side of the cup, and the rice.

What Now?

If the magnetic force can act through newspaper, what other materials can it penetrate? Stock a center with some paper clips, magnetic wands, and a variety of paper squares for students to test. For example, use squares of corrugated cardboard, tissues, waxed paper, aluminum foil, and wrapping paper. Have students place each square over a paper clip and then find out whether the magnetic force will penetrate the paper. Science is best when you have magnets to test!

Explorations

Oh, Buoy!
Plunge into some science fun with this investigation of sinking and floating!

STEP 1
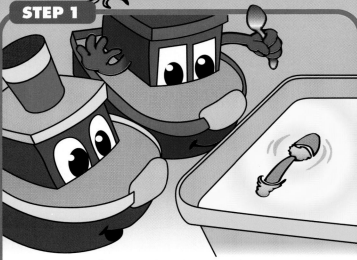

Invite a small group of students to join you at the water table. Illustrate the concept of *sinking* by placing a metal spoon in the water. Then demonstrate *floating* by dropping a plastic spoon in the water.

STEP 2
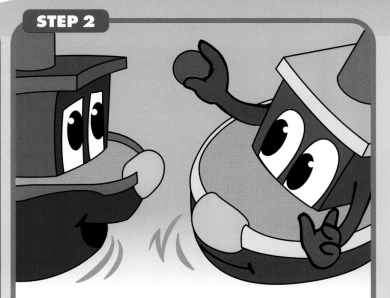

Have students examine a solid rubber ball and predict whether the ball will sink or float.

STEP 5
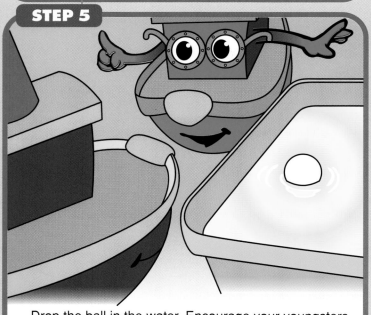

Drop the ball in the water. Encourage your youngsters to observe the ball and then conclude that the ball floats.

STEP 6
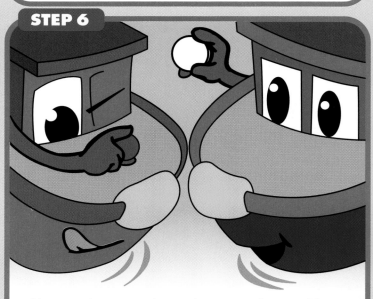

Have students examine and compare the two different balls. Invite each child to explain why he thinks one ball floats and one ball sinks.

Science You Can Do

To learn about sinking and floating, you will need the following:
water table or large container filled with water
plastic spoon
metal spoon
solid rubber ball
Ping-Pong ball

STEP 3

Drop the ball in the water. Direct your youngsters to observe the ball; then lead them to conclude that it sinks.

STEP 4

Have students examine a Ping-Pong ball. Discuss the results of Step 3 and then invite youngsters to predict whether the ball will sink or float.

This Is Why

- The plastic spoon and Ping-Pong ball are less dense than the water. Because they are less dense, the water holds them up and they float!
- The metal spoon and rubber ball are more dense than the water. The water cannot hold them up, so they sink.

What Now?

Gather a variety of balls, such as old golf balls, tennis balls, and baseballs. Place the balls near the water table and invite youngsters to predict and then test the buoyancy of each one.

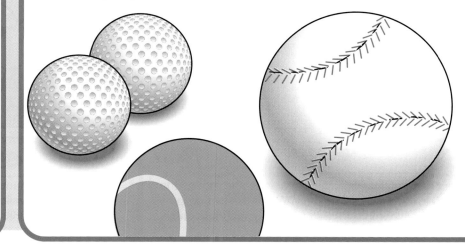

Leaf Patterns
Use with "Sun Power" on pages 260–261.

©2001 The Education Center, Inc. • *THE MAILBOX*® • *Preschool* • Oct/Nov 2001

Head, Shoulders, Knees, and Toes

Head, Shoulders

Trick or Treat!

Halloween is just around the corner! Invite your little ones to practice for the big event with this movement activity. Then send a copy of the song (page 278) home with each child.

(sung to the tune of "Where Is Thumbkin?")

Trick-or-treaters! Trick-or-treaters!	*Point to self.*
Knock, knock, knock. Knock, knock, knock.	*Pretend to knock on a door.*
Happy Halloween! Happy Halloween!	*Pretend to hold out trick-or-treat bag.*
Walk, walk, walk. Walk, walk, walk.	*Walk in place or around a circle.*

Reneé Strock
Helping Hands Preschool
Clifton Park, NY

Step Right Up!

This sensory stomp is a real crowd pleaser! To prepare, gather three small plastic wading pools, or cut three large boxes so that the sides are approximately one foot high. Fill one pool with shredded newspaper, one with Styrofoam packing material, and one with large bubble wrap. Divide your class into three small groups and have each group stand in a different pool. Next, play some lively music and encourage each group to stomp through the material in the pool. Stop the music. Have the groups switch pools; then begin the activity again. If necessary, replenish the bubble wrap in the pool before repeating the activity. To add a seasonal twist, play a musical selection such as "Monster Mash" and encourage youngsters to move like monsters through the pools.

Lori Burrow
Meridian, CA

Pumpkin Roll Relay

Ripen gross-motor skills with this unusual relay race. In advance, have parents donate two small pumpkins that students can easily roll. Then, on a perfect fall day, head outside with your youngsters. Divide your class into two teams and provide each team with a pumpkin. At the start signal, the first child on each team rolls the pumpkin to a designated spot. Then he rolls the pumpkin back to the team and tags the next child in line. The relay continues in this manner until each child has had a chance to roll the pumpkin. On your mark, get set, roll!

Deborah Davis—Three-Year-Olds, First Presbyterian Day School, Deland, FL

From Pumpkins to Pies!

To prepare for this movement activity, create a pretend pie crust by placing a parachute or large sheet on the floor of your classroom. Seat youngsters around the parachute crust. Choose five students to be pretend pumpkins and have them sit on the edge of the crust. As you recite the following pumpkin countdown, direct each little pumpkin in turn to tumble into the crust.

[Five] orange pumpkins sitting on the ground.
One rolled over and tumbled all around.
[He] opened up [his] eyes.
What a big surprise!
My, oh, my!
[He] was in a pumpkin pie!

adapted from an idea by
Merrilee Walker—Three-Year-Old Inclusion
Westbay Children's Center
Warwick, RI

Head, Shoulders

Jug Bands Are Back!

The sound of two empty milk jugs will be music to your ears with this idea! Provide each child with two clean, plastic milk containers. Direct her to hold them by the handles and rub the sides together to create a sound. Have students line up behind you and follow your lead as you march, hop, or skip while playing the jugs. When your youngsters are familiar with this activity, invite each child to take a turn leading the group.

Patricia Moeser—Preschool
U.W. Preschool Lab Site #1
Madison, WI

Jump!

A colorful supply of votive candles is all you need to make the nursery rhyme "Jack, Be Nimble" come to life! Place the candles on the floor around your circle-time area. Then begin reciting the rhyme, using a child's name and identifying a colored candle. For example, you might say, "Sarah, be nimble. Sarah, be quick. Sarah, jump over the blue candlestick!" Repeat the activity several times, giving each child a number of chances to jump over different-colored candles.

Doris Porter
HACAP Head Start
Anamosa, IA

Knees, & Toes

Skating Spree

Youngsters will feel like stars on ice with this movement activity! Have students remove their shoes and stand in a circle in an uncarpeted area. Begin playing some lively music and invite them to skate in their socks around the circle. Periodically stop the music and direct your little skaters to stop and take a bow. Resume playing the music and instruct your youngsters to continue skating—in the opposite direction! Continue the activity in this manner, giving your preschoolers plenty of practice skating in clockwise and counter-clockwise directions.

LeeAnn Collins—PreK
Sunshine House Preschool
Lansing, MI

A Blizzard of Snowballs!

The weather outside may be frightful, but this movement activity is delightful! Lay a large white sheet in the middle of a carpeted area. Invite students to sit around the edge of the sheet. To begin the activity, call out a directive, such as "Brown-haired children, roll like snow-balls!" Have those children tuck them-selves into a ball, roll around on the sheet, and then go back to their seats. Continue the activity in this manner, grouping your little ones in a variety of ways. "Four-year-olds, roll like snowballs!"

273

Head, Shoulders

Stuck on You!

Little feet will be tickled with this sticky sensory experience! Tape strips of duct tape (adhesive side out) around each child's shoes as shown. Play a lively musical selection and invite your youngsters to move to the music. Your preschoolers will enjoy not only the feel of the tape but also the sticky sound it makes as it comes off the floor.

Peggy Wieck—PreK, Litchfield Prekindergarten, Litchfield, IL

Flying Bears

Bring out a parachute and get ready for some high-flying gross-motor fun! Have your youngsters hold the parachute by the edges; then place a stuffed bear in the middle. Invite your students to join you in reciting the rhyme below as they shake the parachute. With each line of the rhyme, encourage your youngsters to shake the parachute a little harder. As you say the last line, have students raise the parachute over their heads and then quickly bring it back down to send the bear flying.

Teddy bear, teddy bear, move real slow.
Teddy bear, teddy bear, here we go.
Teddy bear, teddy bear, start to fly.
Teddy bear, teddy bear, in the sky!

Sarah Booth—Four- and Five-Year-Olds
Messiah Nursery School
South Williamsport, PA

Shamrock Shake

Here's a movement idea that's perfect for St. Patrick's Day! To prepare, cut out a class supply of shamrock shapes, each one large enough for a child to stand on. Use clear Con-Tact paper to adhere each shamrock to the floor of your circle-time area. Have your students stand in a circle around the shamrocks. Begin playing some music and encourage students to shake different body parts. Periodically stop the music and direct students to find a shamrock to stand on. For older preschoolers, use shamrocks that have been programmed with numbers, letters, or shapes and then have each child identify the symbol on his shamrock. Ready, set, shake!

Michelle Packard—Infant–Preschool
The Children's Workshop
Brockton, MA

Roll 'em, Roll 'em, Roll 'Em

Burritos, anyone? Combine dramatic play and movement with a small-group activity that just might make little ones hungry. Have each child in turn lie on a small blanket on the floor. Pretend to sprinkle cheese, lettuce, and tomatoes over him. Then have the child roll over and over as another child wraps the blanket around him, creating a pretend burrito. One burrito, coming up!

Cindy Farnham—Three- and Four-Year-Olds
Boothbay HeadStart
Boothbay, ME

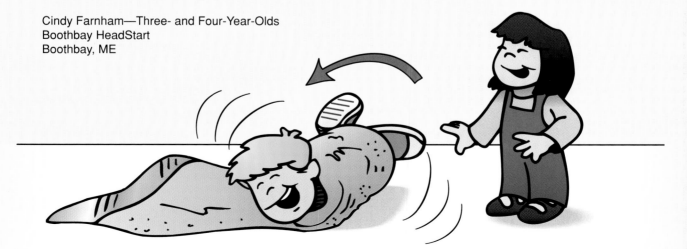

Plant-Part Pokey

What's this Hokey-Pokey adaptation all about? Learning the parts of a plant! To begin, cut out a pair of construction paper leaves and a pair of construction paper roots for each child. Next, make a class supply of flower headbands similar to the ones shown. Have each child wear a flower headband and hold a leaf in each hand. Tape one root to each of the child's shoes, and she's prepared to do the Plant-Part Pokey! "You put your right leaf in...."

(sung to the tune of "The Hokey-Pokey")

You put your [right leaf] in.
You take your [right leaf] out.
You put your [right leaf] in,
And you shake it all about!
You do the Plant-Part Pokey,
And you turn yourself around.
That's what it's all about!

Sing additional verses replacing the underlined phrase, in turn, with *left leaf, right root, left root,* and *flower.*

Sharon Tessier—Preschool
Learning Tree Preschool
Crystal Lake, IL

Float Like a Butterfly

Here's a great movement activity to use with a butterfly unit or as a follow-up to Eric Carle's book *The Very Hungry Caterpillar.* Provide each child with a pair of colorful, lightweight scarves. Then play a lively musical selection. Encourage youngsters to use the scarves to dramatize spinning a cocoon before they curl up on the floor. Briefly stop the music; then resume playing the song as your little caterpillars emerge from their cocoons. Invite youngsters to use their scarves as wings and pretend to fly around the room. Hello, butterflies!

Camilla Canning—PreK
First United Methodist Nursery School
Santa Monica, CA

Ring Around the Puddle

Invite your youngsters to indulge in some muddy movement fun without getting a drop of mud on their clothing! In advance, cut out a large mud-puddle shape from laminated bulletin board paper or from a large piece of brown felt. Use loops of tape to attach the puddle to the middle of your circle-time area. Have youngsters join hands and move around the puddle as they recite the rhyme shown. What should your little ones do after reciting the last line? Fall in the puddle—of course!

Ring around the puddle
Pockets full of mud. Oh!
Splish, splash! Splish, splash!
We all fall in!

Maureen Palladino—Preschool
Bright Horizons Family Center
Andover, MA

It's Raining! It's Pouring!

Get ready for a shower of giggles with this springtime movement activity! In advance, scatter pretend raindrops (Styrofoam packing pieces) over your circle-time area. Invite youngsters to the area. Begin singing the song shown and have youngsters slowly toss the Styrofoam pieces into the air to create a pretend sprinkling of rain. Sing each verse faster and faster and have students toss the raindrops in time to the music. Before long, you'll have a downpour of rain and movement fun!

(sung to the tune of "Are You Sleeping?")

It is [sprinkling].   Rain is [slowly] falling.
It is [sprinkling].   Rain is [slowly] falling.
Drip, drop, drip.   Drip, drop, drip.
Drip, drop, drip.   Drip, drop, drip.

Sing a second verse, replacing the underlined words with *showering* and *quickly.* Then sing the final verse below.

It is pouring!   Rain is all around us!
It is pouring!   Rain is all around us!
Splash, splash, splash!   Splash, splash, splash!
Splash, splash, splash!   Splash, splash, splash!

277

Trick or Treat!
(sung to the tune of "Where Is Thumbkin?")

Trick-or-treaters!
Point to self.

Trick-or-treaters!

Knock, knock, knock.
Pretend to knock on a door.

Knock, knock, knock.

Happy Halloween!
Pretend to hold out trick-or-treat bag.

Happy Halloween!

Walk, walk, walk.
Walk in place or around a circle.

Walk, walk, walk.

©The Education Center, Inc. • *THE MAILBOX® • Preschool* • Oct/Nov 2001

Trick or Treat!
(sung to the tune of "Where Is Thumbkin?")

Trick-or-treaters!
Point to self.

Trick-or-treaters!

Knock, knock, knock.
Pretend to knock on a door.

Knock, knock, knock.

Happy Halloween!
Pretend to hold out trick-or-treat bag.

Happy Halloween!

Walk, walk, walk.
Walk in place or around a circle.

Walk, walk, walk.

©The Education Center, Inc. • *THE MAILBOX® • Preschool* • Oct/Nov 2001

Note to the teacher: Use with "Trick or Treat!" on page 270. Photocopy a class supply of song cards; then send one home with each child. Encourage youngsters to sing the tune with their families.

KIDS IN THE KITCHEN

KIDS IN THE KITCHEN

Put on your apron and step into the kitchen—with your kids, of course! What's on the menu? A generous portion of learning opportunities served up with a batch of fun. Savor the following two hands-on cooking activities perfectly measured for preschool fun and teacher ease.

Here's what to do:

- Collect the necessary ingredients and utensils using the lists on one of the recipe cards below.
- Follow the teacher preparation guidelines for that cooking activity.
- Cut out the step-by-step recipe cards on pages 281 and 282.
- Display the cards on a bulletin board or chart in your cooking area so that the students can see the directions for the recipe you've selected.
- Discuss the directions with a small group of kids; then encourage them to get cooking!

Learning has never been so delicious!

Easy Apple Pie

Ingredients:
miniature graham cracker crust for each child
large spoonful of apple pie filling for each child
1 tsp. instant oatmeal for each child
cinnamon
whipped cream

Utensils and supplies:
2 serving bowls
large serving spoon
1 tsp. measuring spoon
plastic spoon for each child

Teacher preparation:
Arrange the ingredients and supplies near the step-by-step recipe cards (see page 281).

Ghost Toast

Ingredients:
slice of white bread per child
slice of white American cheese per child
2 raisins per child

Utensils and supplies:
ghost-shaped cookie cutter
paper plate per child
aluminum foil square per child
permanent marker
toaster oven (For teacher use only.)

Teacher preparation:
Use a permanent marker to label each aluminum foil square with a different child's name. Arrange the ingredients and supplies near the step-by-step recipe cards (see page 282). Operate the toaster oven.

2 Sprinkle.

Cinnamon

5 Eat!

©The Education Center, Inc. • THE MAILBOX® • Preschool • Aug/Sept 2001

1 Easy Apple Pie

Put.

4 Squirt.

Wash.

3 Sprinkle.

1 teaspoon

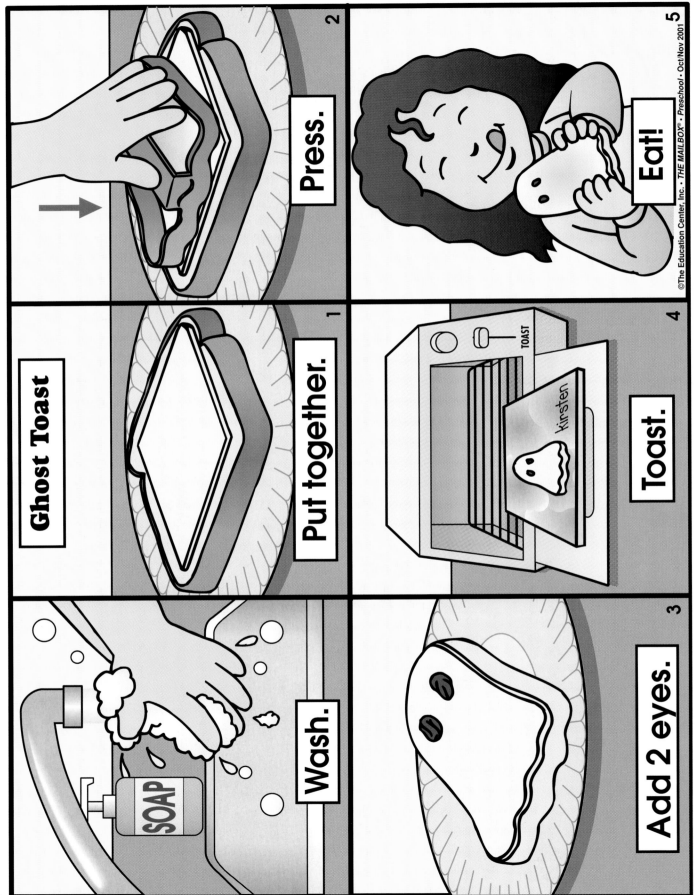

Press. **2**

Eat! **5**

©The Education Center, Inc. • THE MAILBOX® • Preschool • Oct/Nov 2001

Ghost Toast

Put together. **1**

Toast. **4**

Wash. **3**

Add 2 eyes. **3**

KIDS IN THE KITCHEN

Put on your apron and step into the kitchen—with your kids, of course! What's on the menu? A generous portion of learning opportunities served up with a batch of fun. Savor the following two hands-on cooking activities perfectly measured for preschool fun and teacher ease.

Here's what to do:
- Collect the necessary ingredients and utensils using the lists on one of the recipe cards below.
- Follow the teacher preparation guidelines for that cooking activity.
- Cut out the step-by-step recipe cards on pages 284 and 285.
- Display the cards on a bulletin board or chart in your cooking area so that the students can see the directions for the recipe you've selected.
- Discuss the directions with a small group of kids; then encourage them to get cooking!

Learning has never been so delicious!

Chicken Soup 1, 2, 3

Ingredients for one:
½ c. chicken broth, heated
1 tbsp. canned chicken
2 tbsp. cooked rice
3 oyster crackers

Utensils and supplies:
Styrofoam bowl per child
plastic spoon per child
Crock-Pot
1-cup measuring cup
2 tablespoons

Teacher preparation:
Arrange the ingredients and supplies near the step-by-step recipe cards (see page 284). Provide adult supervision near the Crock-Pot.

St. Patrick's Day Spread

Ingredients for one:
whipped cream cheese
green food coloring
crackers

Utensils and supplies:
snack-sized resealable plastic bag for each child
jumbo craft stick for each child
napkin for each child

Teacher preparation:
Arrange the ingredients and utensils near the step-by-step recipe cards (see page 285).

adapted from an idea by
Ann Francioni
New Orleans, LA

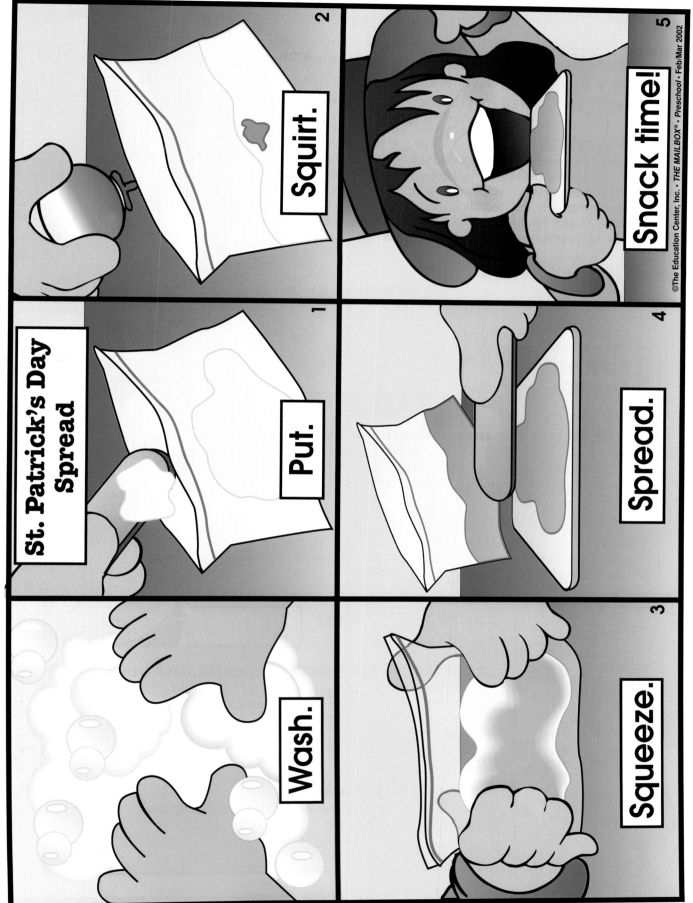

©The Education Center, Inc. • *THE MAILBOX*® • *Preschool* • Feb/Mar 2002

285

Getting Your Ducklings

A Shoe-In for Storage

It's clear—this storage solution makes sense! Hang a shoe organizer with clear pockets over a closet door in your classroom. Fill the pockets with craft items, such as cotton balls, craft sticks, pipe cleaners, and pom-poms. You'll be able to find what you need at a glance!

Elaine M. Utt—Two-Year-Olds
La Petite Academy
Tampa, FL

When's Mommy Coming?

Here's an idea for a little one who needs help adjusting to time spent away from Mom and Dad. Have the child bring in a photo of Mom and Dad. Cut a large construction paper circle. Look through magazines to locate pictures that illustrate parts of your school day, such as art, snacktime, outdoor play, rest, and centers. Glue the pictures around the circle in order, ending with the parent photo. Attach a paper arrow to the center of the circle with a metal brad. Then encourage the child to move the arrow from one activity to the next as the day goes by. Before he knows it, it'll be time for Mom and Dad to arrive!

Angela L. Hupp
Lebanon, PA

breakfast
library
Moms and Dads are here!
free play
creative activities
naptime

Praise on Paper

Here's a quick and easy way to send home a note of praise! Simply tear from a cube of notepaper, add a colorful sticker, and write a few words, s sharing" or "Good listener today." Slip the note into a child's backpack both parent and child will delight in finding it later!

Tiffany Vaughan—PreK, Mays Chapel Children's Center, Timonium, MD

in a Row — Tips for Getting Organized

Name Tees

Try this "tee-rific" way to personalize each child's space in your classroom! Collect a plain white T-shirt for each of your preschoolers. Then use fabric paint and letter stencils to spell each child's name on a shirt. When the paint has set, fit each T-shirt over a child's chair to indicate her place. As an extension, make a name T-shirt for each teacher and assistant; then display these on a clothesline or bulletin board.

Sue Dupree—Four- and Five-Year-Olds
First Presbyterian Child Development Center
Gainesville, GA

Birthday Card Basket

Plan early to celebrate those all-important birthdays all through the year! As you review each child's name and birthdate at the start of the school year, make out a birthday card for her. Print her name and birthday on the envelope; then put all the cards in a decorated basket in your classroom. On each child's special day, present her with her card and your happy birthday wishes!

Nancy Kaczrowski—PreK
ECFE/SR
Luverne, MN

Bulletin Boards by the Book

Can't remember exactly how you made that great bulletin board last year? Avoid the problem by keeping a scrapbook of photos of bulletin boards and displays. Simply take a photo of each board before you take it down. Then compile the photos in a file or scrapbook. You'll never forget, and you'll have a great tool for assistants and parent volunteers when they assemble your displays for you!

Sue Dupree
Gainesville, GA

Getting Your Ducklings

Hold On!

Minimize the mess of painting three-dimensional projects with the help of some well-placed clothespins! Simply clip a wooden clothespin onto the object to be painted; then have the child hold onto the clothespin as she paints the object. Ah…less mess!

Beth Lemke—PreK, Heights Head Start, Columbia Heights, MN

Puzzle Pleaser

Sometimes the perfect puzzle to suit your preschoolers' interests just has too many pieces! Try this trick to make the puzzle easier for your students to assemble. Put together portions of the puzzle (especially from the center of the design); then use a foam brush to coat both sides of the assembled portions with three or four thin layers of Mod Podge water-based glue. When the glue dries, you'll have a few larger pieces, instead of too many small ones.

Lara Flejter, Deer Path School, Cary, IL

Canvas Cover-Up

Here's a tip for a table cover that'll become a work of art all on its own! Purchase a yard of unstretched canvas at an art supply store. Use the canvas to protect a classroom table, floor, or wall before inviting little ones to participate in messy painting or gluing projects. Don't bother to wipe it off or worry about it drying afterward; simply fold it up and tuck it away. It'll be ready to unfold and reuse for your next project. And the more you use it, the more interesting it will look! It may even become a cherished memento of the year's artwork!

Lois Arnold—Three- and Four-Year-Olds
Vermont Hills Family Life Center
Portland, OR

in a Row — Tips for Getting Organized

What's Inside?

If your youngsters are constantly pulling out all the bins in your storage cabinet in order to see what manipulatives are inside, try this trick. Take two or three pieces from each set of manipulatives and hot-glue them to the front of the bin. Your little ones will be able to see at a glance what materials are in each bin. And sorting all the pieces at cleanup time will be easier, too!

Jennifer Padgett—Five-Year-Olds
Little Friends CCC
Indianapolis, IN

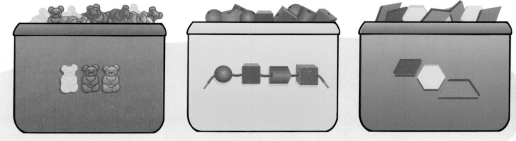

Page Protector Books

You want your class books to last, but laminating all those pages can be time-consuming and expensive. Try using clear plastic page protectors instead! Slip each child's finished page inside a page protector; then assemble all the pages with metal rings or place them inside a three-ring binder. Your class books will look polished and stand up to repeated readings! You can also reuse the page protectors from book to book or year to year.

Jessica Block—Preschool
By Leaps and Bounds
Sauk City, WI

Field Trip Folder

Get organized for your next field trip with the help of a manila folder and a copy of a class list grid. (See page 300.) Glue the grid to the front of the folder; then label the columns with headings such as "permission slip," "money," and "chaperone." Jot down the phone number of each chaperone on the front of the folder as well. As children return their permission slips, place them inside the folder. You can quickly see if any child still needs to return money or a slip, the phone numbers will be handy if there's anything your chaperones need to know, and all of your permission slips will be in one place. Easy!

Mary Jane Henderson
Westside Elementary
Palm Bay, FL

Pumpkin Patch Trip

Name	$	Slip	Chaperone
Allison	√	√	
Ashley		√	
Ben	√	√	Lynn 399-4142
Billy	√	√	
Carly	√	√	
Catherine		√	
Cody			
Dennis	√	√	
Felicia		√	Maria 394-6790
Hien	√	√	
Marcus	√	√	
Mary	√		
Raul		√	Jen 459-3385
Sydney	√	√	
Trey			

Getting Your Ducklings

Six-Pack of Supplies

Soda cartons are perfect for carting around school supplies! Save the cardboard holders from six-packs of soda. Fit a Styrofoam cup into each section; then fill each cup with handy items, such as scissors, glue, markers, or crayons. These lightweight supply holders are a cinch for little hands to carry.

Kimberley Berringer—PreKVE
Clay Springs Elementary
Apopka, FL

Clothes Rack Storage

Rack up the savings in storage space with this idea! Purchase a freestanding clothes rack and adjust it to the lowest height. For each month of the school year, make a fabric bag similar in size to a pillow case but large enough to hold the pieces of your bulletin board displays. Label each bag with the month; then store the display pieces inside and clip the bag to a plastic skirt hanger. Hang all the bags on the clothes rack. To hang flip charts, fit a metal ring into each hole in the top of the chart and then clip the rings to a plastic skirt hanger.

Connie Crocker
Lamar Elementary
Baytown, TX

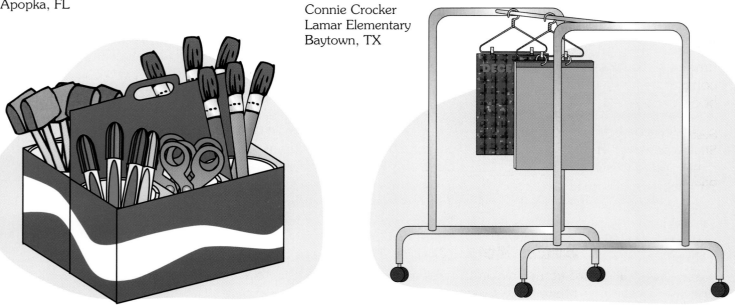

I Spy a Clean Room!

Get your room *really* spick-and-span with a game of I Spy. After most of the toys and materials are cleaned up, move through the classroom and indicate any stray items you see. For example, say, "I spy a red block under the table" or "I spy a paint smock on the floor." Your youngsters will race to clean up your space!

Betsy Fuhrmann—PreK, Dodds School, Springfield, IL

in a Row Tips for Getting Organized

A Dab'll Do It!

Painting something small? Give each child just a dab of paint in a milk jug lid (or other small lid). Less paint will be wasted and cleanup's easy—just toss the lids in the trash!

Mary Kay Ripple—Preschool, Katie's Playhouse Preschool, San Angelo, TX

Dish Drainer Book Display

Move a plastic dish drainer from the kitchen to the class-room for this supersimple display idea! Gather books for the season or for your current theme; then stand them up in a dish drainer. They'll be easy to find at storytime or for your preschoolers to flip through during center time. Use the utensil compartment to store bookmarks, too!

Susan Brown—PreK
St. Joseph Early
    Education Center
Shawnee, KS

Shoe Store

If some of your preschoolers have trouble tying or buckling shoes or get-ting into winter boots, try this tip. Des-ignate a couple of chairs as your "shoe store." Those children who need help with shoes or boots can sit in one of the chairs to let you know they need assistance—without having to say a word!

Cathy Fontana—PreK–6
RNSZ Homeschool
Clifton, NJ

Sticky Note Assessment

Want to make sure you're recording all the exciting new skills your little ones are acquiring? Make an assessment chart similar to the one shown. When you see a child exhibiting a new skill, quickly jot it down—along with the date—on a sticky note. Attach the note next to the child's name on the chart. At the end of each week, move the sticky notes to your as-sessment notebook or other record of each child's individual progress.

Karen Briley and Cathy Barra—Three- and Four-Year-Olds
Stephen F. Austin State University Early Childhood Lab
Nacogdoches, TX

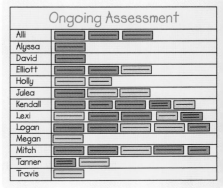

Getting Your Ducklings

CHRISTOPHER

Nap Map—on the Ceiling!

Youngsters will be resting easy with this tip. Write each child's name in large print on a colorful piece of paper. Invite the child to use stickers or stamps to decorate the paper; then tape it to the ceiling directly over the area where the child naps. During naptime, have each child find his name on the ceiling and then lay his mat under it. To help the child settle down, encourage him to silently identify the letters in his name and count the stickers on his nametag. Sweet dreams!

Gayle R. Wells—Two- to Five-Year-Olds
Bright Beginnings Daycare and Preschool
Gillette, WY

A Stockpile of Die-Cuts

Sometimes the die-cutting machine is just not accessible! Try this trick and you'll always have what you need on hand. Cut a large supply of letters, numbers, and shapes; then store them in a hanging shoe organizer. If possible, use an organizer with clear pockets. Or label the outside of each pocket with one of the die-cuts contained inside. When you need die-cuts in a jiffy, simply reach in the pockets and pull out the shapes and letters that you need!

Wendy K. Baize—Director
Pearce 4 Kids Child Care Center
North Chili, NY

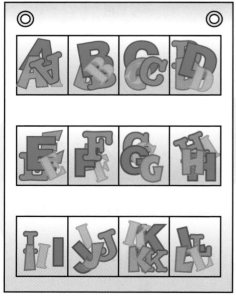

Music Box Cleanup

Encourage a quick and quiet cleanup with this trick. Play a music box to signal students to begin cleaning up. When the music stops, have students finish cleaning and come quietly to the next activity.

Rosa Wilson—PreK, Wee Care, New Carlisle, OH

in a Row   Tips for Getting Organized

Toweling Off

Cleaning up after messy art projects can be so simple with this tip! Cover your work area with a large beach towel and then tape it to the underside of the table with duct tape. The towel absorbs glue and paint, and best of all, little fingers can be wiped off on it! When the projects are through, untape the towel and throw it in the wash for a thoroughly easy cleanup!

Janet Zupetz—PreK, A Creative Playschool, Dublin, CA

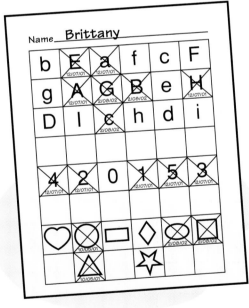

Assessment Made Easy

It's almost too good to be true—an assessment tool that is simple to make and *also* keeps track of student progress! To make one, program each block on a grid with a different letter, shape, or number. Photocopy the grid to make a class supply and then label each one with a different child's name. To assess letter, shape, and number identification, point to a box and have a child name the symbol. If the child identifies it correctly, mark the box with an X. For further documentation, also write the date in the box. The grids will help you monitor student progress and make a perfect conversation piece for parent conferences!

Sarah Booth—Four- and Five-Year-Olds
Messiah Nursery School
South Williamsport, PA

Organize Those Window Clings!

What's the best way to store your decorative window clings? In a photo album! Obtain a large photo album with peel-and-stick pages. Instead of peeling back the plastic on each page, place the clings directly on the plastic page protector. Your window clings will stay pressed, organized, and ready to go!

Heather Armstrong—PreK
Kathy Dunn Cultural Center
Hasbrouck Heights, NJ

Getting Your Ducklings

A Class Portfolio

You may have individual work portfolios for each of your students, but why not make a class portfolio? For each theme your class explores, place a number of clear page protectors in a large binder. Add samples of art projects, records of books you read (along with students' comments), photographs of activities or displays, anecdotal notes, and even suggestions for improvement or further exploration. Allow students to add to the binder along the way. Keep the book in your class library and make it available for students to check out and take home to share with their families.

Peggy Wieck—PreK, Litchfield Prekindergarten, Litchfield, IL

Field Trip Hats

Want to make sure parents remember the next day's field trip? Send youngsters home wearing a field trip reminder hat! Give each child a sentence strip cut to the right length for a headband. Have him decorate the strip with stickers or cutouts related to your field trip. For example, fish stickers will help remind parents of a trip to the aquarium. As students work on their hats, go around the room and print "Field Trip Tomorrow" on each strip. Staple each child's strip to fit his head and send him home wearing the reminder!

Sharon Horn—Head Start
Knights Elementary
Plant City, FL

Is It My Turn Yet?

It can be *so* hard to wait for a turn, especially on something as exciting as the classroom computer! Make it easier for little ones with this idea. Print the question "Is it my turn yet?" on a paper plate. Post the plate near your computer and keep two baskets or coffee cans nearby, one labeled "Next" and one labeled "Done." Write each child's name on a separate clothespin. Clip three or four of the clothespins to the plate to show which children are in line for the computer. Place the remaining clothespins in the "Next" basket. As a child has a turn, move her clothespin to the "Done" basket and clip another name from the "Next" basket to the plate. When everyone has had a turn, move all the clothespins to the "Next" basket and begin again. Hey, I'm on the plate—great!

Sister Barbara Flynn—PreK, St. Raphael School, Bridgeport, CT

in a Row — Tips for Getting Organized

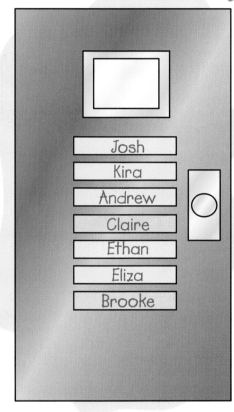

Josh
Kira
Andrew
Claire
Ethan
Eliza
Brooke

Names in a Line

Fill a few extra minutes with a game that will help little ones recognize their own and their classmates' names. To prepare, print each child's first name on a separate sentence strip. Add magnetic tape to the back of each strip. At a transition time, put all the names on your classroom door or doorframe; then challenge youngsters to line up in matching order.

Debby Moon,
Wichita Falls, TX

Rain	yes
Rainy Robert	no
Just a Rainy Day	yes
It's Raining, It's Pouring	yes
	*it's a favorite
Rainy Day	no

Reading Log

Can't remember which stories were a big hit the last time you taught a theme? Keep a reading log this time! Make a list of all the books you read to your preschoolers during a theme study. At the end of the study, take a class vote on each book. Which ones did students especially like? Which weren't so well received? Then file the log with your theme materials and you'll have a great reference when you gather stories next year.

Gabrielle Bohinski—PreK
Tots Landing Learning Center
Murfreesboro, TN

Hooray for Page Protectors!

It's clear—plastic page protectors will help you keep papers neat and organized! Slip original reproducibles into clear plastic page protectors to keep them looking new. You won't even need to remove them to make photocopies! In addition to reproducibles, use the page protectors to file poems, book lists, samples, photos of bulletin boards, and other materials related to a theme unit. Then place all the protected pages inside a three-ring binder and you'll have a one-stop reference for each of your themes!

Amy Drake—Preschool, Westview Child Care Ministry, Fort Wayne, IN

Karen Rhodes—Special Needs Preschool
Columbiana County Educational Service Center, Lisbon, OH

Name			

OUR READERS WRITE

Our Readers Write

Family Fun Bags

Extend learning into the home with thematic family fun bags. To prepare a bag, plan a few simple activities relating to a specific theme. Write the instructions on index cards; then place the cards and needed materials in a canvas bag. Add a related story book and a journal so families can write about their experiences with the bag. If desired, write a thought-provoking question on the cover of the journal and invite families to record their responses in the journal. When the child returns the bag to school, share the journal entry with the class, replenish the supplies, and then send the bag home with another child.

Mary Koczan—Three- and Four-Year-Olds
Christ Child Academy, Sheboygan, WI

Color Check

Need a creative way to assess color recognition? These beaded bracelets are just the thing! Collect an assortment of beads in a variety of colors. Show a child the beads and have him identify the different colors. Each time the child correctly identifies a color, invite him to choose a bead in that color and string it onto a pipe cleaner. When he has earned a bead for each color, twist the ends of the pipe cleaner together to form a bracelet. Encourage the child to wear the bracelet home and identify the colors for his family.

adapted from an idea by
Ann Rand—Three-Year-Olds
The Principia Preschool
St. Louis, MO

Lace a Placemat

If you have some old vinyl placemats, use them to make durable lacing cards for your preschoolers. Cut the placemat into desired shapes and then punch holes around the edges of each shape. What a simple and inexpensive way to lace up some learning!

Jill Beattie—Four- and Five-Year-Olds
Apple Place Nursery School
Chambersburg, PA

Eye Spy

This eye idea covers graphing *and* napping! In advance, make a pair of eye patterns for each child. After discussing each child's eye color, have her color the patterns to resemble her eyes. Instruct the child to place her patterns on a graph similar to the one shown; then discuss what the graph reveals. To display the graph, mount it on your ceiling above an area where students rest and then add the title "Here's Looking at You." Your little ones will quickly settle down as they count, examine, and study the eyes above.

Kimberly Calhoun—PreK
Children's Discovery Center
Raleigh, NC

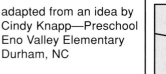

My eyes are...			
blue	green	brown	hazel

Daily Activity Display

Use this idea and little ones will learn your daily schedule to a T. To prepare, cut out a supply of construction paper T-shirts. Write the name of a different daily activity or special event on each one; then add a corresponding photograph or picture to each T-shirt. Mount a length of string on a bulletin board to resemble a clothesline. Then add a laundry basket cutout to the display. Each morning, use clothespins to clip the shirts onto the line to show the sequence of the day. When an activity is over, remove the corresponding T-shirt from the clothesline and place it in the basket cutout.

adapted from an idea by
Cindy Knapp—Preschool
Eno Valley Elementary
Durham, NC

Names on Puzzles

Here's a simple way to keep track of which preschoolers can complete which puzzles. Cover the back of each puzzle board with a sheet of Con-Tact paper. When a child has completed a puzzle, use a permanent marker to write her name on the Con-Tact paper. Your little ones will be proud to see their names on the puzzles and will be motivated to complete even more puzzles! At the end of the year, replace the Con-Tact paper on each puzzle to get ready for a new group of students.

D. Carroll
A New Beginning Preschool
Cleveland, GA

A Big Birthday Box

There's nothing more exciting than opening a big box on your birthday! So make each child's birthday extra special with this birthday box idea. Wrap a large lidded box in birthday wrapping paper. Be sure to wrap the lid and box separately. Fill the box with unwrapped, inexpensive toys and treats. Add a large bow to the lid and then place the lid on the box. When a child has a birthday, present him with the box. Invite him to open it and choose one of the items inside as his gift. How exciting!

Terry Incerto—PreK
Paul Revere School, Revere, MA

Judy Botte—Preschool
Irish-Hills Co-op Nursery School, Onsted, MI

Snip, Snip, Snip!

Refine fine-motor skills with this cutting edge craft idea. To prepare, cut out a class supply of brown construction paper paintbrush handles. Glue a piece of colorful construction paper to the flat side of each handle; then have each child cut his paper into strips to resemble bristles. For younger students, draw lines on the paper to help guide each child when cutting. Finally, have the child glue a personalized strip of construction paper across the middle of the brush. If desired, mount each child's brush near a paint can cutout and you've got a display that's a cut above the rest!

Amy Drake—Preschool, Westview Child Care Ministry, Fort Wayne, IN

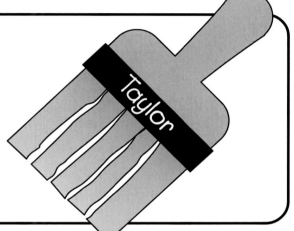

Inside an Apple

This minibooklet gets down to the core of apple science! To make one, fold a 9" x 6" piece of red construction paper in half; then trace an apple shape onto the paper as shown. Cut the apple shape through both thicknesses of paper, leaving part of the fold intact. Provide a child with the apple cutout and an apple half. Invite the child to examine the inside of the apple. Then direct her to open the apple cutout, dip the apple half in white paint, and then make prints on the insides of the cutout. When the paint is dry, have the child glue seeds onto the apple prints. What's inside an apple? Open up the booklet and "see-d"!

Donna Pollhammer—Three-Year-Olds
YMCA Chipmunk Preschool
Westminster, MD

An Apple a Day

Taking attendance is easy with this red, ripe display! To prepare, collect a class supply of small lightweight apple ornaments; then place a piece of self-adhesive magnetic tape on each one. Write each child's name on a small paper leaf; then tape each leaf to an apple stem. Mount a laminated tree cutout on a wall or on a door at children's level. Attach strips of magnetic tape to the tree so the apples can be mounted onto it. Place the apples on the tree and then set a basket near the display. As each child comes to school, direct him to pick his apple from the tree and place it in the basket. When taking attendance, a quick glance at the tree will tell you which of your little apples are absent!

Diane Kelnhofer
Hoover Elementary
New Berlin, WI

Pumpkin Pops

Use this idea to transform a lollipop into a pretend pumpkin! Wrap an orange napkin around a Tootsie Roll POP. Tie a length of green curling ribbon around the napkin to hold it in place. Set the Tootsie Roll POP on a table with the stick pointing up; then use a marker to draw jack-o'-lantern features. Ta-da!

Beverly Walton—PreK
Jacksonville Heights Elementary, Jacksonville, FL

A Treat for the Whole Family

Families will be giving thanks for this sweet turkey treat made by your little ones. To make one, have a child place a Little Debbie Creme Pie on a paper plate. Then help him use frosting to attach five Swedish fish candies to the pie to resemble turkey feathers. Have him add a vanilla wafer head, pretzel-stick legs, a candy corn beak, and an M&M's Minis eye. Cover the turkey cookie in plastic wrap and have the child take the treat home for his family to gobble up!

adapted from an idea by
Robyn Rogers—Preschool Special Needs
Tri-County School
Murphysboro, IL

Party Pumpkins

Here's a "kool" carry-all for fall treats and party favors! Remove the label from a 19-ounce plastic Kool-Aid container. Mix a little liquid dish detergent with orange tempera paint. Then have a child use the mixture to paint the outside of the container. When the paint is dry, invite the child to use a black permanent marker to draw jack-o'-lantern features on the container. To fill the container with treats, simply twist off the top! Trick or treat!

Christa Strickland—
Preschool
Mt. Vernon, OH

Painted Pinecones

Invite your youngsters to express themselves with paint and pinecones! To prepare, set a supply of tempera paints and brushes on a newspaper-covered table. Provide each child with a pinecone and invite him to paint it as desired. Then have the child set his pinecone on a personalized sheet of paper to dry. Later, tie a length of ribbon around the pinecone to create a fabulous fall ornament!

Dayle Timmons
Jacksonville Beach, FL

Laminated Leaves

Here's an inexpensive way to dress up your fall calendar. Use real leaves to display the days of the month! In advance, collect a supply of leaves, making sure that each one is small enough to fit on your calendar. Laminate the leaves and then cut them out. Label each leaf with a different date and then use them on your calendar. The laminated leaves will retain their beautiful colors and add an authentic autumn touch to your calendar!

Virginia Soulier—Preschool
Red Cliff Tribal Head Start
Bayfield, WI

Shoe-Tying Incentive

This cute ghost is the perfect treat for a child who has learned to tie his shoe. To make one, fold a piece of poster board in half and then cut out a ghost shape as shown. Place a piece of red shoestring licorice in a snack-sized resealable plastic bag; then tape it inside the ghost cutout. Punch a hole in the bottom of the ghost through both thicknesses and then tie a length of ribbon through the holes. Draw a face on the ghost and then tape a copy of the poem shown onto it.

Sarah Booth—PreK
Messiah Nursery School
South Williamsport, PA

This little ghost says,
"Good for you! You know how to tie your shoe!"
Untie the bow and find a treat,
A red shoelace for you to eat!

Circle-Time Seating

Do you have a class supply of extra large foam lacing shapes or interlocking mats with numbers and letters? If you do, then give them a new use with this idea! Remove the laces from the shapes and separate the mats into individual pieces. Place an adhesive label on each mat; then write a different child's name on each label. Arrange the mats on the floor of your circle-time area. Invite each child to find the mat with his name and then sit on it. When your group time is over, call out a shape, number, or letter, and have the child sitting on that mat leave the area and put his mat away.

Debbie Hamm—Preschool
Bristol Preschool Child Care Center, Bristol, CT

Gourd People

Get ready for fall with a decorating idea that adds character to your classroom. Glue paper facial features onto a dry gourd. Then use hot glue to attach yarn hair. Next, dress up the gourd by wrapping a scarf or fabric remnant around the "neck" and then tying it in place with a length of string. Add other craft items to the gourd as desired. Create several gourd people; then display them around a pumpkin with a supply of silk leaves. Or place the gourds in a wheelbarrow filled with straw. However you show off these characters, visitors to your classroom are sure to say, "How cute!"

Martha Briggs—Four-Year-Olds
Rosemont School, Fort Worth, TX

Under Construction

"Do I have to tear it down?" Here's an idea that will help your little ones break down their elaborate block creations and then put away the blocks. Use an instant camera to photograph the student and her structure. Provide the child with the photograph to help her rebuild a similar structure on another day. Or display the photos in the blocks area to inspire other visitors to the center.

Dayle Timmons
Jacksonville Beach, FL

Forecast Fun

Did you know that you have access to a free resource that will help teach your youngsters about weather? What's the resource? The great outdoors! In advance, modify your weather chart so that it can be easily taken outside. During your group time, designate one child to be the weather person and provide her with the chart. Then have your class head outdoors to experience the day's weather and record it on the chart. On cold, rainy, or snowy days, have your little ones wear their coats and then check the weather from a covered porch or stoop. The forecast for this idea calls for 100 percent chance of learning!

Courtney Sears—Head Start
Independence Elementary
Manassas Park, VA

Dotty Over Dalmatians

Seeing spots? That's just the dots on these cute Dalmatian headbands! To make one, have a child make black thumbprints on a long white paper strip and on a pair of white paper dog ears. When the prints are dry, staple the strip to fit the child's head. Next, have the child glue the dog ears and a firefighter hat cutout to the strip as shown. Then have the child glue on a personalized construction paper shield. Invite your little ones to don the headbands and sniff out pretend fires. Fire dogs to the rescue!

Sarah Booth—PreK
Messiah Nursery School, South Williamsport, PA

The Itsy-Bitsy Line Leader

Use this spout-and-spider display to ensure that every child has a turn as line leader. To begin, cut out a class supply of construction paper spiders and then label each one with a different child's name. Laminate the spiders for durability. Mount a laminated waterspout cutout near your door, or use PVC pipes to create a three-dimensional spout. Next, use self-adhesive Velcro to mount the spiders in a line on the spout. The child whose spider is at the top of the spout is the current line leader. When her turn is over, "wash the spider out," place it at the end of the line, and then move the other spiders up the spout.

Cris Edwards—PreK, Helena United Methodist Church, Helena, AL

Here's a Story...

Celebrate a child's birthday with a creative-thinking idea that produces a priceless keepsake for parents. Prior to his birthday, send home a note requesting photos of the child as an infant, toddler, and preschooler. On the day of his birthday, display the photos in sequence. Invite your class to use the photos to help create a story about the child. Record the story on a sheet of paper and then send it home with the photos for the child and his parents to enjoy—year after year after year!

Rebecca Fisch
Hirsch Yeshiva
Brooklyn, NY

Wash 'n' Go

This sudsy song will help your tots thoroughly wash their hands in a timely manner. Sing the song as each child begins to wash her hands. When the song is over, her hands will be squeaky clean and ready to go. Next!

(sung to the tune of "Row, Row, Row Your Boat")

Wash, wash, wash your hands.
Wash them every day!
Wash your fingers.
Rinse the soap.
Now you're on your way!

Shay Stufflebean—Preschool, Special Needs
Graham Road Elementary
Reynoldsburg, OH

HAPPY BIRTHDAY TO YOU!

Birthday Display

Make note of each child's birthday with this festive display! Cut out a class supply of musical notes in a variety of colors. Program each note with a different child's name and birthday. Mount the notes on a poster board musical staff. Then add construction paper balloon cutouts and the title "Happy Birthday to You!"

Lori Maiello and Beth Klidonas—Preschool
First Step Preschool, Niagra Falls, NY

Character Cutouts

It's a fact—favorite books become torn. But before you toss out those books, cut out the characters, laminate them, and then use them in this creative-thinking activity. Provide each child in a small group with a character from a different story. Invite the child to tell a new story involving the character. Or encourage the group to create a story in which all the characters interact with one another. With this idea, you just might hear an entertaining tale called "Goldilocks and the Three Pigs"!

Nissa Evans—Preschool
Bright Beginnings
Bend, OR

Twist and Shout

Here's a shapely twist to the classic game Twister. Tape laminated cutout shapes to each colored circle on the Twister mat. Add the same shapes to the spinner and then twist away! For younger students, play the game without designating *right* or *left*. "Foot, circle!"

Andrea Henderson—PreK
Jefferson Brethren Preschool
Goshen, IN

Index